HOW WAR CAME

An American White Paper;
From the Fall of France
to Pearl Harbor

BY

FORREST DAVIS

AND

ERNEST K. LINDLEY

1942

SIMON AND SCHUSTER

NEW YORK

Second Printing

CONTENTS

FOREWORD

This is an informal report to the American people. It tells how, with no aggression in their hearts, they found themselves fighting at the end of 1941 on all the continents and all the seas. It deals with the men and events, the ideas and impulses, that shaped American policy during the immensely significant months between the battle of Sedan, in May, 1940, and Pearl Harbor.

In compiling this report, the authors have sought reliable information wherever it could be obtained. They had, to begin, the voluminous day-by-day record chronicled in the press by seasoned Washington correspondents, including alert and discerning reporters assigned to the White House, the State Department, and other divisions of the government with duties bearing on foreign policy. In reviewing these fateful months, the authors have been impressed by the earnest and persevering efforts made by responsible officials to take the American people into their confidence, to acquaint them fully with the policies and methods of American diplomacy as well as the vital issues at stake.

There were, of course, facts which could not be revealed currently without damage to the national interest. With the passage of time, certain of these can be disclosed. In particular, when the Japanese spread sudden death over the island of Oahu, they brought to an end some of the most delicate negotiations in the history of American diplomacy.

The authors, of course, have examined the official records to the extent that they are available. But a true report cannot be founded upon documents alone. The hurried conference, the telephone conversation of which no record exists, the backgrounds and ways of thinking and moods of the men who made the day-by-day decisions, the political climate in which they work, the chance happening that at the moment seemed irrelevant—these, too, are the essential stuff of history. The authors have searched the still fresh recollections of the men who directed American policy in the most perilous and difficult year and a half since Appomattox. For the patient and painstaking responses of these men, the authors are deeply grateful. Their attitude bespoke clear consciences, as well as an unflinching commitment to free expression and the sturdy, eighteenth-century principle of "public enlightenment."

How War Came *is an independent venture, critical, unofficial, and bearing no imprimatur. The authors worked as journalists with a definite assignment. They have sought to be as accurate and as objective as possible. For such interpretations and judgments as seemed appropriate, the authors alone are accountable.*

The new facts thus made available cast additional light on the period and give new point, color, and meaning to the record as it was currently chronicled. It will be seen that during the eighteen months in which the people of the United States, endlessly debating and confused by angry counsels, sought their true relationship to the great conflicts of interest and principle overseas, American foreign policy came to form a unified, strategical pattern.

The writing of contemporary history has its obvious drawbacks as well as the advantages already suggested. There remain gaps which can be traversed only by conjecture until, if ever, they may be solidly spanned by matter now concealed in the archives of our enemies. Moreover, the period under review is still too close for final, dogmatic judgment. For these and other shortcomings, the authors can only plead the limitations of the time factor and of their own capacities, and beg indulgence.

Washington, D. C.   FORREST DAVIS AND
July 11, 1942   ERNEST K. LINDLEY

How War Came

CHAPTER ONE

When War Came

THE BLOW that was about to fall cast no shadow into the unseasonably warm sunshine of December 7, 1941. At midday Washington was the capital of a people technically at peace, psychologically at war: a "white" war against overseas aggressors and, at home, among themselves on the question of how far to pursue the war abroad. The first note of menace reached the capital almost inadvertently at 1:45 P.M. It came by way of an alert, intercepted at Mare Island and relayed to the Navy Department, which read:

> From CINCPAC (Commander in chief Pacific fleet) to all ships present Hawaiian area: Air raid on Pearl Harbor. This is no drill.

In the final sentence, Admiral Husband E. Kimmel was correcting the incredulous reaction of Hawaii, which had accepted the first Japanese bombs as evidence of a particularly realistic maneuver.

At the Navy Department, Secretary Frank Knox, about to depart on a routine visit to the Washington Navy Yard, received the message from one of his companions, Admiral Harold R. Stark, Chief of Naval Operations, who had it from a panting Communications officer. By a rueful irony, the Secretary's annual report, attesting the Navy's fitness, had appeared in that morning's Sunday newspapers, which now lay strewn through millions of American living rooms. Handing the message to Knox, Stark failed to comment.

"What," demanded the Secretary, "does this mean?"

"It's the beginning," replied Stark, somewhat vaguely,

3

whereupon Rear Admiral R. K. Turner, of War Plans, standing alongside the Secretary, broke in with the definitive: "By God, sir, they've attacked us!"

Back into his private office hurried the Secretary. In private life a Chicago newspaper publisher, he nevertheless keeps his office as nautical as a man-of-war's wardroom. Behind his desk stands a bank of telephones, one a direct wire to the White House. He lifted that receiver and jiggled the hook. The color had drained from Knox's loyal, good-humored, and eupeptic features. Forty-two hours later, at 8:00 A.M. on Tuesday, the Secretary, conscious of his share in the blame for the surprise at Pearl Harbor, was flying to Hawaii to see for himself the extent of the disaster. On Monday he had notified the President he thought it was his duty to go, overcoming mild objections from Mr. Roosevelt, who privately applauded the decision. The Secretary of the Navy regarded his mission as an expiation.

At the moment when Knox lifted the White House phone, half of Washington was lingering over Sunday midday dinners. Such was the case with the President, who was eating from a tray on his desk in the oval study, a large, littered, intensely personal chamber on the second floor of the White House. With him were his friend, Harry L. Hopkins, lounging on a couch in a V-necked sweater and slacks, and the President's Scottie, Falla, expertly pouching morsels from the tray. After an exhausting week with the Far Eastern crisis, aggravated by clogged sinuses, Mr. Roosevelt had dedicated this day to rest. Saturday he had worked late, clearing his desk while the White House staff took a half day for Christmas shopping. Today, tieless and in shirt sleeves, he hoped to catch up with his neglected stamp collection. After a late breakfast, Hopkins, whose health is poor, had strolled in from his bedroom down the book-lined corridor for some relaxed talk. The President might have been any one of a million Americans putting in a loafing Sunday afternoon with a crony and a hobby.

There was this difference: the imminence of war could not be banished wholly from the President's study. Mr. Roosevelt expected war—but not this week end. Only yesterday he had cabled Emperor Hirohito, immured behind his moat in Tokyo, to solicit his help in "dispelling the dark clouds." The overnight cables had reported a large movement of Japanese transports toward the Gulf of Siam, but the President held on to a faint hope that even yet the Emperor might restrain the war party. In any case, there had been no warning. The Japanese had not even answered Cordell Hull's comprehensive note of November 26, and the President did not anticipate that afternoon a thrust to the heart of United States sea power. If war did come, he assumed, along with 132,000,000 other Americans, it would break first in Siam, the East Indies, or the Malay Peninsula.

The White House, therefore, was, like the country, at peace. Elsewhere in the great Regency-Georgian mansion, Mrs. Roosevelt was giving a luncheon for an American radio commentator recently home from London, but the President's calendar was bare and the executive staff scattered. A "do not disturb" order had been confidently placed with the switchboard. Mr. Roosevelt was topping his dinner with an apple when his desk telephone jangled disobediently.

The President lifted his receiver on an apologetic operator agitatedly saying that Secretary Knox had insisted on being put through . . . the call was most urgent. The President cut the operator short: "Put him on," and then, "Hello, Frank."

In a tone and at a pace the President still regards as a model of casualness on the brink of crisis, Knox began: "Mr. President, it looks like the Japanese have attacked Pearl Harbor. . . ."

"NO!" the President interrupted.

"It's true," said the Secretary. "I'll read you the message," which he did.

The hands of the brass ship's clock on the President's desk

stood at 1:47. The message, which was, as we have seen, a service alert to the fleet and not an official report to Washington, did lack explicitness, and its terse language gave no insight into how the attack was being met, no hint as to the extent, weight, or gravity of the air raid. Yet its meaning was plain to the President: the flag had been fired upon, Hawaii, not Siam, had been subjected to the overt act, and the war, so long dreaded, so exhaustively debated, had come to America. Directing that Knox see at once to safeguarding the Panama Canal and the Alaskan bases, and to doubling the guards at all Naval establishments against sabotage, the President rang off, bidding the operator get him Secretary Hull. Thrice that afternoon he lodged anxious inquiries about the Canal with the Navy Department.

Just before Hull lifted his receiver at the State Department, Hopkins said: "This is it." For a long while the President's *fidus Achates* had predicted that World War II would overtake America in the Pacific rather than in the Atlantic.

By coincidence the Japanese Ambassador, Admiral Kichisaburo Nomura, and Saburo Kurusu, the last-minute "peace envoy," were due at that moment at the State Department with Tokyo's answer to the note of the 26th, an answer rendered superfluous by the happenings in Hawaii a half-hour earlier. (The first bombs fell on Pearl Harbor at 1:20 P.M., Washington time.) At 1:10, the Japanese Embassy had telephoned for an appointment to deliver the answer: 1:45 was the hour set, but the diplomats were not yet at the State Department when the President telephoned.*

---

*The Japanese asked that the appointment be for 2 P.M. Mr. Hull's personal assistant, J. F. Stone, eager that the Secretary should have his lunch, suggested that they come immediately. The Japanese said that the typing of the translation was not yet completed, but agreed to appear at 1:45 P.M. Actually they did not arrive until 2:05 P.M. If the note had been delivered at 1 P.M., in accordance with what the Japanese envoys told Mr. Hull their instructions had been, the first bombs would have fallen on Oahu just about the moment Mr. Hull finished reading it.

To Mr. Hull the President said: "Frank Knox has just telephoned a report of an air raid over Pearl Harbor. We haven't confirmed it yet." The Secretary, a man of fire and storm under a gently benign manner, uttered a profane comment. In his graphic phraseology, the Japanese war party had, for some time, been succinctly characterized as "Dillinger."

Of all the ranking officials in Washington, Mr. Hull should have been the least surprised. Five weeks earlier, before the arrival of Kurusu, he had warned the Army and Navy that the Far Eastern crisis, having passed outside the bounds of diplomacy, was now in their lap. A fortnight before he had been more precise. Reminding his War Cabinet colleagues of Japan's proclivity for beginning wars by stealth, he had suggested that all hands in the Pacific be on watchful guard lest a shock attack on a wide front "stampede the hell out of our scattered forces."

But with Mr. Hull foresight never lapses into imprudence. He is not, by nature, a jumper at conclusions. The President had said the report was unconfirmed. So little did the Secretary relax his customary caution that he withheld from his associates the news that the country constructively was at war and the next day, at a press conference, recalled only that an "unconfirmed report" had reached him from "an official source" before the arrival of the Japanese envoys. Because the report lacked corroboration, he had elected to see them.

In turn the President telephoned Henry L. Stimson, Secretary of War; General George C. Marshall, Chief of Staff; Viscount Halifax, the British Ambassador; and Sumner Welles, the Under Secretary of State. Ten years earlier, Stimson, as Hoover's Secretary of State and Hull's immediate predecessor, had labored to arouse the Western World against the explosive implications of Japan's "Manchuria incident." Today he observed the cycle of aggression begun at Mukden conclude its march around the globe.

General Marshall and some of his staff had been at his office all morning. Shortly before one o'clock he went to his quarters at Fort Myer and was at dinner when he was called to the telephone by Lieutenant Colonel (now Colonel) John R. Deane, then assistant secretary of the War Department General Staff. A messenger from the Navy Department had just handed Deane a penciled note, apparently a brief bulletin from the Navy radio operator at Pearl Harbor, stating that an attack was in progress. General Marshall directed that all the key officers of the War Department be informed. He immediately returned to his office. Soon afterward, a second message came from the Navy Department. This one was typed and of a more formal character than the first, although it contained little additional information.

Halifax, the stooped, bony, melancholy, and conscientiously useful British Ambassador, was reading in the library of the huge Georgian Embassy building on Massachusetts Avenue. With the Ambassador were William Hayter, first secretary of legation, and Angus Malcolm, His Lordship's private secretary. After talking sympathetically with the President, Halifax directed Hayter to put in a call for London and himself began telephoning ranking officers of the Embassy and other leading Britons in Washington that America, at long last, was in the war. In an admirable demonstration of British composure, Malcolm continued at the stint he had set himself for that afternoon, addressing Christmas cards to catch a pouch for London.

The London connection could not be had until about three o'clock (9:00 P.M., London wartime). It being Sunday night, a lone duty clerk at the Foreign Office received the news and at once telephoned it to Winston Churchill, the Prime Minister, and Anthony Eden, the Foreign Secretary. Meanwhile, the radio had carried the news to America, and a pickup by the British Broadcasting Corporation had beaten the telephone report to the Prime Minister.

—2—

A little later the President made a historic call to Mr. Churchill at the country place where he week-ends in wartime, a spot unidentifiable because of the war. The President said that he would ask Congress for a declaration of a state of war on Monday; Mr. Churchill volunteered to obtain a like pronouncement from his Cabinet on the same day in fulfillment of the pledge of war "within the hour" he had voiced publicly upon returning from the Atlantic Conference the preceding August. Neither statesman knew as they spoke that Hirohito was at about that time announcing war with both Britain and the United States. Actually, because of the time difference, the British declaration preceded the one in Washington.

The transatlantic exchange of views reminded the President of a difference over Far Eastern policy that had developed between him and the Prime Minister when they met in a "Newfoundland blight" for the Atlantic Conference. In July, the United States had frozen Japanese funds, inducing an embargo on shipments to Japan, its possessions, and its subjugated territories. This Government, moreover, knew from sources of proved reliability that Hitler at the moment was pressing the Japanese with all vigor to validate a secret protocol of the Axis pact of September, 1940, calling for war on the English-speaking Powers under specified circumstances. Consequently, anxiety over the Far Eastern prospects weighted the sessions on the American cruiser *Augusta* and the *Prince of Wales*.

Churchill wished to meet the issue head on. He asked the President (as the Australians, the Dutch, and his own people had repeatedly besought his own Government) to join in an ultimative declaration to Japan. For some time the other Pacific powers had sought to establish a dead line in the Far East, serving notice on Nippon that so far, and no farther, might they go: a dead line political as well as geographical, setting bounds to pressure on other States as well as to the enlargement of Japanese forces in Indo-China. While such a move entailed the risk of war, Churchill, mistrusting further procrastination, believed it might cause the Japanese to halt further aggression. In any case, it should, in his opinion, retain the initiative in the hands of the Western powers. Disregardful of Japanese "face," that Asiatic procedure for conserving self-esteem, the Prime Minister advocated making the admonition public.

Unlike the Prime Minister, Mr. Roosevelt lacked the Constitutional capacity to make a commitment involving the possibility of automatic hostilities. Only Congress can declare war; nor can the President decree a war if, as, and when. There were, moreover, other considerations. Mr. Roosevelt feared in August that war in the Pacific was a matter of weeks or months. Yet he knew the country's unreadiness, he was under solicitation from the armed forces for "more time," and, besides, he felt that every day of peace was a day gained to American concentration on supplying the British, Russians, and Chinese. Actually, on December 7, this Government by emergency order canceled shipping orders for six hundred out of eight hundred airplanes consigned at the moment to the British, the orders later being restored. Parenthetically, up to that date only two hundred of the several thousand aircraft shipped the British had gone forward under lend-lease, the others being purchases.

Back in August, therefore, the President had temporized.

"Wouldn't we be better off in three months?" he asked. Churchill agreed, still doubting, however, that the respite would be forthcoming without immediate concerted action.

"Leave that to me," said the President. "I think I can baby them along for three months." *

* The verb "to baby" often is used by the President to mean to pacify or to nurse. By the quotation given here, the President did not imply that he had given up all hope of more than a respite in the Pacific.

Of course, Mr. Churchill and the British Government were as ardent as the President and the American Government in their desire to avert war in the Pacific. Mr. Churchill told the President plainly that the British Government needed more time to prepare for resistance against any Japanese attack. The President knew this; and, of course, the same consideration applied to the state of our defensive preparations in the Philippine Islands. The difference of opinion between Mr. Churchill and the President was solely as to which tactic would have the better chance of deterring the Japanese from further aggression. The British favored the issuance of a stern warning; the President believed that would precipitate the action that the Western powers desired to avert or, if that proved impossible, to postpone until their defensive positions could be strengthened. The course agreed upon at the Atlantic Conference, and subsequently followed, was this: (1) the American and British Governments would take parallel action in making it clear to Japan that these Governments could not be expected to sit idly by if Japan continued in its course of aggression in the Pacific area; and (2) the United States, in response to the requests repeatedly made by Japan, would resume its conversations with the Japanese with a view to exploring all possibilities of finding a peaceful adjustment of the entire Pacific situation.

In entering into the conversations with the Japanese this Government realized that the prospects of success were very slight. It was actuated, however, by a sincere desire to bring about a peaceful, fair, and progressive settlement of the situation throughout the Pacific area. This desire was entirely consistent with the traditional belief of the American people. It was also consistent with the need of having as much time as possible to carry forward the defensive preparations of the United States, which were vital not only to this country but also to many other countries resisting aggression.

The effort to persuade Japan to accept a reasonable and just alternative to military conquest failed. But on December 7, Mr. Roosevelt could reflect that he had gained precious time: that he had "babied" the Japanese along for almost four months, not three. Naturally he suspected that the Japanese concurrently were "babying" along the Western powers. The Japanese, readying us for the kill, needed time to mature their treachery. In its unremitting search for peace, the American Government had followed every trail to its end. But in the light of their Atlantic conversations, neither Roosevelt nor Churchill was surprised on December 7, although both were taken aback by the foulness, force, and widespread nature of the blow. With his instinct for tactics, the President may also have reflected on that day upon the different turn that events would have taken had it been possible to accept Churchill's counsel. The initiative might not have been so completely in Japanese hands.

—3—

At the Navy Department, Knox's first order directed Stark to telephone Admiral C. C. Bloch, Commandant of the Hawaiian naval district, the assumption being that Kimmel would be too busy fighting ships and planes to talk. Bloch disclosed the worst. The dull roar of the bombardment reached Knox through the telephone as he learned that the Japanese had struck in force. The battle still raged, damage already appeared heavy, but officers and men were fighting with the utmost courage against the overwhelming odds imposed by surprise.

The bleak report went at once to the President, who by now had transformed his study into the G.H.Q. of a nation at war. In this homey room, filled with books, ship prints, family portraits, and mementos, the only reminder of rank was a brightly lacquered cigar box on the desk, bearing the words THE PRESIDENT OF THE UNITED STATES in a gilt line running around all four sides. From these unlikely headquarters the United States already had been ordered on a war footing.

Here the President received the Secretaries of State, War, and Navy, generals and admirals, and, later, the full Cabinet and Congressional leaders. Here he had word of the raid on the Philippines, which arrived at about two o'clock, but by mystifying chance could not be confirmed until six. Here he spoke with Governor Joseph B. Poindexter of Hawaii, getting firsthand information of the devastation wrought on Oahu. Here he penciled releases to the press, dictating a first draft of his war message to Congress, a draft beginning with a phrase of high survival value: ". . . a date which will live in infamy."

The President's associates maintain that he works under extreme pressure with precision, clarity, and economy of effort. Recalling the night of March 5, 1933, when, amidst a welter of conflicting counsels, dubieties, and alarms, the President closed the country's banks, they put his performance of the afternoon of December 7 on the same high plane. No recriminations escaped him. That would come later. This day he engrossed himself in the battle of Hawaii, the fate of the forces in the Philippines, and the safety of installations and concentrations nearer at hand in both oceans. He did allow himself the luxury of one heartfelt characterization of the sneak attack, remarking to Hopkins that it had been neither "decent nor Christian." *

Meanwhile the Japanese envoys reached the State Department at 2:05. The murderous bombardment of Pearl Harbor, the airfields and barracks of Oahu, had been under way for forty-five minutes. Already, hundreds of American soldiers

---

* One of the high officials who saw much of the President that day offered this comment upon reading the above: "It does not seem to me that there is emphasized sufficiently the extraordinary vigor, energy, calmness, and complete control over men, policies, and even the smallest details which characterized the President's handling of the situation. I cannot say more than that I have never more deeply admired the President as Chief Executive than upon that occasion."

and sailors had perished on the decks of ships, in engine rooms, in water coated with blazing oil, and trapped in barracks. That was war. There were, however, no intimations of war in the State Department, an architect's heavy-handed evocation of French Renaissance applied to the United States in the 1870's. On their final visit, Nomura and Kurusu, clad in street clothes, went as usual to the diplomatic anteroom, a dingy chamber opposite Mr. Hull's office. Either the room or the errand depressed Nomura, who relaxed on a sofa, paying only scant attention to Kurusu, when, pacing the floor, he stopped now and then for a whispered word.

Mr. Hull kept the envoys waiting fifteen minutes.

All morning the Secretary had been uneasy, scenting something in the air, with the prevision of a frontiersman. As usual, he arrived at his office at 10:15 for the Sunday-morning roundup of the Department's ranking officers which had become a fixture as the world crisis deepened; a gathering partaking somewhat, despite the momentous subject matter, of the nature of a cracker-barrel session in a back-country store.

The conference this morning was deferred. Stimson and Knox, calling to discuss the alarming movement of Japanese transports toward Siam, remained an hour and a half. The Cabinet members agreed that war would not be long in coming. It might, Hull ventured, come any moment. Stimson, a soldier, an eminent New York lawyer, and a rather formal statesman, shared with Hull and Knox a detestation of Nazism, extending to the whole Axis and international brigandage in general. Since 1936, Hull steadily had stigmatized the Rome-Berlin-Tokyo aggressors in private as the "gangster nations." Less picturesque, Stimson and Knox were no less wrathful. It occurred to none that the blow was even then making up. As they separated at a little after twelve, Japanese carriers lay within effective radius of Pearl Harbor, with bombers already winging over the unwatched Pacific toward their objective.

Upon the departure of Stimson and Knox, Mr. Hull called
in Welles, Assistant Secretary Adolf A. Berle, Jr., and experts
of the Far Eastern division, headed by Stanley K. Hornbeck,
a political advisor. Likewise present was Green H. Hackworth,
the State Department's legal advisor, a knowledgeable counselor, and during the session Norman H. Davis, president of
the American Red Cross and "roving Ambassador" to Europe
under both Hoover and Roosevelt, dropped in. Mr. Davis
hails from the same end of Tennessee as Mr. Hull and frequently employs the same vernacular; the Secretary relies on
his estimate of situations. Mr. Hull communicated his own
trepidation: there was an atmosphere of waiting for a blow to
fall somewhere.

This group had broken up for lunch when the request for
an appointment came from the Japanese Embassy. Mr. Hull
at once called back his principal advisors on Far Eastern affairs,
Mr. Hornbeck and Maxwell Hamilton; and they were soon
joined by Michael J. McDermott, Chief of the Bureau of Current Information. Together they conjectured on the content
of the message the Japanese emissaries were about to submit.

At 2:20 Mr. Hull admitted the Japanese. He bowed un-
smilingly, bade them be seated. Upon Kurusu's arrival in
November, the Secretary had allotted him lesser rank than the
Ambassador, and Nomura had a seat on Mr. Hull's right. The
Secretary's office is a large, shabby room bearing the marks of
long use, but impersonal as a railway-station waiting room.
None of the Secretaries who have occupied this room since
Hamilton Fish moved in during the latter seventies has left a
mark of his own upon it. Along the far end is a huge map of
the earth, brightly colored and showing the pencil marks of
strategical discussion. The walls near the ceiling are lined with
steel engravings of Washington, Lincoln, Grant, and the Jefferson who, in an earlier time of international upheaval, bade
the United States "marry the British fleet." Of John Quincy

Adams also, who crustily warned President Monroe against
embracing Canning's proposal for an English-speaking league
safeguarding the New World for fear the United States might
become a "cockboat in the wake of the English man-of-war."

Facing the Secretary as he regarded his country's enemies
was a spirited engraving of another fiery Tennessean, Andrew
Jackson. Behind Mr. Hull stood the flag of the United States
and the Secretary's standard. At his left, reaching to the ceiling,
was a gaunt rubber plant, furnishing a surprising spot of color
in the room and testifying to the Secretary's constancy. The
gift of a friend, it has remained here since March, 1933, when
the Secretary moved into this office, and he has cherished its
growth from three feet to eleven.

Nomura apologized for their tardiness. Their instructions
were to present the note from their Government at one, but
the decoding had gone slowly. "Why one o'clock?" asked Mr.
Hull. Nomura professed not to know. He handed the Secretary the translation, which Mr. Hull, affixing his pince-nez,
proceeded to read. The note ran to twenty-five hundred
words. As Mr. Hull's eye took in the bellicose farrago of insults, couched in an English sometimes bordering on pidgin,
his jaw tightened. The note was absurd as well as insolent,
charging the United States at one and the same time with
impossible idealism and "scheming for the extension of the
war."

When Mr. Hull had finished the paper he arose. The Japanese stood also. Ignoring Kurusu and eyeing Nomura, the
Secretary said with the restraint of an anger too deep-seated
and righteous for truculence:

"I must say that in all my conversations with you during
the last nine months, I have never uttered one word of untruth. This is borne out absolutely by the record. In all my fifty
years of public service I have never seen a document that was
more crowded with infamous falsehoods and distortions; in-

famous falsehoods and distortions on a scale so huge that I never imagined until today that any government on this planet was capable of uttering them."

Nomura opened his mouth to make some reply, but the Secretary, his dark countenance reddening, cut him short. Raising his right arm, he pointed to the door.

"Good day," said the Secretary, with considerable finality.

The Japanese Ambassadors walked out of Hull's office into a battery of news photographers, but, instead of stopping as usual for posed pictures, they hurried down the corridor, Nomura flinging noncommittal phrases at correspondents hurrying along beside him. In his office, Mr. Hull began dictating to M. J. McDermott, Chief of the Division of Current Information, his recollection of the rebuke for the press. The White House telephone on his desk rang. It was the President, asking for the Secretary's own version of the incident. Mr. Hull reviewed the encounter and quoted his remarks, with interruptions of gratification from Mr. Roosevelt.

"That's grand, Cordell," the President ended.

As his indignation abated, Mr. Hull doubted that Nomura had been privy to the stealthy attack, although he recalled grimly that both envoys had "cowered" under his blast. When Welles and Berle re-entered the Secretary's office, he grinned: "I'm afraid I was pretty rough on those Japs." In their intimate association—Hull and Nomura held sixty conversations between March, 1941, and December 7, most of them at night in the Secretary's apartment—Mr. Hull had developed a fondness for the Admiral, referring indulgently to him as the "old codger," although Nomura was his junior. For "that other citizen," Kurusu, Mr. Hull had entertained only mistrust from the time of his presentation by the Ambassador. It was Kurusu who had signed, on behalf of the Emperor, the tripartite pact in Berlin on September 27, 1940. Mr. Hull—an ex-judge skilled in testing the credibility of witnesses—found it hard to believe that Kurusu, who had left Japan only a month before, had not been aware of the scheme.

The episode in Mr. Hull's office lasted twelve minutes, the Japanese leaving him at 2:32.

—4—

Seven minutes earlier the black news had been broken to the public. Satisfied beyond any shadow that the blow was all-out, deliberate, and warlike, after Knox reported his talk with Admiral Bloch, the President penciled a brief announcement —the first American communiqué of the war. His principal secretary, Stephen Early, was at his home, six miles from the White House. In pajamas and dressing gown, Mr. Early was deep in the Sunday papers when his White House telephone rang. It was the President.

"Have you got a pencil handy, Steve?" he asked.

"Do I need it?" Early countered, half suspecting a Presidential jest. The President was serious. "Yes, I have a pretty important statement here and it ought to go out verbatim," he said. Mr. Early was in his library, no pencil was within reach, so he called for Mrs. Early, who had been a stenographer, asking her to take down the President's words as he repeated them. After reading the communiqué, the President inquired of Early: "Have you any news?" Early said he had none other than that which had just quickened his breathing.

By Early's wrist watch the time was 2:22. While Mrs. Early transcribed her pothooks into longhand, the President's secretary instructed the White House switchboard to set up a three-way hookup into the offices of the Associated Press, United Press, and International News Service. Within three minutes the bulletin, telephoned by the wire services to broadcasting clients, had reached the air, interrupting network programs throughout North America.

Scrambling into street clothes, Early started for the White

House in his own car, intercepted a White House limousine on its way to pick him up, commandeered a traffic policeman, and made a record run through red lights and the sparse Sunday traffic to the Executive Mansion. He found the President and Harry Hopkins in the oval room, decks cleared, and Secretaries Stimson and Knox just arriving.

At 3:20 Secretary Hull crossed to the White House, entering the oval room with General Marshall. Vice-President Henry A. Wallace, calling from New York, announced he was taking the next plane for Washington. Meanwhile the Executive Mansion's switchboard lights danced, as calls arrived from Administration officials, from Senators and Representatives, Governors, retired statesmen, admirals and generals, and plain citizens in all corners of the land. The callers prevailingly offered their services.

The news dazed Washington. At first incredulity was widespread. Not in the eighty years since Sumter had this country been propelled into a war without notice. The phenomenon observed in every capital on which World War II has descended was likewise observable in Washington: the public accepted hostilities without demonstration. This war was an ordeal, not an adventure. No crowds gathered except for small knots of curious persons clustered around the west gate of the White House, which was promptly closed. In these groups, wearing uniforms, were enlisted men in town on week-end leave from near-by camps. Some had not been quite certain whom they were to fight. Now they knew. Many Washingtonians, grouped around loud-speakers in restaurants and hotel lobbies, wondered hopefully if this would not turn out to be another "Orson Welles hoax." *

A factor in the capital's apathetic response was the time. It

* Three years before, an actor of that name had driven many thousands of persons in the East to the verge of panic by an inherently implausible but blood-curdling radio playlet that affected to depict the invasion of New Jersey by warlike creatures from another planet.

being Sunday afternoon, much of Washington, heedless as
yet of wear on tires, had streamed into Maryland and Virginia. The population was scattered; the downtown streets,
except for queues at the movie theaters, were virtually empty.
A record crowd of 27,000 watched the last professional football game of the season at Griffith Stadium, oblivious of the
carnage at Pearl Harbor. Although the loud-speaker presently
was calling Army and Navy officers to their respective departments, no war news issued from it to disturb the game. Nor
did the moving-picture theaters enlighten their audiences.

Few incidents arose. In a barroom two overheated patriots
insisted on purchasing beer for all men in uniform. Uniden-
tified, and no doubt deranged, miscreants hacked a couple of
Japanese cherry trees on the banks of the Tidal Basin. A
group of Sunday strollers gathered outside the fence of the
long white rectangle of the Japanese Embassy on Massachusetts Avenue, watching more or less good-humoredly as Washington police mounted guard, as attachés arrived hurriedly
by taxicab from other parts of the capital, and as other aides
in the back yard ceremoniously burned Embassy documents
in a succession of flame bursts. Occasional insults reached the
ears of the Japanese, penned behind their ornamental iron
fence—jesting invitations to "come out and fight, you so-and-
sos." Generally, it was observed that the Japanese had committed hara-kiri in a dastardly, if rather enterprising, manner.

The lethargy of the Washington populace contrasted with
the stir and hum of the great State, War, and Navy Departments as they passed from peace to war. Soldiers wearing steel
helmets, equipped with gas masks, and armed with ball ammunition took up sentry duty around the southern confines
of the President's park. At the War Department, guards iden-
tified all who sought to enter. Marines promptly took post at
the Navy Department. An early order issuing from the endless twin buildings of the War and Navy Departments on
Constitution Avenue ("temporary" structures dating from

World War I) required all officers to shed mufti and appear at once in uniform.

These buildings quickly came to life—by nightfall they were blazing with lights—as officers and civilian personnel hurried past the guards to their desks. Naval communications and the Army's Signal Corps labored at clearing messages to all the far-flung military and naval establishments and ships at sea, invoking orders already particularized to the last detail for war when it should come. Orders were issued for troop and plane movements to the West Coast and to other vital areas, and arrangements were made for the immediate reinforcement of Hawaii, Alaska, the Caribbean Defense Command, and other outlying garrisons.

So it was also at the frowning gray bulk of the State Department: personnel hastening to work, orders already agreed upon going smoothly into execution, dispatches long ago drafted and typed being committed to the cables. Welles, in general, supervised the external activities, the outreaches to our missions everywhere around the globe and to friendly nations. Berle pushed buttons effectuating measures drawn in advance for domestic security. Berle it was who, in concert with the Department of Justice, ordered Japanese diplomats, both Embassy and consular, confined to their residences, directed their isolation from communication by telephone, cable, and wireless, and set in motion steps for their protection.

Berle and J. Edgar Hoover, Director of the F.B.I., extended the restrictive orders to the German and Italian Embassies, those Embassies being without telephone service until Monday, when James L. Fly, Chairman of the Federal Communications Commission, revoked the deed as premature. The German and Italian declarations of war later that week again deprived those Embassies of their communications. Orders went out calculated to stop all Japanese aliens in their tracks, forbidding them to travel by train, bus, or airplane and advising them to remain close to their homes.

Breckinridge Long, Assistant Secretary of State, the only ranking officer in the Department who had served in the same rank during World War I, motored in from the country to direct the closing of the borders to enemy aliens. Messages went forward formally requesting the Swiss Government to represent this Government in Japanese territories along lines specified in advance. Our representation of anti-Axis belligerents in Axis countries likewise was shouldered onto the willing Swiss.

A first concern of the Far Eastern division was the well-being of American Foreign Service officers in the path of the Japanese. A message expedited to Ambassador Joseph C. Grew in Tokyo actually reached him. Cables would come from him as late as next day. The broadcast news brought a storm of telephonic inquiries from relatives and friends of persons in the Far Eastern war zones, as well as from Americans with property interests in those places.

A circular telegram from the Division of the American Republics ordered the twenty other republics informed that this Government had made effective all war measures, both military and economic, against Japan and her allies. Soon messages of support began pouring into the State Department from the Presidents and Foreign Ministers of Latin-American states, as well as from their missions in Washington. Meanwhile, in conjunction with the Treasury Department, curbs on commerce with the enemy, drafted beforehand, were placed in effect. Goods on ships consigned to Japanese anywhere were ordered unloaded. All commodities of Far Eastern origin, notably rubber and tin, were ordered withheld from shipment to any destination outside the British Empire, Russia, and such Latin-American countries as declared war on Japan.

In the matter of strategic materials, the Department moved promptly into new ground. Cables drafted beforehand by the

Division of Defense Materials sped to consuls in the great arc of the East Indies and the Indian Ocean from Singapore through India and down the east coast of Africa to Durban in Natal, directing them to report at once on critical materials available in port, in warehouse, at the mine head or planta- tion. The replies went to the Inter-Departmental Shipping Priorities Committee for transmission to the Maritime Com- mission. Many thousand tons of raw materials were snaked out of the path of war in its early weeks, some cargoes being deposited (for later shipment home) in India and other coun- tries regarded as safe. Dr. Herbert Feis, economic advisor of the Department, estimates that 85 per cent of all the raw materials that could be had in that part of the world safely reached our own and Allied ports.

The shift to a war footing proceeded along preordained lines and without hitch at the State Department, testifying to thoughtful planning by the professional personnel in the final months of peace. In a sense, the arrival of war at the State Department was anticlimactic, the Department having lived with crisis for so long that the rupture brought what amounted to a sense of relief.

"The other shoe," as Berle put it, "has been dropped."

Mr. Hull quit the scene fairly early, going to his apartment at the Wardman Park Hotel at 10:45 P.M. when a conference of Cabinet members and Congressional leaders broke up at the White House. Past seventy, the Secretary is still fairly rugged, yet he must constantly guard his resources of health. The President turned in at midnight, Mr. Welles being his last caller. Together they went over the war message, to be read on Monday.

The day had been black, one of the most disastrous in American history. Yet, both the President and Mr. Hull could reflect that night that they had preserved America's moral position throughout the difficult prewar years. Under their guidance this country had not wavered in opposition to the

dark forces; time and again they had called America as witness
to the abhorrence which free men felt toward despotic aggressors. And they had resisted the temptation to fight evil
with evil: the blood was not on their hands.

—5—

The State, War, and Navy Departments remained alight
until daybreak. The foreign and service departments, however, functioned with a difference, subjective and intangible.
The armed forces were only beginning a mission. The future,
for an unpredictable period, belonged primarily to them. As
for the State Department, it was concluding a mission. For
eighteen months, since the reduction of the Low Countries
and the defeat of France placed the Nazis on the Atlantic
shore, the State Department, under the President, had constituted this country's main line of defense.

In June, 1940, the United States, with its tempting wealth,
its hemispheric commitments, and its profound stake in the
survival of the classical, Christian, liberal tradition of the
West, found itself in grave peril. France, a cornerstone of
the West, lay crushed. Of the Continental powers only Russia
stood erect, her position anomalous. The citadel of England
remained untaken, yet her capacity to resist all-out war from
the air was as yet untried. Who could be sure that we might
not soon be left to fight in the Atlantic area a last-ditch war of
survival? Mr. Roosevelt, addressing the Pan-American Scientific Congress which met in Washington while Panzer divisions swept through the Low Countries, accepted as a "dim
and unpleasant possibility . . . that the Americans might
have to become the guardians of Western culture, the pro-
tectors of Christian civilization. Today that fear has become a
fact."

To the westward lay dangers equally great. In 1940, Japan
was coiled to strike whenever the distraction of the West af-

forded hope of success. With England subdued, with Germany in command of the Atlantic coasts of Europe, and with the American fleet withdrawn to the Atlantic, nothing would stand between Japan and hegemony over eastern Asia, the Indies, and, in all likelihood, Australia, New Zealand, and India. The vast dreams of the samurai military state would then be realizable. Moreover, the other great Pacific power, Russia, was an enigmatic quantity. Only China, shut off from effective use of the sea, inhibited by lack of industrial power, fighting a defensive war with pathetic, persistent gallantry, blocked Japan's career of conquest in Asia. The United States, as the great American power-philosopher, Alfred Thayer Mahan, had disclosed a half century ago (and as the Axis powers have made evident since December 7), was an island, open to attack from all quarters.

In such swift, broad strokes was the strategical situation sketched in June, 1940, by the leaders of this Government. The United States faced isolation in a hostile world; not the self-sufficient, negative isolation advocated by the Continental school of American historians and the politicians who vulgarized them, but a sinister condition flanked by formidable enemies. Unless we intelligently resisted we stood in danger of losing our national identity, our character as a free society, and our political independence. To the men who principally shaped American foreign policy, a half dozen, headed by the President and the Secretary of State, this country's potential isolation was real in June, 1940. Cables that hourly streamed into the State Department's decoding room confirmed and emphasized it.

Increasingly in the years preceding 1940, America had been conditioned by the behavior of the aggressors. This country had not rested easy since the rape of Ethiopia and the "China incident" of 1937. Spain, Austria, Czechoslovakia impinged with mounting intensity on our thought, our sympathies, our economy and political relationships. The European war, open-

ing in September, 1939, with the advance into Poland, produced an immediate reaction in favor of England, France, and
their allies. The President and the Congress promptly abandoned a Chinese-wall type of neutrality, saddled on the country by influences both parochial-minded and fearful, and
prepared to assist our friends of the West.

Thus was ushered in the first of two phases in the national
attitude toward the war. In the first phase, beginning with
Poland, progressing through the long winter *Sitzkrieg* to the
reduction of Denmark and Norway, and culminating with the
attack on the Low Countries, France, and England, we played
the role of benevolent neutral.

The industrial plant of America was opened, on a "cash-
and-carry" basis, to France and Britain—an opportunity they
were slow to grasp—and American sympathy and voluntary
assistance flowed in rising volume toward the Atlantic powers.
Yet the war still seemed remote to many Americans. The Atlantic mentality which regarded that ocean itself, and not the
command of it, as a screen sheltering this country from European aggression, still widely prevailed, and the President had
not wholly abandoned his "quest for peace," pursued so vigor-
ously between Munich, in September, 1938, and Poland.
Sumner Welles' tour of the belligerent capitals in the spring
of 1940 had for part of its motivation the President's desire to
see if a spark of desire for peace still existed in the warring
hearts. No such spark was found.

A sailor and an amateur geographer, the President has been
a student of power problems since, at the age of fourteen, he
had encountered the great systematic works of Admiral
Mahan. With Mahan, the President understood the supreme
importance to the United States of sea power, a concept embracing all elements of strength—surface, undersea, and air
ships, as well as bases and shore support—and not, as some
profess to believe, merely men-of-war. Not since John Quincy
Adams have we had a President with such balanced under-

standing, the sure, unillusioned grasp of international situations. Besides, more than Adams, Roosevelt has a flair for the management of foreign policy.

Mr. Roosevelt's hemispheric policy, conforming to new realities, enlarged our declared and immediate responsibilities, but it also widened this country's capacity to defend itself at a distance. Defense at a distance was a salient point with Mahan, who in his lifetime steadily propagandized for bases, including Hawaii, which he termed the "Gibraltar of the Pacific," as a means of keeping war as far as possible from the home shores. The hemispheric policy, which bore splendid fruit in the period under review, took form through the foresight of Mr. Roosevelt in 1936 in the Inter-American Conference for the Maintenance of Peace, at Buenos Aires. There the principle was established that a nonhemispheric act of aggression against any one of the American republics was to be considered an attack on all. Believing a world war imminent in 1936, the President conceived that the time to lay the foundations for inter-American military solidarity was in days of peace and before the exigencies of actual war complicated the issues. The advantages of this policy to the Americas when a world war did come cannot be exaggerated.

Mr. Roosevelt's acquisition, discussed hereafter, of bases in the British offshore islands, in friendly Latin America and in Greenland and Iceland and his watchful guard over North and West Africa and the Atlantic islands constituted, of course, the soundest Mahanism. So too was his recognition of the interlocking interests of the United States and Great Britain, sea powers with like languages, political institutions, and cultural traditions, besides roughly complementary economies. Their collaboration was inevitable if an alien and predatory land power would seek to subdue the European Continent as a means of breaking out into the Atlantic.

Before the *Reichswehr* swept, in Churchill's phrase, like a "sharp scythe" through the Low Countries, bringing a foreshadowing disaster to the French at Sedan, Mr. Roosevelt and his circle had not contemplated a swift German victory in the West. The President, as he confesses, was slow to see the immediacy of our defense problem. Like so many Americans, he relied on the Maginot Line, the highly regarded French Army, and the British fleet. True the Nazis had air superiority but that, provided the Maginot Line and the British fleet held, could be overcome by time and the industrial output of the Atlantic powers. In the spring of 1940 this seemed to the President a satisfactory formula for the restraint of Nazism in Europe: a trinity of French land power, British sea power, and American industrial power, expressed chiefly in terms of aircraft re-enforcement of the European Allies. Three contingencies dominated Administration anticipations: (1) allied victory, (2) stalemate, and (3) a slow beating back of the Allies by the Germans, retarded enough to allow this country's industrial assistance finally to turn the scale.

A fourth alternative, a prompt German victory in the West, failed to impress itself on the President and his associates. In the light of Welles' interview with Hitler, during which the *Führer* boasted of victory in the West by July, and the weight of intelligence reports on the mechanized might of the German land and air forces, the Administration's blind spot toward this fourth alternative must be put down to that wishful thinking which persistently underappraised the naked power of the evil forces besetting the democracies in 1940.

Whatever the precise reasons, the fact of present significance is that the *Blitzkrieg* of May, 1940, wrought an instant transformation in American attitudes toward the war, introducing, as the second phase of American participation, a year and a half during which American energy increasingly became absorbed in defense of the country and hemisphere. Gradually, the United States was to evolve into the role of non-belligerent ally of the peoples resisting aggression. At first, emphasis centered on our own neglected defenses. That was the period of conscription and of appropriation bills that poured billions into the task. Slowly, with many slips and halts, this country began to forge a modern war machine. Then, as the British bulwark held, the Royal Air Force repelling the *Luftwaffe*, the effort broadened.

By the end of 1940, with the development of lend-lease and the open acknowledgment that America had a stake in World War II wherever fought, this country became, in the President's words, the "arsenal of democracy." It had grown apparent to a substantial majority of Americans that their prestige, well-being, and survival depended upon activity that might not stop short of war. In the hot fires of a historic American debate, ranging across the country, often reckless but essentially democratic, the issue had been resolved long before Pearl Harbor in favor of global defense—of defense at a distance. Meanwhile, the men charged with executing national policy abroad had gone steadily forward, fending off hostilities, actuating alliances, acquiring bases, furthering American interest in the remotest islands of the seas, and, above all, "purchasing time" during which the giant forces of the country might be mobilized for its military defense.

This book deals with what may be termed the defense period, with the broad policies and the men who, for the first time in American history, were obliged to organize this country's foreign relations on a planetary scale. In World War I our diplomacy was chiefly preoccupied with Europe, only slightly with the Far East, with only casual reference to Latin America. The diplomatic problem was as rudimentary as the military, which called for the relatively simple re-enforcement of the Atlantic powers on a stabilized line in the West. In 1940, the hostile, aggressive power of Japan, the new importance of South America, the ambiguities of Russia, and the terrifying demonstration of Nazi might in the West vastly magnified the problem. Moreover, the necessities of June,

1940, required deployment of American influence and interest not only on a world-wide scale but according to a consistent
pattern—a sort of master plan. It is only by reference to this
pattern in its entirety, and as circumstances forced it into new
applications, that prewar policy may be understood.

—6—

An ordinary globe provides a reliable and objective guide
to this planetary story, as well as to America's world relationships in general and specifically her role in World War II.
Such visual aid clarifies and separates the political and strategical problems that confronted this Government in the prewar
period.

Look first at the Atlantic basin. Note how North America
faces Europe, that fated, combative peninsula of Asia, across
a relatively narrow ocean. Observe what Adolf A. Berle, Jr.,
has termed the North Atlantic bridge, an easy air path to
America, with the spans resting on Norway, Iceland, Greenland, and Canada. Southward lies the other half of the American hemisphere, the whole of which constitutes that New
World which, since Monroe spoke in 1823, the United States
has been sworn to shield against the Old. Note that all of
South America, except its West Coast, and including the
Isthmus of Panama, linking the American continents, lies
east of New York, nearer to Africa at one point across the
South Atlantic Narrows than New England is to Europe.

Spin the globe to the Pacific and you detect a geographical
circumstance that still strikes many of us with the force of
novelty. The nearest neighbor of the United States to the
West is not Japan, but Russia. If you proceed toward Asia
by the Great Circle route, the first land you encounter upon
leaving the Aleutians or the Seward Peninsula of Alaska lies
under the flag of the Soviet Union. Nor is that all. Across the
Arctic wastes beyond the top of North America, wastes already

traversed by Russian airmen, our nearest neighbors are the Soviet Union and Scandinavia.

So much for geography, which underlies a nation's history, its strategical necessities, its economic development, and its political relationships with other powers. The complementary nature of geography, strategy, and history is well exemplified by the Monroe Doctrine, the oldest and most cherished of American foreign policies. The Monroe Doctrine rests on the geographical division between Old and New Worlds dictated by the Atlantic Ocean. That geographical separation allowed for a different political evolution in the Americas. History teaches that the Monroe Doctrine's strategical interests have been best served by co-operation between the American republics and whatever power commands the eastern Atlantic and the great sea exits from Europe: the North Sea, the English Channel, and Gibraltar.

The Monroe Doctrine and the theory of the "opposite shore," a synthesis made articulate by German navalists, have made the dignity and security of the Americas depend in large degree on who controls those exits. In the hands of a friendly power, the Atlantic is an inland sea, and has been with British collaboration for a century and a quarter. In hostile hands, the Atlantic becomes a high sea (to use the terminology of the "opposite shore" theorists), the mastery of which would, in all likelihood, be determined only by one or a series of life-and-death struggles. We can thus see why the United States has not remained indifferent, since Napoleon, to any war in Europe that threatened to transfer command of the eastern Atlantic from a politically congenial and satisfied power to an aggressive, potentially inimical power.

From the Monroe Doctrine and its strategical projection, the Atlantic policy of the United States has developed. Twice within a generation that policy primarily has involved us in what many Americans mistakenly regarded as purely European wars.

In our other ocean, the Pacific, the strategical pattern has been the reverse of that in the Atlantic. The western shores of the Pacific are controlled by the Japanese, who for a generation have exhibited imperialistic ambitions hostile to our interests and ultimately to our security as a nation. In other words, the Pacific has been a high sea with an importance that has grown steadily clearer since last December 7. For more than a generation our strategical interest in Asia has required the support of the great continental power, China, against the great sea power, Japan, a situation exactly the reverse of the one we occupy toward Europe. Moreover, sentimental inclinations have followed national interest, creating a strongly sympathetic bond between the American and the Chinese people.

The air arm has developed during this war with such bewildering speed and its potentialities remain so hazy that the strategical lessons of air power still remain fluid. We know enough, however, to conclude that air power confirms and strengthens the validity of the Atlantic policy and its Pacific corollary. Indeed, air power makes it even more necessary for us to maintain some measure of control, either military or political, over distant bases from which this hemisphere may be threatened. Thus, one lesson at least is clear. Air power, added to sea power, widens the defensive overseas arc to which we must give unremitting attention in the future.

The strategical aspects of a country's position, as well as the related long-term policies, are fairly well fixed in the mold of geography. More fluid are the influences of civilization, or the ideological points of reference, as some prefer to call them. The warlike behavior of nations may be determined almost altogether by the fixed factors, yet modern man fights in the name of ideas. This war, many thoughtful observers assert, differs from its predecessors, notably the last one, in that it is a conflict between great, revolutionary movements and not strictly between or among nations. The tides of Communism,

Nazism, and democracy, it is said, strike across national boundaries, giving to World War II some of the aspects of civil strife, making this a "horizontal" as well as a "vertical" struggle and minimizing the importance of nations and national ideas.

We may admit the observations upon which that conclusion rests without accepting the uniquely revolutionary character of these times. The era of Napoleon was also revolutionary. The Corsican conquered partly in the name of the universal, "rights of man" revolution, partly with the aid of "fifth columns," although the term had not been applied, and partly, of course, through the Grand Army. That revolution was more inclusive than the racial sectarianism of the Nazis and the class particularism of the Communists. Moreover, the slogans of that time—"all men are created equal," "life, liberty, and the pursuit of happiness" and "liberty, equality, fraternity"—contained more yeast, they inspired a wider hopefulness throughout the world, than anything yet disclosed by the counterrevolutionaries of Berlin and the doctrinaires of the Kremlin.

In the last war, the West contended against "autocracy," specifically the remnants of that type of political organization under which kings ruled by divine right; and three ancient dynasties, in Russia, Germany, and Austria-Hungary, went down. The soldiers and sailors in this war, moreover, wear the uniforms of national states and do battle under national flags, and, as the war intensifies, we hear less of the peculiar ideologies professed by Germany and Russia and more of those nations as nations. In 1917, we also had enemy aliens active at sabotage, we had conspiratorial diplomats from the Central Powers—Franz von Papen and Dr. Dumba, to name only two —and for the Communists and the New York *Daily Worker* (of the pre-Russian invasion days) we had the "no war" Socialists, the I.W.W., and Victor Berger's Milwaukee *Leader*.

It may be noted also that Germany acts toward the outside

world in much the same way under the Nazis as under the Pan-German Hohenzollerns, although with more unabashed ruthlessness. Russia, exchanging the rigidities of monarchical despotism for the dictatorship of the proletariat, still yearns for warm-water ports, longingly regards the Dardanelles, and hopes for elbow room in the Baltic. Italy remains, under Fascismo as under a parliamentary system, unwarlike, individualistic, and rational, painful as that may be to Mussolini.

Apart from surface change, the United States and Great Britain also remain much the same: loosely organized politically but each tightly knit in national sentiment, proud, stubborn, accustomed to having their way in the world, with a genuinely due regard for the rights of others, and proposing to continue to have that way. There is a hard core of will in the American and British national states, harder and less perishable, it may be, than in any of the others. So much for the vitality of the idea of the national state as against the competing concepts of Hitler's racial state and the class state of the Bolshevik revolution.

In 1939, when the West responded to Hitler's challenge, the Great Powers of the Atlantic basin stood erect, although enfeebled by the undigested, badly administered victory of 1918 and by a crisis in their traditional economic system. Great Britain was a sea power, France was amphibian, and the United States, unchallenged in its hemisphere, stood in relation to the outside world as a sea power.

Of the three other Great Powers of 1939, one was in Europe, one in Asia, and one lay astride both continents. Japan, a samurai state, which had imperfectly applied the political and social lessons of the West, was rapidly returning to *Bushido,* the way of the warrior. Primarily a sea power, Japan also was based on the continent of Asia in Korea, Manchuria, and occupied China. Russia's taproots ran not to the West, but to Byzantium. Since 1917 that great, diversified world of its own known as the Soviet Union had been transforming itself from the absolutism imposed by czarism into a new kind of absolutism arising from below, a huge, all-embracing state organism. The "rights of man" revolution never had gained sway in Russia, which remained in 1917 the most backward of the Great Powers, and the Revolution of that year abandoned the political democracy of the West in favor of the Marxian dogma of the dictatorship of the proletariat. Russia and Germany, both continental powers, had surpassed the sea powers in their development of military aviation.

But Germany was also a special case ideologically, having roots in the West but also in the Teutoburger Forest. Germany never had foresworn her pagan heritage. Incompletely developed, according to the political standards of the West, the German people did not achieve national unity and the modern concept of the nation until 1870. And in 1933, the Nazi party under the zealot Hitler rejected Western culture and tried to bring the German *Volk* back to the atavistic mores of the Saxon tribes.

On the one hand, the laws of geography, strategical necessity, and economic survival still dictate national behavior. On the other hand, civilization is the product not only of material conditions, but also of ideas, and different concepts of civilization created the great divisions of the wartime world of 1940. The West behaved in one way, Japan in another, Germany and Russia in still others. What do we mean by the West? The phrase applies to the civilization descended from Greek rationalism and Roman law, modified by western Christianity and developing through the "social contract" revolutions of the eighteenth and nineteenth centuries into the generally humane, politically free, and socially elastic regimes prevailing in the countries bordering the Atlantic. But in 1939 it seemed that an organic civilization, which recognized certain eternal moral values, had lost its proselytizing, dynamic character. Nevertheless, its inertia in the face of the rude assertiveness of Fascism was not complete enough to justify the epithetical charges of degeneracy hurled from Berlin and Rome.

The primary custodians of that civilization were the Atlantic powers, France, Great Britain, the United States, the Scandinavian countries, Holland, Belgium, the republics of Latin America, and the British Dominions. Italy had forsaken its Western tradition, but all these other peoples professed political democracy and the common religion of the West, whether derived from Rome, Geneva, Canterbury, or Wittenberg; they used the same cultural language and their values were, generally speaking, interchangeable. A certain unity, therefore, linked the Atlantic peoples, a broad harmony of outlook and interest observed years ago by Thomas Jefferson and Simon Bolivar and finally defined in 1906 by Henry Adams as "the Atlantic system."

When sharply challenged, the towering values of the West regained their positive qualities. The free man in the free state, the sovereignty that resides in the citizen, political democracy as the best of social compromises that permits the easy, bloodless play of forces and interests within the state— these things came back into their own. The West took the counteroffensive sometime about 1940. With liberty perishing in wide areas of Europe, with Asia under the heel of reactionary and despotic conquerors, the simple concept of the dignity of the individual which once moved our ancestors stood forth again in its original luster. It is this pattern of civilization to which this book refers when it speaks of the West; it is this to which Mr. Roosevelt and other leaders of the American people appeal in public utterance.

These values are by no means confined to the Atlantic basin. It simply happens that in the Atlantic nations, the civilization of the West has had its freest development and its longest sway, but the ideas informing it have permeated most of Europe, including the Balkan states, where they are again flourishing. In Poland also, which accepted the lessons imperfectly, the ideals of the West have a new meaning. And in Asia, the national state of China, drawing its wisdom and strength from a civilization far older than our own, finds at this moment of its ordeal a far deeper affinity with the civilization of the West than with that of its unneighborly neighbor, Japan. In all countries of all continents, men who prefer liberty to subjection belong to the Western cause.

—7—

The chance that brought Mr. Roosevelt, with Mr. Hull as his principal coadjutor, to the management of foreign policy in time of overweening danger to this country, may be called fortunate. Together they had implemented the Good Neighbor policy. The whole course of American foreign relationships under Roosevelt had been nonaggressive and reassuring to other powers, large and small. Abandoning whatever traces of imperialism, military or financial, lingered in American policy toward the Latin Republics, the Administration withdrew our shadowy protectorates over Cuba and Panama and witnessed the statutory relinquishment of sovereignty over the Philippines at a specified date in the future.

In personal attributes, Mr. Hull's prudent judgments, often expressed in the homely vernacular of the Appalachian frontier, complement the daring self-confidence of the President. If the President has a sure grasp of strategy and international relations on the political plane, the Secretary has given a lifetime of thought to world trade. A modified free trader, a Jeffersonian liberal, Mr. Hull has never foresworn faith in the unhindered movement of goods and persons that contributed to nineteenth-century prosperity and enlightenment. His reciprocal-trade formula was an attempt to beat back the totalitarian tide on the economic level and, although the times overcame some of Mr. Hull's hopes, they failed to shake his faith that the free exchange of goods helps to soften interna-

tional asperities and promotes peaceful ways. He has also an
abiding faith in international law as an essential foundation
of a peaceful world order. By circumstances inexplicable in
terms of Hull's background as country lawyer, judge, Congress-
man, and United States Senator, he has likewise a shrewd understanding of military strategics.

The President takes advice where he finds it, but not all
advisors are equally influential, and the decisions are the President's. During the defense period, the circle of advisors shifted
to meet the changing foreign situation. Henry Morgenthau,
Jr., for example, exerted weight in matters dealing with pro-
curement of supplies for the Allies, being a prime mover in
lend-lease. The Secretary of the Treasury (Henry the Morgue)
also championed the cause of the Chinese in season and out.

Certain advisors, however, remained fairly constantly at
the President's side when foreign policy was uppermost. These
were the regulars and included Mr. Roosevelt's "gray eminence," Harry Hopkins, known as "Buzz" in White House
informality, the Iowa harness maker's son who rose, via a
career in social service, to become a Cabinet member and the
intimate friend of two of the greatest statesmen of his time,
Roosevelt and Churchill. Hopkins, whose judgments are disinterested and delivered to the President with clarity, force,
and corn-belt pith, approximates the role of Colonel Edward
M. House in Woodrow Wilson's time. The frailness of his
health is a source of extreme regret to Mr. Roosevelt. Another
foreign-policy regular was William C. Bullitt, a scion of the
Philadelphia Main Line, a onetime foreign correspondent,
self-assured, brilliant, inclined to dogmatism and the *beau
geste,* but a capable and loyal observer.

At the State Department, Mr. Roosevelt also relied on
Welles and Berle. The Under Secretary, who went directly
from Groton and Harvard (Mr. Roosevelt's schools) to the
State Department, was born of New England stock into the
New York City brownstone aristocracy of the 1890's. His

grandfather's cousin was Senator Charles S. Sumner, of Massachusetts, the intellectual gadfly of the Abolitionists. A diplomatic technician of the first rank, Welles, by his unvaryingly formal manner and his unfailingly correct address, suggests a statesman of the eighteenth rather than the twentieth century —John Jay, for example—and conceals the warmth with which he holds to democratic convictions.

In contrast to the steady-paced Under Secretary, Berle has a far-ranging, inventive, intellectual compass matching the President's in boldness. A product of the German immigration of the middle of the last century, the "blessed forty-eighters," Berle (known to the White House as Dolf) is the son of a Congregational clergyman with advanced ideas on education. The rigid intellectual discipline of his days as a youthful prodigy at Harvard, when he had to wait a year after finishing the work until old enough to qualify for his bachelor's degree, was deepened and mellowed by several years in New York municipal politics as aide to Fiorello H. LaGuardia. One of the last members of the original "brain trust" remaining near the throne, Berle still thinks almost visibly.

But it is Mr. Hull's spirit that informs the State Department. In a foreword to Harold B. Hinton's recent biography of the Secretary, Mr. Welles ranked Mr. Hull among the greatest of America's foreign ministers, the other elect being Jefferson, Madison, John Quincy Adams, Elihu Root, and Charles Evans Hughes.

Behind a rather reserved façade, Hull has a homespun, kindly nature. Like Hopkins, and unlike the four other principal fabricators of foreign policy, Hull springs from the common people. Although his father, "Uncle Billy" Hull, became a man of substance, Cordell was born in a log cabin and grew up in small towns of the Cumberland foothills far from the centers of sophistication. The racy speech of that region and that period still comes easily to Hull after thirty-five years of public service in Washington, and he uses the idioms of "down yonder" by preference when at his ease. It is probable that not one of his predecessors, except possibly Daniel Webster, ever applied such unabashedly forceful and Elizabethan language to the problems of the State Department, and one turns to the John Hay of the *Pike County Ballads* for a similar preoccupation with folk speech.

As for example, Hull assuring the Siamese Minister when he called to express his shame and sorrow over his country's fall: "Never mind, we'll whip the hell out of those fellows yet." In his *mémoire* of the conversation, the Secretary observed that the Minister had called, at his own request, to express his sentiments about the unhappy turn in his country and had been "consoled in appropriate terms." Asked to send a certain diplomat to a troubled spot in Europe, Hull declined on the ground that, amid so much tumult, the man would "twirl around like a goose hit on the head with a corncob."

There is also the favorite White House story about the day on which Mr. Hull startled the Cabinet and disillusioned the President about his sanctity. From the beginning the Roosevelt Cabinet sessions were lighthearted, the President and the members exchanging banter when the business at hand was not too pressing. In this interchange, Mr. Hull took no part, sitting gravely apart, his fine features composed, until the President began to think of him as "saintly, the only saint in the Administration." That impression abruptly was banished one day when a point of foreign policy arose, touching on an evil act of the Nazis. The Secretary stiffened in his chair. "Jesus Kwyst!" he exploded, prefacing an incisive and derogatory comment. The Secretary's lisp and general air of benignity lend an unprofane, otherworldly quality to phrases of the utmost emphasis. On that occasion the President concluded that he had no saint for Secretary of State.

Mr. Hull is at his most warming in the Sunday cracker-barrel sessions. There, among trusted subordinates and friends, he unbends, his dry and subtle humor playing with remarkable appositeness over situations confronting the State Department. When one first hears Mr. Hull expanding a subject, it appears that he is circumlocutory. It is only later and upon examination that the underlying lucidity of his thought patterns becomes apparent. Actually, his method is economical; he dispenses with the obvious and the already understood. As he speaks, his sensitive hands trace their own patterns in the air before him. The motion reminds Berle of weaving; he fancies that the Secretary is weaving the strands of his disquisition carefully into a stout fabric of thought.

Hull's illustrations, almost invariably taken from his Tennessee experiences, go directly to the point. There is his apt comment on sea-power strategy expressed in the classic story of the red flannel undershirt. Mr. Hull used this story—in the best vein of Lincoln in wartime—at a Sunday conference to illuminate a discussion of strategy on two oceans.

"You boys," said Mr. Hull, "remind me of a lawsuit I tried down yonder. It was a will case. One of the lawyers was in the unfortunate position of representing both the legatees and the devisees. When he made a point for the legatees, he was likely to harm the case of the devisees, and vice versa. He got pretty well tangled and when he sat down his opponent announced that he wouldn't put in testimony or make a summation. Instead, he wanted the court's permission to tell a story.

"The story was about a friend of his, who was traveling on a Mississippi river steamboat one night when the boiler blew up. The traveler was thrown from bed, ran on deck, and committed himself to the river, where he swam manfully for the Arkansas shore. As he pulled himself up on the river bank, he discovered to his dismay that he was clad only in a red flannel undershirt. The noise of the explosion and the sight of the burning vessel had drawn a great concourse of men, women, and children to the river bank. The traveler was a modest man. Seeking to hide his seminakedness, he pulled his shirt down in back. But as he did so, it rode up in front, disclosing his

legatees. He then pulled his shirt down in front and it rode
up in back, disclosing his devisees. 'The plight of my unfortunate friend,' said the lawyer, 'reminds me of the difficulties
into which my learned colleague has fallen.'

"It reminds me, gentlemen, of your dilemma: plotting the
strategy of a two-ocean war with a one-ocean navy."

In the division of Department labors, Mr. Hull assumed
primary responsibility for the Far Eastern situation. He conducted the delicate, protracted negotiations with the Japanese. His guidance extended, however, to all fronts of the far-
flung diplomatic campaign of the period. He likewise interpreted foreign policy to this country in speeches and statements, also waging with considerable moral fervor and great
skill political warfare in other countries. From 1934, when
Hitler's intention to rearm became unmistakable, the Secretary steadily warned the nation of the danger of another major
upheaval. Always he deplored "extreme nationalism" and
competitive armaments.

As early as June, 1935, when addressing the graduating class
of the University of Michigan, Mr. Hull cautioned his hearers
that the United States lay in the path of a general war, saying:
"I cannot with a good conscience tell you that as Americans
you are immune from the effects of a possible conflict by being
far removed from its locus, and that you may look without
concern on the darkening clouds around the magic circle of
the United States."

As time passed and aggression spread to Ethiopia and civil
war drenched Spain with blood, Hull's admonitions took on
a sterner tone and in September, 1936, addressing the World
Power Conference, he said fervently: "I spoke . . . of the
great responsibility of governments and peoples to preserve
the peace. In all history, the weight of that responsibility has
never been so great as at this hour." In a succession of speeches
thereafter, condemning the lawlessness of the aggressor nations, he called for military preparedness and avowed this

country's willingness to fight for the survival of its political and cultural values as well as its independence. A man of peace, Hull, who had served in Cuba as a captain of volunteers, has never shrunk from the hard alternative of war if all else failed.

—8—

In submitting this report on the currents and policies culminating in the black Sunday of December 7, we recur to the events of May, 1940, when this country was jarringly awakened to its peril, and what had been in geographical terms a European war became in actuality World War II. The fall of France, as Churchill has indicated, marked one of the great climaxes of the war and one which was scarcely less significant in its effects on the United States than on Europe itself. In the organization of the report, which is not strictly chronological, the story of the American reaction to the defeat of France comes first. Next, in keeping with American preoccupations at that moment, come the measures undertaken in support of this country's determination to keep Britain afloat. As 1940 wore along, other and wider anxieties bore in on the policy makers as well as on the popular consciousness and as wartime foreign policy widened to include Latin America, Russia, the Balkans, Africa, and Japan, this report also broadens its boundaries.

In the last half of 1940, the realities of a global diplomatic strategy assumed form. At that point (Chapter Four) all aspects, all fronts, and all flanks are caught up to sweep along chronologically to the end of the book and the beginning of war. First France, then England, then the world-wide front including France and England: that is the sequence of progression in the story of how war came to America.

CHAPTER TWO

Atlantic Frontier—The Vichy Policy

ON MAY 10, 1940, Hitler opened the war in western Europe, tramping brutally into the Low Countries. That day also Neville Chamberlain, who had misinterpreted Disraeli's prognosis of Europe after the Treaty of Berlin as a promise of peace for times infinitely more complex and tragic,* surrendered the seals of office to George VI, Winston Churchill kissing hands as his successor. Four days later, on May 14, the *Reichswehr* veered into France, making mincemeat of the French Fifth Army at Sedan, and that evening William C. Bullitt guardedly notified President Roosevelt from Paris that, saving a miracle, the jig was up with the Third Republic. Until that moment and before the stark meanings of Sedan were unveiled to the Western world, the deluded democracies still were counting upon the Maginot Line and the French army to absorb and deflect the Nazi *Wehrmacht*.

The road to Paris and German victory in the West, as Bullitt perceived, stood open, and his conclusion rested on exact, expert, and confidential information. All that afternoon the American Ambassador, closeted at the War Ministry with his friend, Édouard Daladier, the Minister, had surveyed the debacle at Sedan through dispatches each more appalling than its predecessor.

Two days later—May 16—before the French Government

---

* In 1878, Lord Beaconsfield had only been required to match skills with Prince Bismarck, a Prussian but also a great European, a man of limited objectives and tinged with the civilization of the West.

had quite worked up the courage to make a clean breast of the disaster, Mr. Roosevelt drove to the Capitol in a drizzle of late spring rain. There, solemnly addressing Congress in emergency session, the President enjoined the American people to "recast" their thinking about defense. From a sobered Congress he asked a mechanized army, setting a distant goal of 50,000 aircraft, with provision for an annual production of like size.

Significantly, the President suggested the necessity of bases from which we might "attack an aggressor on his route before he (himself) can establish strong bases within the territory of American vital interests." Through the address ran intimations of a preoccupation which would grow stronger with Mr. Roosevelt during the prewar period—keeping war at a distance. In effect, the President was announcing that the frontier of the Americas had been beaten back from the Rhine, that now, after Sedan, the Meuse also was gone, and that the line of defense had come to rest somewhere in the Atlantic.

Thus promptly were the implications of Sedan and *Blitzkrieg* in the West reflected in American policy.

Bullitt had gone to the War Ministry at the urgent bidding of Daladier. This was no novelty, the American Ambassador standing on such intimate terms with prewar ministries that certain diplomatic wits insisted he should have a portfolio. Since his transfer from Moscow in 1936, Bullitt had diligently pursued the romantic pattern of American diplomatic behavior in France first traced by his fellow Philadelphian, Benjamin Franklin. Like Thomas Jefferson, he cultivated philosophers. If the aristocratic, peg-legged Gouverneur Morris ineffectually plotted with Marie Antoinette for her escape from the guillotine, the equally aristocratic Bullitt conspicuously dined royalties, including the Duke and Duchess of Windsor. Nor did he neglect the other ranks, for like Franklin, Bullitt had an eclectic circle of friends, knew everyone, went everywhere on both banks, and "meddled" heartily in French politics. So it was that he shared with the War Minister, the melancholy ex-Premier, a former history professor known to his admirers of the Leftist press as the "little bull of the Camargue," the tragic insights of May 14.

The news was unrelievedly bad. From the broken Gamelin at Allied Headquarters and from poor, fat General Corap at Vervins came the now familiar story of *Blitzkrieg*: of Stukas screaming down to the treetops with sirens open, of tough Skoda-built tanks resisting gunfire and spewing white flame, of fifth columnists and a shattered command—an Apocalyptic version of warfare, "hell and sheet lightning," as Mr. Hull divined it to be from a distance of three thousand miles.

As Bullitt and Daladier, surrounded by frightened aides, read dispatches, it was apparent that France for whatever reasons—national fatigue, internal strife, corruption, industrial weaknesses, and obsolete military thought—would not long resist this invasion. The Maginot Line had been flanked in fact as well as spirit, and French ineffectuality in arms, morale, and discipline stood disclosed in every syllable of the reports. At 6 o'clock Gamelin telephoned that he had nothing left— not even reserves—in the 125 miles between the Nazis and Paris. Daladier wept. He knew that Hitler, if he so elected, could take Paris in a day's march before swinging to the sea.

Leaving the War Ministry a little after eight, Bullitt drove dejectedly across the Seine to the Embassy on the Place de la Concorde, through a Paris unaware of its impending fall. To Bullitt that night it seemed that the French had been as much disadvantaged at Sedan as medieval crossbowmen upon first encountering gunpowder. He was struck by the symbolical role of Sedan in the Third Republic, the regime which had arisen seventy years ago out of a French defeat in that locality now being marked for doom after a second Sedan. A month later to the day, the Nazis would be marching, with wooden discipline, down an unscarred Champs Élysées, but tonight no implication of fate touched the terrace cafés, crowded in the warm twilight; traffic was, as usual, dense and noisy, and the news vendor cried only brief and evasive communiqués.

Tomorrow Churchill, fuming over from London, would learn to his horror that the French Army had no "mass of maneuver, or general reserve." Two days later, Paul Reynaud, "the Gamecock," the volcanic little Premier with the face of an Oriental, would take to the air with a partial admission of the devastating implications of Sedan, place Paris under martial law, and deny that the Ministry meditated flight. On the third day, Reynaud was to dismiss Daladier, his deadly rival, from the War Ministry, taking that post himself and installing an enemy of the Third Republic, Marshal Henri Philippe Pétain, as Vice-Premier and military consultant. The next day the demoralized Generalissimo Gamelin, a loyal son of the Republic, would give way to Maxime Weygand, recalled from Syria in the vain hope of staving off military defeat.

All that was veiled tonight, Bullitt bearing secrets shared by few in Paris as he considered how best to place Mr. Roosevelt in possession of the portentous news. Its implications, thought Bullitt, made it too delicate for transmission in the usual coded cablegram, for he had no doubt that somewhere along the line our codes were being broken. Manifestly, the Germans would give much for intimations that members of the French Government were in despair, and, however good their intelligence reports, the Nazis might not yet be certain that Paris lay open to them. Nevertheless, and in spite of the obstacles, the Ambassador thought it imperative to present a definitive picture to Washington without delay.

Too delicate for the cables, the news could not even be entrusted to the "code within a code," which the President and the Ambassador had worked out, proudly believing it all but unbreakable, for transatlantic telephone conversations. A masterpiece of improvisation, the code was based on com-

mon knowledge of facts thought unlikely to be within the
ken of a European "black chamber." *

At length, the Ambassador determined to make use of both
media, cable and telephone, "scrambling" the first by means
of the second. He dictated to Carmel Offie, a legation secretary, a message presenting the situation at Sedan in virtually
its reverse proportions. In this report, the engagement was a
victory for France: the Germans had been hurled back, French
morale, staff work, and fighting effectiveness were of the high-
est, the road to Paris was blocked, and should the Nazis break
through anywhere, they would promptly find themselves
trapped. A faint note of exaggeration informed the vivid, detailed story, which, being coded, went through normal channels to the President.

Bullitt then telephoned the White House, first informing
the President that he had just dispatched an important report
and suggesting that it be studied at once upon receipt. The
Ambassador thereupon began a long, apparently aimless and
lighthearted conversation that seemed to have no serious import. In course of the talk, he managed subtly to convey the
idea to Mr. Roosevelt that his cable should be read precisely
in reverse. The President understood, but it is unlikely that
an unwelcome listener-in could have done so. Thoroughly
alarmed, Bullitt continued to press home the implications of
Sedan. On the next day he cabled the President: "Berle's name-
sake intends to be where you are by Christmas." The Berle in
point was, of course, Adolf A. Berle, Jr.

—2—

The depressing word from Sedan found the President
plunged already into anxiety. The country had watched the

---

* For example, the codemakers at one time made use of a Yale-Harvard base-
ball score; again employing the combined ages of several of the President's
elderly relatives as a means of conveying a quantitative measure.

swiftness of the Nazi advances with vague alarm. Mr. Roosevelt's news was more specific, hence he was more disturbed. Into the oval room poured a stream of messages from the invaded nations and England. All testified to one thing: the weight of the machine at war. Supplementing the dispatches were digests from G-2 (Army Intelligence) of the lessons of Norway and Holland. The Navy, too, had submitted its disquieting studies of the victory of air over sea power at Namsos. Moreover, with the recent Allied withdrawal from Norway, the Nazis were left in undisputed possession of the eastern bridgehead of the North Atlantic bridge by way of Iceland and Greenland.

The President's emergency message of May 16 was a fighting speech, military and strategic rather than political. He first portrayed the nature of war as it had been exhibited to the Scandinavians, the Low Countries, and the French: land war at the rate of two hundred miles a day, lightning attack, parachute troops, plane transports, dive bombers, formidable tanks, and treachery in front and rear, with the fifth column beguiling and betraying the civilian population. It was clear to him that "so-called impregnable fortifications no longer existed."

Moreover, the speed of air warfare, three hundred miles and better an hour, rendered this hemisphere unsafe from a European aggressor. The President drove this home with graphic if hyperbolical illustration, disclosing the vulnerability to air attack of points on this continent. He reckoned that St. Louis, Kansas City, and Omaha were only two and a quarter hours by air from Tampico; from Bermuda a hostile bomber could reach our coastal cities in less than three hours. The Florida coast was a mere two hundred minutes from the outer West Indies. And on the Pacific, Vancouver, Seattle, and Portland lay only four or five hours from our sparsely settled outpost of Alaska. Although Mr. Roosevelt overstressed the speed of war aircraft at the time, there was warrant for believing that the span of bombers might easily approximate these figures if the war lasted two or three years longer.

Underlining this speech, whose historic implications are only now apparent, was the unexpressed fear that France was about to fall. And with France gone, what of England? The call was for aggressive preparedness on the Atlantic line. In February, 1939, the President had confounded a group of Congressional leaders by suggesting that the United States had an interest in the security of the Rhine frontier. Some of his hearers could not digest this bold conception, and, when they whispered the Presidential utterance in garbled form, he issued a brisk denial.

On May 16, the country's strategics were no longer speculative. The President's address revealed our hemispheric responsibility. Only implicit then was the subsequent acquisition of bases in the Atlantic and Caribbean from the British, the Danes, the Icelanders, and the Dutch with which to project our strength offshore. One thing the President was driving home: in the type of war now being fought you could not afford to wait for the enemy to knock at the door.

To effect his recommendations Mr. Roosevelt asked Congress for $1,182,000,000. The President had executed a sharp reversal since January, when his military requests in the annual budget had been the result of compromise, based, he said, "not on panic but on common sense." He had then asked for $1,840,000,000, a median between the "vast sums" sought by "enthusiastic alarmists" and the reductions craved by "unrealistic persons claiming superior private knowledge." Himself anything but an "alarmist" in January, with the European war stalemated, Mr. Roosevelt a bit self-assuredly felt his recommendations "a sufficient amount for the coming year." It was not Mr. Roosevelt who changed between January and May, but events. Before the year was out his requests for defense would exceed ten billion dollars, with Congress hastening to pass each new appropriation as it was evoked by encroaching circumstances.

The President's exigent note matched the popular mood. Partisanship had diminished under the impact of Hitler's invasion of western Europe. At the end of the message of May 16 Representative Joseph W. Martin (R., Mass.), House Minority Leader, announced flatly: "We're for the program." The prevailing view of the press was that Mr. Roosevelt had not gone far enough. Citizens, reading that the War Department could muster only 68,000 troops, without mechanized equipment and with few modern planes, for the "most extensive maneuvers ever held," agreed with the press. It was being said that the Army had only one adequate antiaircraft gun, and Mayor LaGuardia vowed that we could not even defend Coney Island.

While Mr. Roosevelt had refrained from mentioning the dire prospects for France and England, much excited speculation went on at other levels. The possibility that the British Crown and Government might escape to Canada, with the fleet, aroused mixed feelings as rumors spread that a survey of Toronto's office and housing space already was under way. Suddenly multitudes of Americans became conscious of the British and French fleets and of their significance to our defense, and in the columns of military and political commentators talk began to appear of the desirability of offshore bases.

"These," said the President, "are ominous days." It was generally so agreed. The "Munich mood" swiftly was vanishing in the light of the day's headlines. Late in 1939 Bullitt, home on leave, found irritating the country's indifference to events abroad. "The United States," he complained, "is still in the state of mind of England before Munich." There was little of Munich or of the "phony war" cynicism of the preceding winter in evidence when the President, patently weary, read his defense message to the joint session. The moment was so fraught with decision that women in the packed galleries wept, and members of both houses seriously applied themselves to the words of warning as the President, himself a sinner, called the country to repentance for its slackness and frivolity.

There were, quite naturally, dissenting voices. United States Senator Burton K. Wheeler (D., Mont.), addressing an antiwar rally in Washington, deplored what he termed the "mad hysteria [which] grips many of our people, a hysteria created in New York and . . . Washington." And Colonel Charles A. Lindbergh, in a radio address, charged the Administration with inspiring a "hysterical chatter of calamity and invasion," observing that the outcome of the European war was no business of ours. To which *The New York Times* retorted that Lindbergh was "a blind young man if he really believes we can live on terms of equal peace and happiness 'regardless of which side wins this war.' "

As for the public, there could be no doubt which way the wind blew. The instruments for measuring the winds of public opinion devised by Dr. George Gallup estimated (1) that 84 per cent of the citizens sampled wished England and France to win the war, only 1 per cent favored Germany, and 14 per cent had little or no preference; (2) that 65 per cent believed Hitler would carry the war to us should he destroy the sea power of the western European powers; (3) that majorities of 86, 88, and 91 per cent supported enlargement of the Army, Navy, and Air Force respectively; (4) and that by June 65 per cent expected the United States to be in the war before its end.

By an understandable dualism encountered throughout the prewar period, fewer than 10 per cent, however, thought we should send an army to Europe to affect the war's outcome, although 64 per cent recognized that a Nazi victory would affect their personal fortunes. As recently as March only 32 per cent had seen themselves personally involved. The people, manifestly, had no illusions regarding the identity of the enemy or his nature, although, when given the chance to vote on the abstract issue of war or peace, they overwhelmingly expressed a preference for peace, much as they would have plumped for health over sickness, riches over poverty. In every test of sentiment on concrete alternatives the same public invariably supported concrete measures in behalf of the warring democracies and to extend defenses outside our borders. Some of these were warlike. The public-opinion polls always reflected a substantial majority, usually about two to one, opinion in favor of the Government's foreign policy. This difference between the subjective and objective will of the people baffled and finally discountenanced the isolationists.

Alive to their danger, the people plainly wished something "short of war" done about it. Fortunately, something was being done, abroad as well as at home.

—3—

Once convinced of French doom, Bullitt looked about in Paris to salvage what he could for his own country. An intense partisan, the Ambassador loved France, and, happily for him, the interests of the Third Republic coincided, in defeat, with those of the United States. His post-Sedan cables and telephone talks with the President hammered, therefore, on the three great assets that might still be retained by the Republic. These were the fleet, virtually unharmed by battle and the second in Europe; the overseas empire, capable of being screened by sea power, even if the mother country were overrun; and, thirdly, such gold bar and bullion as remained in the Bank of France, a potential loot of incalculable value to a blockaded conqueror.

The fleet was mobile. It could be placed out of reach of the landlocked Nazis; it could enter the service of the ally Britain or take refuge in American ports.* Whatever move this power-

---

* These ports were repeatedly to be offered.

ful armada made, the balance of sea power would be gravely altered. In German hands, united with their fleet and the, as yet, untested and uncommitted Italian Navy, the French Fleet might rob England of her command of the Atlantic, set aside the blockade, and accomplish British defeat. To Bullitt and the Administration such a prospect was highly disconcerting. And, taking a longer and more frightening view, if Britain surrendered, entering the Axis bloc, and her vast fleet were to be added to the aggregate weight of the Continental powers, the United States might not find harbors remote enough in which to shield her battleships.

As for the overseas empire, it included excellent ports suitable for naval operations, such as Casablanca in Morocco, fronting the open Atlantic, and the first-rate stronghold of Dakar in West Africa, opposite the bulge of Brazil across the South Atlantic narrows. By a tradition dating back to the Algeciras conference in 1906, we have opposed having Germany as a transatlantic neighbor. To continue with the dread possibilities of May, 1940, it was clear that French North Africa in Nazi hands would destroy British control of the western Mediterranean.

Urgently, the Ambassador besought the President to take steps to preserve these assets for the Atlantic cause or, at least, to keep them out of Axis hands. Fortunately for the enterprise, the same considerations had been moving the appropriate parties in Washington. The Navy high command was exhibiting a healthy concern. At the State and Treasury Departments, both sensitive to the economic aspects of total war, the midnight oil was being burned over the statistics of colonial France. All spring this Government had watchfully encouraged the movement of gold in bulk out of the Allied war zone to New York, to Montreal, and to a cache in French West Africa. In the first half of 1940, a half-billion dollars had come to this country for safekeeping and to meet war bills. At the White House, the President and those of his advisors who think strategically had been conning maps, noting where French possessions flanked shipping routes, and spotting harbors on which submarines might be based.

It should not be thought that in May the defense councils were perfectly articulated. Although on May 16 Mr. Roosevelt had committed this country to the "protection of the whole American hemisphere against invasion or control or domination by non-American nations," some sections of the Army General Staff still shrank from taking responsibility below the equator, holding defense of the "quartersphere" to be the limit of our military capacity at that time. In Congress and elsewhere men were beseeching the Administration for "a plan." What and where were we to defend?

Indicative of the opaque thinking of the moment, Treasury experts thought themselves bold for suggesting that the Government might have to spend as much as ten billions for defense by the end of 1942.

The defense program was to evolve, slowly and pragmatically, out of circumstances. Today Mr. Roosevelt is the first to observe that the magnitude of the impending task dawned on him only by degrees. Except for his recommendation for 50,000 aircraft on May 16, which he jocularly regards as somewhat inspired, the major steps came as events forced re-evaluations of the Axis power. All hands, however, toward the end of May agreed on the advisability of saving that which might be salvaged out of the disaster in France.

So on May 26 the President cabled Bullitt to acquaint Premier Reynaud and Foreign Minister Daladier with this Government's profound concern over the French Fleet and bases in the unhappy contingency of defeat. This was three weeks before Pétain sued for a truce. Our interest, it was pointed out, arose from sympathy with the cause for which the French were bleeding. We presumed to speak because of the claims of ancient and unbroken friendship. The message was both precise and firm.

Bullitt needed no prodding. The task of obtaining from an embattled Government promises predicated on its imminent defeat would ordinarily be most delicate—a good bit like approaching a man moderately ill about what to do with the remains. But France's malady was more than moderate. On the day of the President's telegram, Reynaud was in London pleading for a "miracle." Two days later Leopold was to surrender the Belgian Army, ending effective resistance in the Low Countries, and the ordeal of Dunkirk, though not its glory, was in sight.

Moreover, the French Ministry had been considering these questions more intensively than any non-Frenchmen. With President Albert Lebrun, Reynaud, and Daladier, Bullitt had no need to labor his case. Pétain, whose negative influence was being felt more and more as the clouds darkened, readily agreed when the Ambassador pointed out that France, with her Navy, whether still at war or having yielded to the blows, was still virile; and that without a Navy France would be a "eunuch." Likewise in agreement was Admiral Darlan, the Minister of Marine, who still loved the Navy more than he hated the British.

From all these—Reynaud, Daladier, Lebrun, Pétain, and Darlan—came categorical pledges, oral but solemn, promptly transmitted by Bullitt to Washington. Within the month the first three were to vanish from power, with Daladier facing trial, but the others remained. All pledged their personal honor. None placed a higher value on his word than Pétain: none was more explicit than Darlan, who vowed that he would himself scuttle the vessels first. "And you may tell your President that," the Admiral added by way of emphasis.

So much for the fleet.

On May 29, the U.S. cruiser *Vincennes* sailed from Norfolk, Virginia, with the destroyers *Truxton* and *Simpson* for Casablanca, under orders to pick up a cargo of gold and return to New York. The squadron, under command of Captain (now

Rear Admiral) J. R. Beardsall, later the President's naval aide, reached Casablanca on June 9, took on $241,000,000 in metal, and departed the next day. A fabulous cargo, the gold had been sent out of harm's way at the suggestion of Bullitt. A sizable political nest egg, which, along with gold held to French account in Canada, London, and elsewhere and the quarter of a billion dollars sequestered in the harbor of Martinique,* awaits the establishment of a government acceptable to the United Nations. It may be surmised that this foreign-held gold, which may amount to two billion dollars, is never wholly absent from the calculations of such patriotic statesmen, factionalists, and adventurers as dream of organizing postwar France.

These paragraphs have disclosed the genesis of United States policy toward France since Sedan: a policy which, subsequently labeled the Vichy policy, has been among the most difficult ever pursued by this Government and one of the most widely misunderstood. It began, as we have seen, in a desire to salvage for the Atlantic powers what might be left within France's grasp. It has remained, as we shall see, in large part a salvage operation.

—4—

The disintegration of French hopes and spirit went on rapidly after Dunkirk. Having cleared the Low Countries and established command of the Channel shore of France, Hitler could now strike at Paris and the south. The respite for Paris was about at an end, a circumstance well known to the Ministry. On the first of June, Reynaud and Lebrun asked Bullitt if he would stay behind if and when the Ministry fled and hand over the capital to the Germans whenever they reached a dangerous proximity, should the Government not elect to defend Paris.

* This shipment also was bound for New York at Bullitt's urging, when the armistice brought new orders.

Bullitt received the proposal hospitably. It gratified the romantic part of his nature; furthermore, it accorded with tradition. No American envoy ever had deserted Paris in an urgent hour. Gouverneur Morris braved the Terror, being the only chief of mission to do so. Minister Elihu Washburne endured a horse-meat diet and the excesses of the Commune in 1871, and Myron T. Herrick, of course, had refused to leave when the Ministry hurried, unnecessarily as it turned out, to Bordeaux in 1914. Bullitt cabled the request, along with a suggestion that Anthony J. Drexel Biddle, the Ambassador to Poland, then in Paris as a refugee, be designated to follow the French Government. Contrary to reports published at the time, the White House and State Department did not forbid Bullitt to remain in Paris, hence he did not disobey orders; but the judgment of Mr. Roosevelt and Mr. Hull opposed that procedure. Both felt that Bullitt should hang on to the Ministry until all hope of keeping it in the war, either at home or in the colonies, had vanished.

On June 3 Paris was subjected to its first air attack, 240 lives being lost and bombs dropping near the American Ambassador, who, at luncheon with the Air Minister, went to a roof balcony to see the show. Five bombs struck within a radius of one hundred yards of the building, and another bomb lodged in the ceiling of the room where the Air Minister and Ambassador were, exploding an hour later and wrecking the room. Two days later the awaited drive on Paris began. Meanwhile, the Ambassador had been forwarding appeals for assistance from Reynaud to the President, the pitch of which arose in intensity with the state of panic in Paris.

In Washington, Berle and others, at the President's instance, were figuratively scraping the barrel of reserve war materials for dispatch to the beleaguered Allies. On the 5th, the day the Nazis headed for Paris, the White House announced the availability of "vast stocks" of World War rifles, field guns, and ammunition. Also under way was the technique for the "trading in" of Army and Navy aircraft to its makers, for immediate resale to Britain and France. Actually, only 500,000 rifles (Lee-Enfields) with one hundred rounds apiece, fewer than a thousand .75's, and a couple of hundred planes were dispatched as a result of this emergency pressure, and France fell before even this scanty help could arrive.

This contribution had its value, no doubt, as a gesture, and the willingness to perform a neighborly act in time of distress may have heartened the hard-pressed English. As for the United States, the hurried provision of weapons out of our small store marked another step on the road from neutrality to involvement in England's war with the Nazi-ruled Continent.

By an arresting coincidence, the White House announcement of the surplus arms sale followed by one day Winston Churchill's magnificent burst of defiance to the Germans in his report to the House of Commons on Dunkirk, wherein he concluded:

> We shall defend our island whatever the cost may be; we shall fight on beaches, landing grounds, in fields, in streets, and on the hills. We shall never surrender and even if, which I do not for the moment believe, this island or a large part of it were subjugated and starving, then our empire beyond the seas, armed and guarded by the British fleet, will carry on the struggle until in God's good time the New World, with all its power and might, sets forth to the liberation and rescue of the old.

This speech, so inspiriting to the English-speaking world in general, carried a special implication to the United States, and Churchill's promise to withdraw the fleet and fight on overseas was taken here at face value. It served to relieve American anxiety and, as much as any one utterance of the war, encouraged a sense of solidarity with Britain. In the Government the declaration had the standing of a unilateral pledge and only three months hence, as we shall see, its renewal was

confidently asked for by Mr. Hull. Incidentally, the Prime
Minister's faith in the eventual re-enforcement of his cause by
the New World grew, it may be stated here, out of a conviction that would not vary or weaken after the reduction of the
Low Countries.

—5—

On Sunday, June 9, the Germans, proceeding deliberately
toward Paris, were only a half-hour away by motor. Sometime
before this date the American Ambassador had asked the Archbishop of Paris, Monsignor Beaussart, to consecrate a new
altar in the church at Domremy adjoining the birthplace of
Joan of Arc. Funds for the altar had been provided by Bullitt
and Catholic and non-Catholic friends in the United States.
Conceiving that it might be his last demonstration of Franco-
American cordiality before the inundation, Bullitt was determined to carry through. The Archbishop likewise wished to
persevere. Accordingly, over the protests of the War Ministry
but with a motorcycle escort provided by Reynaud, at 6 A.M.
the Ambassador and Archbishop, with their staffs, motored out
of Paris for Domremy, where Bullitt made a speech attesting his
faith that France would survive her trials. Reynaud had been
fearful that the Nazis might swoop down on Domremy during
the visit, but they did not arrive until 1 A.M. of the 10th.

Upon returning to Paris at nightfall of June 9, the Ambassador found the Cabinet discussing its early departure.
Joining the Ministers at the Élysée Palace, he passed most of
the night there as the debate raged, receiving the instructions
that were to guide him during the transition period when he
was to embody the Third Republic's civil authority in the
capital. A decision was reached early in the morning, and on
the 10th the Government, accompanied by truckloads of official papers, streamed out of Paris for Tours. A number of
ministers and subordinate functionaries of state found time

to bid their adieus at the Embassy. The last to call was Léon Blum. This was at 5:30 P.M.

Before setting out for Tours, Reynaud addressed to President Roosevelt the first of two despairing, last-minute appeals for help. The message, imploring the President for a public declaration of "material support by all means 'short of an expeditionary force,'" referred to Italy's declaration of war. "This very hour," said the Prime Minister, "another dictatorship has stabbed France in the back." Like a ghoul, Mussolini had struck that morning.

The sincerity of Reynaud's plea has been called into account by friend and foe. Did he believe there still was a chance to stay the invasion? Or was his Macedonian cry an attempt to shift part of the responsibility for disaster upon Roosevelt and, by implication, Bullitt? Was it merely diversion politics, designed to sustain the home front? Reynaud still insisted he would carry on the fight, assuring the President:

> We shall fight in front of Paris; we shall fight behind Paris; we shall close ourselves into one of our provinces to fight and if we should be driven out of it, we shall establish ourselves in North Africa to continue the fight, and, if necessary, in our American possessions.

Those words, reminiscent of Churchill, disclosed no dilution of will. Reynaud had sent General Charles de Gaulle, his protégé at the War Office, into Brittany to survey the probabilities of a successful defense of that peninsular reach into the Atlantic. At the moment Reynaud and De Gaulle may have believed a retreat and last-ditch stand possible there, with another Dunkirk at Brest if they failed. This explains the reference, hitherto unspecific, to Reynaud's promise "to close ourselves into one of our provinces. . . ." But the General Staff was to veto the Brittany venture, as Pétain and Laval were to block the retirement to North Africa.

In the hasty bustle of departure, Reynaud found his own

facilities for coding and transmitting the message unequal to the task and he asked the American Embassy to perform the chore for him. The message, timed at 6 P.M., Paris, was delayed, reaching the White House at 10:13, being handed to the President on his return from Charlottesville, Virginia, where, in addressing the University of Virginia graduating class, he had uttered the famous and startling condemnation of Mussolini: "On this tenth day of June, 1940, the hand that held the dagger has stuck it into the back of its neighbor."

Awaiting the President at the White House were Hopkins and Berle. The Assistant Secretary of State had taken to the White House the draft of a neutrality proclamation covering the new war situation. Upon Mr. Roosevelt's arrival, Hopkins and Berle joined him in the doctor's office in the White House basement, where Rear Admiral Ross T. McIntire, the President's physician, administers remedies to the White House family and staff. While Admiral McIntire sprayed the President's throat to ease an irritation brought on by speaking, Hopkins commented on the parallel reference to a stab in the back in Reynaud's belated appeal. Mr. Roosevelt was in high spirits, rejoicing that he had "for once said exactly what I think of an evil action." Sumner Welles vainly had sought to excise the phrase from the speech, but Mr. Roosevelt, his patience exhausted, his Dutch up, had insisted on retaining it.

Welles wished to keep ajar a door he himself had helped to open in a manner not heretofore divulged. On his final visit to Rome in March the Under Secretary had re-established direct contact between the President and *Il Duce,* renewing communications broken since November, 1938. From March until June 10, Roosevelt and Mussolini had been steadily in personal and secret contact. Welles brought back from Rome a characteristic message from Mussolini, boasting that because of his determination not to enlarge the conflagration, two hundred million persons in the Mediterranean basin still were at peace, and the President had labored long and earnestly to hold the Italian dictator in the path of rectitude. Offering his mediation to London and Paris on behalf of Italy's aspirations and grievances, he had further pledged this Government's influence to bring Italy to the peace table with the same weight and authority as a neutral as she might have as a victorious belligerent.

All these generous attempts at appeasement, and others, had been outbalanced by the thuggish might of the Germans, Mr. Roosevelt's olive branch failing to carry the same conviction as Hitler's club. A part of the President's anger on June 10 stemmed from his intimate knowledge of the sheer unreasonableness, the senselessness of Mussolini's war; the President being so well aware that *Il Duce* could have obtained every legitimate advantage for the Italian people without war. Welles' reasons for withholding the insult were purely pragmatic. He saw a certain advantage in having the President still able to communicate directly with Mussolini at the moment of French defeat and when Britain's fate was still unresolved: an advantage he was unwilling to exchange for a phrase. To Welles, as to Roosevelt, it was obvious that the "dagger" sentence would automatically break the line.

In Rome, William Phillips, our Ambassador, had seen *Il Duce* for the last time on June 8. The news Phillips brought from a forty-five-minute interview and committed to the cables was bad. A cautious and correct career diplomat, he had reviewed the President's placatory proposals, including his pledge to work for "a more liberal international economic system, assuring equality of opportunity in world markets." Mussolini, while cordial, was remote. He made it clear that he had certain aspirations to consider, certain promises to redeem. When the Ambassador spoke of America's potential might, *Il Duce* smiled condescendingly. The United States, he was indifferently sure, had neither the arms nor the will with which to oppose the Axis. Phillips felt certain Mussolini intended moving at once.

"You do not appreciate," the dictator protested, as he had to Phillips before, "the power of the Germans. They are the most formidable people in the world." The American Ambassador was not again to be received at the Palazzo Venezia. Mr. Roosevelt's searing characterization of Italy's entrance into the war was withheld from the Italian people, and among the Fascist hierarchy only Count Ciano, the Foreign Minister and *Il Duce*'s son-in-law, commented loftily to the Ambassador. "That was rather a harsh reference of your President's," was all he said.

Over that week end the President's determination was hardened, his enormous energies stimulated by the blow he saw about to descend. With Italy, one of the rich, primary sources of Western culture, about to link forces with the enemies of the Western World, the future took on an even darker hue. Nor was it relieved by the realization at the White House that the Italian people themselves had no stomach for war. Austria, Czechoslovakia, Poland, Denmark, Norway, and the Low Countries had gone down. Now France, and soon the full wrath of the Nazis would be visited on England. The President dictated a draft of his Charlottesville speech on Sunday, conscious of the death toll of the European countries of our tradition, in full expectation that Italy would march against that tradition. On Monday morning, the expectation having been turned into reality, he added the finishing touches.

Although it was the damning "dagger-in-the-back" phrase that splashed across the headlines, sharpening the public consciousness, the rest of the Charlottesville speech contained more meat for students of the prewar period. At Charlottesville, the President first committed the country to wholehearted assistance to those fighting the "gods of force and hate," identifying their cause with ours. Up to that time there had been generalized approval: ways had been opened for the purchase of supplies; the President had promised Reynaud publicly and the British through diplomatic channels to redouble production on their orders. Now he was sending forth "our prayers and our hopes to those beyond the seas who are maintaining with magnificent valor their battle for freedom," but he also pledged now a full effort, saying:

> In our . . . American unity, we will pursue two obvious and simultaneous courses; we will extend to the opponents of force the material resources of this nation and, at the same time, we will harness and speed up the use of those resources in order that we in the Americas may have equipment and training equal to the task of any emergency and every defense.

With the entrance of Italy, "once more the future of the nation, the future of the American people," was at stake. The President had come a long way since May 16, when he merely expressed the wish in passing that the people would not demand a curtailment of the munitions flowing to the Allies. The seeds of lend-lease were in the Charlottesville speech, and soon Virginio Gayda, Mussolini's mouthpiece, would be proclaiming this "an Anglo-Saxon war."

During the talk in the White House doctor's office with Hopkins and Berle, it was suggested that at Charlottesville the President had taken a fairly firm grasp on the leadership of the democratic world. The situation might rapidly evolve, said Berle, into a clear-cut world division, with Roosevelt confronting Hitler as the leader of the free, civilized peoples, and with all other national leaders as *Gauleiters*. The President regarded this thought seriously. "That would," he said, "be a terrible responsibility." There are those among the Presidential circle who believe that the decision to run for a third term may have crystallized that night.

—6—

General Henri Dentz, military governor, and Ambassador Bullitt delivered Paris to the Germans on June 14. General

von Studnitz, commanding the second German forces to occupy the city within seventy years, arrived at the Porte de Saint-
Denis, the northwest gate, on the night of the 13th. There he
was met by a representative of the Ambassador, asking him to
delay his entrance until dawn. Studnitz, whom Bullitt had last
met at a dinner party in Warsaw, agreed—to the Ambassador's
surprise.

At 10 A.M. on the 14th, the arriving general, booted, spurred,
staffed, and exuding *Junkerissimo,* called at the embassy. Bullitt had prepared his requests under three headings: (1) those
which had clear sanction of international law; (2) those with
shadowy legal standing; and (3) those he preferred solely on
humanitarian grounds. Studnitz put his O.K. on all three lists.
His behavior and that of his forces, just then pouring along
the Champs Élysées, lacked nothing in correctness.

Bullitt's lot from the 10th to the 14th had not been a happy
one. The British Embassy and consular officers had followed
the Ministry to Tours, leaving a good proportion of the seven
thousand Britons in France under the protection of the American Embassy. Foreseeing the emergency, the Ambassador had
provided $25,000 in gold from his personal funds and a million
francs in Embassy funds for the relief of the stranded, both
British and American.* A volunteer staff supplemented the
American Foreign Service officers in the job of helping the
British toward the coast and home.

But this, after all, only consumed time and energy. There
was a far more grievous strain on the civil authority. On the
morning of the 13th General Hering, the French military commander, declared Paris an open city, withdrawing his troops.
General Dentz remained as military governor, but with no
forces, his staff consisting only of a captain and a sergeant. Only
the *gendarmerie* and police were left and, after consultation

---

* Through the intervention of the Marquess of Lothian, Ambassador to the
United States, he was subsequently reimbursed by the British Government
for expenditures in its behalf.

between Bullitt and Roger Langeron, prefect of police, those peace officers were disarmed.

The white batons of the police thereupon became the only symbols of authority in all Paris. At this moment a secret radio station, purporting to speak in the name of the outlawed Communist party, began to broadcast each half-hour a blood-chilling appeal to the "citizens of Paris" to arise, seize weapons, slay the *bourgeoisie,* and pillage their houses and shops. Langeron ordered a fruitless search for the station as Bullitt, suspecting that it might be a Nazi device to make the appearance of their forces less odious, prepared to defend the Embassy. Whatever the source of the incitement to insurrection, the Ambassador's observations of fifth-column activities by French Communists during the month-long battle of France left him with a deep aversion to the conspiratorial talents of the Third International. Happily, Paris did not take to the streets, and the final hours of Bullitt's custodianship passed without civil disorder. The Ambassador remained in Paris until June 30, caring for Americans and stranded British and other Allied nationals. In those troubled days, the flag over the American Embassy furnished to such Frenchmen as mourned the Republic almost the sole reassurance in all Paris.

Twice Bullitt was able to telephone Ambassador Biddle in Tours: once on the 13th, after Reynaud's final appeal to President Roosevelt, in which Churchill collaborated, for "clouds of airplanes," with which to stem the military defeat that everyone in France now felt in his bones. Reynaud, cruelly offering his people a final ray of hope he must have known to be false, read this message on the radio. Bullitt's second call came, through a lapse in Nazi efficiency, after the occupation.

The little Touraine city was by no means suitable for a capital. The Ministry huddled in a château on the Loire while in the city hapless government functionaries, diplomats, refugees, enemy agents, and their consorts milled about under occasional bombings. Mr. Churchill arrived on the morning of the 13th with Viscount Halifax, the Foreign Minister, and Lord Beaverbrook, Minister for Aircraft Production. They found the airport deserted in fear of the *Luftwaffe* and no official present to receive them.

Reynaud had promised to produce the Prime Minister at the château for a conference with the Cabinet, but they conferred instead, on Reynaud's motion, secretly in the town. The French Premier was seeking release from the Anglo-French treaty forbidding a separate peace, which he had himself signed a few weeks earlier. Churchill temporized, proposing that Reynaud again solicit help from America; if that proved fruitless, the Premier might again raise the point. The British Ministers made strong representations regarding the disposition of the fleet, on behalf of themselves and the United States, the two Governments having largely concerted their interest in this matter. At Tours, the diplomats accredited to the French Government saw Ministers with difficulty, but Biddle continued, as he could, to remind them of the pledges of Paris.

The bombings drove the Ministry to Bordeaux: a hot, dusty motor pilgrimage across France to the Atlantic. Here and there the highways were thronged with other pilgrims: hungry, tired refugees from the Netherlands, Belgium, Paris, and northern France. As motorcycle details made way for Reynaud's car, flying the tricolor, some of the refugees cheered, crying: "We'll fight on!" But Camille Chautemps, a former Premier and with Pétain then a Vice-Premier, observed that others clenched their fists and spat in the road as the official cars passed. As Chautemps recalls it, the journey to Bordeaux was an unhappy experience. Unhappier ones were to follow.

All the reactionary forces in France seemed concentrated in Bordeaux. The men of the Third Republic, the Leftists, from the bourgeois Radical Socialists through to Blum's fractional Socialists, were in eclipse, as were the stanch nationalist Rightists. Most in evidence were the notorious friends of the enemy, the "hooded men," the proto-Nazis such as Pierre Laval and the onetime Socialist mayor of Bordeaux, a dentist named Adrien Marquet.

Within the Ministry, meeting at the prefecture, Marshal Pétain renewed his threat to resign unless an armistice was sought at once. Chautemps, a clever parliamentarian with the subdued, bookish presence of a country schoolmaster, reports that he countered by proposing that the Ministry ask President Roosevelt or the Pope to sound Germany independently on its disposition toward France in case of surrender. Pétain overrode that compromise. He and Laval preferred to approach the Nazis through the Marshal's friend and former pupil at Saint-Cyr, General Franco.

The resolve of certain stalwart leaders to carry on the war in northern Africa collapsed finally on the 16th. Lebrun, ex-Premier Édouard Herriot, then President of the Chamber, and others, had papers and effects packed for departure for Algiers. There were military men, of De Gaulle's rather than Pétain's generation, ready to go with them. A number of politicians already were in the colonies or en route. It was then that Laval produced a coup. Recruiting a dozen or more defeatist Senators and Deputies, he waited upon Lebrun, threatening the President of France, in effect, that if he led a Ministry to Africa he might never again set foot on his home soil. The perverse moral force of Laval then and there broke the back of the African venture. Reynaud, the aggressive little Premier, earlier had lost heart for northern Africa, the corrupting influence of his constant companion, Countess Hélène des Portes, and her defeatist clique, having paralyzed his will in the last days.

A body of opinion in high American circles, including Hull and Welles, maintains that Bullitt, had he retired with the Ministry to Tours and Bordeaux, could have prevented that decision and the suit for an armistice. Bullitt's influence with the Ministry was profound, the secret forces motivating French political behavior lay open to him, and, above all, he would have had behind him the still enormous prestige of the United States, which was so unmistakably on the side of continuing the war. These authorities believe that Bullitt, as no other non-Frenchman might, would have been able to surmount the evil counsels of Laval and the moral exhaustion of Pétain. Certainly Bullitt's decision was historic and fateful.

Churchill's offer to merge the British and French Empires, with common citizenship and a Frenchman at the head of the united war effort, was rejected on the 16th almost without discussion. Reynaud telephoned the British Prime Minister, pronouncing Roosevelt's reply to his final message of the 13th unsatisfactory and renewing his request for release from the treaty. The President, in a sympathetic cable dispatched on the 14th, had bespoken the admiration of the American people for the "resplendent courage" of the French armies, had recalled the inadequate but not inconsiderable flow of aircraft, guns, and munitions which had gone forward to the Allies, and had promised that if France continued to resist this Government would "redouble its efforts." Included was a significant pledge that the United States would "not consider as valid any attempts to infringe by force the independence and territorial integrity of France." "Only the Congress," the President reminded Reynaud, could make military commitments—a fact well known to the French Government. Yet, the collaborationists, during the long diplomatic struggle revolving around Vichy, were to charge Mr. Roosevelt with "betraying" France in her final hours.

On the 16th, Churchill and the Cabinet agreed to a breach of the treaty on condition that the French Fleet "be dispatched to British ports and remain there while the negotiations [for an armistice] are conducted." The Prime Minister was on a train, beginning a land-air journey to Bordeaux, when word reached him that Reynaud had resigned, Pétain succeeding. Returning to London, he telephoned Pétain at Bordeaux, reminding him of the above condition. Churchill thereupon sent

A. V. Alexander, First Lord of the Admiralty; Admiral Sir
Dudley Pound, First Sea Lord; and Lord Lloyd, Colonial Minister, to Bordeaux to watch over the British stake in fleet and
colonies.

At Bordeaux, with everything "fusing into collapse," in
Churchill's phrase, the British Ministers received "many
solemn assurances" that the fleet never would fall into German hands: assurances similar to those being conveyed through
Biddle to Washington, but without the background carefully
established by this Government in May. Believing that "the
safety of Great Britain, and the British Empire's, is powerfully,
though not decisively, affected by what happens to the French
Fleet," Mr. Churchill was downcast by the paper character of
the assurances. He gravely doubted that the Germans would
refrain from seizing the French vessels within grasp.

To the French, beset by panic, the British and American
concern may have seemed academic. Pétain sued for a truce
on the 17th in the profound conviction that England also
would yield to superior might. Cheerfully, Laval assured everyone that Britain soon would be a "grease spot." In Bordeaux
it was taken for granted that the War in the West would be
at an end by midsummer. In which event, what did it matter
about the fleet? Only let it be in French ports and manned
by Frenchmen? This belief in the impending fall of England,
a pessimistic view conforming to Pétain's nature, was at Tours
and Bordeaux an implement of persuasion in the hands of the
Lavals, already cogitating plans for a partnership with Berlin.

At Bordeaux, the substitute Ambassador, "Tony" Biddle,
never lost sight of this Government's objectives—the fleet and
bases. Periodically, he saw Reynaud and Darlan. "Our people," as Mr. Hull once put it, "kept calling on them, hour by
hour." On the 17th, Biddle transmitted to Pétain and Darlan
a strong reminder from Washington of this Government's
concern, together with a hint that the French Admiralty dis-
pose its strength at the ends of the Mediterranean so that,

should the Nazis prove intractable, the ships might easily escape into the Atlantic and Red Seas. Again the hospitality of New World harbors was tendered the French.

Pétain assured Biddle that the armistice commissioners would, under no circumstances, allow physical control of fleet and bases to pass from French hands. This allayed but did not remove the apprehensions of London and Washington. In 1918, Germany's fleet was interned; in 1919, delivered by order of the Versailles treaty to the British, it was scuttled by them at Scapa Flow. Who could be sure that the Germans, in memory of that, might not demand the fleet at once on pain of ravaging all France?

For whatever cause, whether or not as the result of Biddle's representations, on June 22, when the armistice was signed in the historic railway car in the forest of Compiègne, the fleet was disposed at the ends of the Mediterranean, at Mers-el-Kebir (Oran) in the west and at Alexandria in the east, with only nominal strength in the home base at Toulon.

—7—

Although concern over the French Fleet loomed first in the thought of London and Washington, the fate of the overseas empire was scarcely less engrossing. From a strictly American point of view, the colonies in northern and western Africa were of major strategical importance, with French Indo-China, flanking the Japanese path to Singapore, the Indies, and the Indian Ocean, second. But from a wider view of the Atlantic powers' global necessities, the French mandate over Syria and Lebanon had likewise to be taken into urgent account.

A glance at a map will show the pivotal position of the French Levant, lying, roughly, between Turkey and the British strongholds of Palestine and Egypt, in any Nazi scheme for capture of Suez and the oil fields of Iraq and Persia. Syria in Nazi hands would vastly enhance Britain's Middle Eastern difficulties and, it was then thought, should Japan enter the war and gain command of the Indian Ocean and Red Sea, the Levant would almost certainly be the junction point at which Germany and Japan would aim. Syria, as well as the North African French colonies, lay on the British life line to India.

In Syria the diplomatic weight of the United States went into the scale for the Allied cause, although it would prove insufficient. Weygand's Levantine army, upon which Allied hopes for a Balkan front had been built, was now under command of General Eugène Mittelhauser, who, despite a partial German ancestry, was firmly loyal to the Western cause. Mittelhauser was in Beirut, Lebanon, his headquarters city, when France asked for peace. There also was General Puaux, High Commissioner of the mandate. Both wished to fight on with the British. In this they had the vigorous support of Cornelius van H. Engert, the American consul general at Beirut, a stanch friend of the British, passionately devoted to the war on the Axis and influential in the Levant.

With State Department consent, Engert maintained close contact with the French officials from June 17 until June 27, when their decision was announced. Mittelhauser and Puaux hesitated to act alone, preferring a concert of the Mediterranean colonies. This seemed to them more essential after the home Government abandoned the projected retreat to North Africa. To that end, the Frenchmen communicated with General Noguès, Resident General of Morocco, the trusted senior functionary in French North Africa.*

The negotiations between Syria and Morocco continued until the 26th, when Noguès finally reported failure to obtain a united front with Tunisia and Algeria. Without that, neither

---

* The French commanders in Syria banked on Noguès. As the son-in-law of the great Théophile Delcassé, the Foreign Minister who helped fabricate the *entente cordiale* with England in 1904, Noguès was expected to bear in mind that Kaiser Wilhelm and Prince von Bülow had forced Delcassé from public life and that before resigning the statesman warned the French that Germany could not be "appeased by concessions."

Noguës nor the Levantine authorities wished to take the plunge. Accordingly, to Engert's regret, Mittelhauser on the 27th proclaimed throughout Syria and Lebanon a cessation of hostilities, subscribed to the armistice, and concluded: "The French flag will continue to fly over this territory, and France will pursue her mission in the Levantine States."

Among opponents of this country's French policy, it has been widely charged that Syria was lost, necessitating its re-conquest by the Free French and the British in 1941, because this Government recognized the Pétain regime, thereby dis-heartening Puaux and Mittelhauser. There seems little ob-jective ground for such a supposition. The armistice terms were accepted on June 22, France laid down its arms on the 25th, and Mittelhauser acted two days later. Up to the 27th no declaration of policy had been made by Washington, this Government's intentions consequently had not been com-municated to Engert, and the so-called Vichy policy was not to assume form for some weeks.

It has been suggested that due diligence on the part of the British at Cairo might have withheld Syria from the Vichy yoke. London recognized General de Gaulle as chief of the Free French on June 18, and it might have been assumed then that the Syrian administrators needed encouragement. They might even have required assurances that money to pay the troops and other expenses would be forthcoming if they broke the tie with the homeland. But this also may be sheer conjec-ture, and the unwillingness of the North African proconsuls to unite under De Gaulle's banner was, at least, the overt rea-son for the temporary loss of Syria.

—8—

All the way to the Vichy border on June 30, Ambassador Bullitt and his party were impressed by the military ubiquity of the Nazis. At intervals of five hundred yards German soldiers stationed by the roadside watched the motorcade of five cars, one a station wagon piled with luggage, whirl past. The distance from Paris to Moulins, where the party crossed the border into unoccupied France, is about 190 miles.

More impressed was Bullitt by the attitude of the French. On this bright Sunday, all the village streets through which the motorcade passed were crowded with strollers and loungers, men and women. Robert Murphy, the Embassy counselor, and Carmel Offie had dreaded the experience of passing through the heart of France. Reynaud's flamboyant appeals to Roosevelt had been without visible results, Nazi propaganda had created a mistrust of the English in French hearts, and the Foreign Service officers feared that this mistrust might also embrace the Americans.

In the villages the French and Germans had divided the main streets into two zones, as France itself had been divided, the invaders taking one side, the residents the other. As Bullitt's leading car, flying a small American flag, appeared at the head of village streets, the French began to demonstrate. Cries of *"vive l'Amérique"* arose, followed, as the people recognized Bullitt from frequent photographs of him in the press, by *"vive l'ambassadeur!"* Bullitt read into the cheers, spontaneous and startling to the Nazi soldiers, an additional meaning. They were, he thought, a vehicle for expressing resentment at the presence of the Nazis, and one unlikely to provoke retaliation.

At Clermont-Ferrand the Ambassador learned that Laval was drafting a new, authoritarian constitution; that he proposed, with Pétain's full agreement, to destroy the Third Republic, cast down the tricolor, erase the watchwords, "liberty, equality, fraternity," once so dynamic throughout the Western World, and install a regime that Laval basely hoped would gratify the cynical barbarians now ruling at Paris. For the first time since June 13, the Ambassador had unhampered communication with his Government and he filed graphic reports on the impending death of the Republic.

In sentences etched with caustic, Bullitt reported to Washington on the wreckers: on Laval, Marquet, Count Fernand de Brinon, whose work for Hitler was to be rewarded with the Vichy Embassy to Paris; on Marcel Déat, a journalist notable for the query, "Why die for Danzig?" and the others. To a man steeped in Western, humane, liberal civilization these men were, of course, traitors. At Clermont-Ferrand, as at Bordeaux and later in Vichy, the opportunistic, cunning Laval was assuring Pétain, Darlan, and their associates that France must yield now, like the sapling before the wind, in order to assure her future destiny. A masterpiece of sinister rationalization, Laval's argument, which shocked a highly placed American when Laval repeated it (at dinner in Paris a year later), ran like this:

> You will see, we will be the gainers in the end. We shall become the Number One ally of Germany in the new order for Europe. Italy? The Germans have only contempt for the Italians. Nothing can stop the Germans. They will have the English on their backs in a few weeks. America is fat, rich, lazy, and ignorant. They will not resist. The Russians even now are shivering in their boots. We must pretend to collaborate in good faith with the Germans but the French are a much cleverer race. Within ten years it will be us, not them, who shall be ruling Europe. We shall accomplish this with the formidable German army. True it is not a French army, but what of that? Any army will do, as long as it serves our purposes. Our loins have failed us, but not our wits. As for France, she needed this lesson. She needed a strong fist to restore discipline and order. But now we must begin to repair our losses with guile.

The argument of the dark little schemer with the "mustaches of a gendarme" struck responsive chords in Pétain and Weygand. It had a spurious patriotism, throwing a sop to national vanity; it accorded the old generals' mistrust of the people. Neither truly had ever made his submission to the

Third Republic. Weygand, broken by the failure of French arms, had retreated into mysticism, muttering to callers about the "sins of France," about retribution and the hard, penitential days ahead. The reputed natural son of the Emperor Maximilian of Mexico, General Weygand is a deeply pious man and a clerical, who shone in the reflected glory of Marshal Foch, but singularly, in a debauched country, is a man of his word. He had been Foch's Chief of Staff. It was Foch (and Clemenceau) who saved France in 1917 and 1918 when Pétain, pessimistic, self-absorbed, and afflicted with a nostalgia for the unequal union of peasant and aristocrat which once characterized France, would have given in.

Worldlier than Weygand, Pétain was no less unsympathetic with the Republic. The France both men felt most at home in was the France of Louis XIV, a France orderly, compact, self-assured, with the masses, the peasant, bourgeois, and town worker, securely placed in a hierarchy ascending to the noble, the archbishop, and the king. Both generals were men of the *ancien régime* but they were also nationalists to the core, and they differed as much from the Nazi lackeys on the one wing as from the proletarian internationalists on the other. Both had taken part in the bloodless civil war, preferring, in their egotism, to destroy France as she was in order to re-create her in their own image. To Pétain and Weygand (who, incidentally, had sustained a longtime rivalry) the Nazis were savage upstarts. The generals' brand of Fascism was clerical, approximating to that of Dollfuss and Schuschnigg in Austria, Franco in Spain, and Salazar in Portugal.

Two passions imbued Darlan: one a pride in the fleet he had helped to create; the other a hatred for England that developed into derangement after the British attack on fleet units at Mers-el-Kebir early in July. The little, round, rough-spoken admiral's strongest motivation, it was judged, however, was that of personal advancement. From all three, Pétain, Weygand, and Darlan, Ambassador Bullitt obtained at Clermont-Ferrand renewed oral pledges regarding the fleet and bases, even after Mers-el-Kebir, Darlan again suggesting that his word be conveyed to the President in his own phraseology. Paradoxically, it was Darlan's Anglophobia that had brought about the Mers-el-Kebir incident as much as anything; the British, being highly mistrustful of the admiral's intentions, feared a purge of pro-Allied officers.

By now the French fleet was diminished. Certain units had taken shelter in British ports, and the portion at Alexandria had consented to internment. Of the four battleships under the French flag, three were out of commission, and the fourth, the *Jean Bart*, lay still unfinished at Casablanca. The *Strasbourg* and *Dunkerque* had taken heavy punishment at Mers-el-Kebir, and a daring, small-boat raid had immobilized the *Richelieu* at Dakar. By no means negligible, however, with these capital ships capable of being refitted, the fleet still contained an airplane carrier (the *Béarn* at Martinique), four heavy and ten light cruisers, twenty-five large and twenty-eight small destroyers, and fifty submarines. Added to Italy's strength, these vessels in Nazi hands might have broken British command of the Mediterranean in 1940—the command which enabled the British to hold Egypt and the approaches to the Suez.

At Clermont-Ferrand, Bullitt relieved Biddle, who departed for home. Disinclined to outlast the Republic in France, he then arranged to quit Vichy immediately after the death decree. On the morning of July 9, therefore, Bullitt paid a farewell call to Marshal Pétain, who lived on the third floor of the Hôtel du Parc. Bullitt did not stop at the suite of the infamous Laval, which was directly below. (In those days Pétain summoned his second in command by thumping on the floor with his cane.) Accompanied by members of his staff, Bullitt attended the session of the National Assembly in the Grand Casino, where, heretofore, nothing more valuable than francs had been put to the hazard. Bullitt showed strong disapproval as Laval called for a "new regime . . . bold, authoritarian, social, and national," adding:

> There is no other road . . . than that of loyal collaboration with Germany and Italy. I experience no embarrassment in speaking thus . . . for even in peacetime I favored such collaboration.

With the public excluded, the parliamentarians of the Republic voted authority for a new constitution; the deputies by 395 to 3, the senators by 225 to 1. His voice choked, tears streaming down his venerable face, Jules Jeanneney, President of the Senate, ordered adjournment. Whereupon the single outspoken dissenter, Pierre, Marquis de Chambrun, a great-great-grandson of Lafayette and a former counselor of Embassy in Washington, cried: "Long live the Republic, forever." Chambrun was seventy-five and an uncle of Count René de Chambrun, the husband of Laval's daughter, Jose.

In departing, Bullitt pointedly ignored Laval, who stood, grinning broadly, amidst a milling group of place seekers.

—9—

Upon his return to America via Clipper, Bullitt reported first to the President, over a week end at Hyde Park, and then to Secretary Hull. He made two major recommendations: (1) that the United States continue normal relations with the Vichy Government, and (2) that we distribute milk and other essential foods to children and their mothers in the unoccupied zone, using American personnel for the distribution and carrying it out under the American flag. Bullitt rested his recommendations on considerations of national interest as well as on his own and America's concern for the French people.

The United States, Bullitt reasoned, would be the only Western power represented at Vichy—the only great force standing counter to the pressure of the Axis. Pétain had broken with the British after Mers-el-Kebir, and, although Mr. Hull strove mightily to prevent a complete break, the rupture ran deep.

The returned Ambassador did not, as reported at the time, represent the Vichy regime as independent and non-Fascistic. On the first heading, Bullitt knew too well the truth of Pétain's words that the Germans have a "halter around my neck and can pull the rope at any time." Also, the Ambassador understood and detested the Fascistic coloring of Vichy. He actually reported that the regime did not see eye to eye: while Laval sought servility to Germany, Pétain was not a Nazi and, being sensitive to the claims of personal honor, might be relied upon to keep his pledged word up to a point. Bullitt believed that maintaining relations with Pétain constituted an inexpensive form of insurance against the eventualities we most dreaded: the surrender of the fleet and naval bases and, at the worst, acts of war by France against her recent ally.

In short, Bullitt had a qualified faith in Pétain and in the French people, too, believing the people had faith in the United States. Mindful of the warming receptions in the villages from Paris to Moulins, recalling also the evidences of affectionate regard shown him by simple people in Paris and Vichy, the Ambassador saw in our flag a symbol of hope to the French. Pétain, he considered, needed public support if he were to resist the Nazis and their agents in the tug of war Bullitt envisaged developing over Vichy, with Berlin at one end, Washington at the other. Hence, he wished the flag shown wherever possible, especially in association with American good works.

The Vichy policy by no means sprang full-blown from Bullitt's reports. Evolving slowly through conversations in the oval room and during long deliberative sessions in Secretary Hull's office, the policy surmounted controversial obstacles. Certain individuals, in and out of the Administration, ob-

jected to recognition of a French regime they considered a
mere puppet of Berlin. Yet, it was pointed out, we maintained
diplomatic relations with Germany itself, with Italy, Japan,
and Russia—all of them ranged in some degree or other against
the democratic world. The cause of the Free French was gallant
and appealing, and the President, Mr. Hull, and their consultants were drawn emotionally to the standard of De Gaulle
vastly more than to the authoritarian regime of Vichy. As
Mr. Hull once put it: "We were willing to help anybody on
the planet who would help fight the Germans and the French
people knew that, and so did Pétain and so did the Free
French." But to recognize De Gaulle would break the last ties
between the West and metropolitan France.

In July, 1940, there were actually three Frances. There was
the France of Laval, a minority accepting German victory
as inescapable and intending to make the best personal terms
with the conqueror. The fortunes and lives of the collaborationists depended upon a German victory over the Western
World. Then there were the Free French. These were *émigrés,*
bearing a stigma historic in France since the great revolution;
bearing, also, the hopes of multitudes of Frenchmen. As the collaborationists had staked their all on German triumph, the De
Gaullists had put their lives and fortunes in the British basket.
Lastly, there were the great body of Frenchmen, peasants,
workers, gentlemen, scholars, freethinkers, and clericals,
bound to French soil, not politicians and not soldiers, who,
in the absence of any alternative, had rallied around the
ancient and arid figure of Pétain. These forty millions, still
numbed by defeat and by no means reconciled, severed from
Britain and the Western belligerents, might feel themselves
wholly alone in an Axis world should the United States withdraw its influence from their midst.

All that summer the American policy toward Vichy remained in flux. Mr. Roosevelt, on the chance of his defeat,
wished to keep it fluid in order not to commit his successor,

and the search for Bullitt's successor did not begin in earnest
until after the November Presidential election. Meanwhile,
the policy was taking form. It should not be overlooked that
the British had an interest at least as vital as our own, and by
now we were committed to British survival. The British, therefore, were consulted. Prime Minister Churchill approved the
diplomatic division of labor by which England backed De
Gaulle and this country contributed toward the Atlantic cause
in Vichy.

The problem could be reduced to simple terms. Vichy had
in its custody a "bloc of sea power and territories" (in Berle's
language) which we wished withheld from the enemy. We believed our security involved in this, hoping that the war might
be confined to Europe and not allowed to break out into the
Atlantic. Pétain and Darlan had agreed to withhold this bloc
from the enemy. Under the armistice terms the fleet and colonies were in their keeping. In our turn, we had agreed not to
recognize changes in French sovereignty procured by force.

At no moment during the long, eighteen-month seesaw were
the policy makers under any illusions. They knew themselves
outmatched in terms of pure power. Germany always had the
military strength to enforce collaboration on defenseless, unoccupied France, and, by invoking the familiar and barbarous
method of hostages, the Nazis might also work their will with
the fleet. The best that Washington might hope for was to
play with the intangible weapons of diplomacy and historical
friendship—plus such real concessions as might prove advisable
—for such time as the fleet could be kept immobilized. The
Vichy policy, when formulated, was a day-to-day attempt to
purchase for the Atlantic powers that invaluable time. We
shall see how it worked.

CHAPTER THREE

Destroyers for Bases—All Aid to Britain

A HOT midsummer afternoon in Washington found His Britannic Majesty's Ambassador, the Marquess of Lothian, conducting a conversation with the President of the United States so delicate that its delicacy, as much as the weather, accounted for the limpness of the diplomat's collar. An affable, plain-speaking man, Lord Lothian had been charged by his skeptical Foreign Office with probing the President's underlying intentions toward the British possessions from Newfoundland to Trinidad and British Guiana, which, under stress of the Nazi menace to the New World, were soon to afford air and naval bases to this country in exchange, approximately, for fifty World War I destroyers.

The day was July 24, 1940. Only that morning Winston Churchill, by telephone from London, and the Cabinet in Washington had approved a method of transfer by which sites for the bases could be leased to the United States. The story of the negotiations ending in the destroyer-bases deal, which was to be hailed by the President at its consummation on September 2 as "epochal" and likened by him to the Louisiana Purchase, constitutes a fascinating and hitherto untold chapter in Anglo-American relations.

The *modus operandi* for the British end of the reciprocal arrangement had been found only the day before. For weeks the two desiderata—destroyers for England, bases for America—had been widely agitated. There were obstacles to both. Statutes of 1883 and 1917, although somewhat ambiguous, threatened to block the way on this side. For her part, England had no wish to cede her American colonies; nor did the colonies wish to be cut adrift from the Empire.

No more did Mr. Roosevelt want title to the offshore islands and the bit of South American jungle involved. In fact, as he discussed the matter on the 23rd with Frank Knox, Secretary of the Navy, the President acknowledged some rather strong views on the subject. The President's voyages in the Caribbean and elsewhere in American waters had afforded him intimate insight into the political, ethnic, and economic problems of the British possessions, and he showed a wholehearted aversion to a transfer of their sovereignty, putting it on the practical ground that he wanted to acquire no "headaches" for this country. Puerto Rico and the Virgin Islands had, he thought, sated our territorial ambitions in the West Indies.

As fortified bases, these same British islands would, however, screen the hemisphere's land mass from overseas aggression. On the 23rd Mr. Roosevelt had propounded to Colonel Knox a solution avoiding the question of sovereignty. Why not ask the British and colonial governments to lease the sites? At the moment, Mr. Roosevelt had not defined the terms, which would come later after talks with Mr. Hull and others, in the form of a swap, a Yankee horse trade: destroyers for leases. England would have her colonies, their sovereignty intact, with fifty stanch convoy craft to boot; this country would gain a chain of bases enabling it the more effectively to safeguard the hemisphere, including the Dominion of Canada and the other British possessions.

The President foresaw no difficulties from Britain over so equitable an exchange. For a long generation the British had acknowledged this country's military seniority in American waters. From the time Lord Salisbury, Victoria's four-time Prime Minister, assured Henry White, the American attaché, in 1898 that his Government regarded Cuba as a strictly American preoccupation, the British had been withdrawing in force from North America. Soon thereafter they dismantled their naval bases on this side, confined the North American Squadron to purely ornamental functions, and resigned their equal treaty rights in a canal at the Isthmus of Panama.

But while one barrier to the destroyer-bases exchange had gone down on the 23rd, the future held another.

Colonel Knox asked leave to discuss the leasehold proposal with Lord Lothian, who, as it happened, was dining with him that night. Knox had only recently joined the Cabinet, with Henry L. Stimson, in response to the President's desire to broaden the Administration's party base for the emergency, and was living on the former Presidential yacht *Sequoia* in the Potomac to escape the city's heat. A follower of Theodore Roosevelt and a disciple of Admiral Mahan, Knox heartily endorsed the President's desire for the offshore bases. The Chicago publisher and Lothian, who had been Lloyd George's secretary and a liberal journalist, were friends of old standing. Dining that night, as they cruised down the river, Knox introduced the lease formula. Lothian at once saw its merits.

When the Ambassador was leaving the *Sequoia,* Knox suggested that he telephone the Prime Minister early in the morning to get his immediate reaction. If favorable, the Secretary promised to communicate the result to the President so that he might, if he wished, lay it before the regular weekly Cabinet meeting that day. Lothian telephoned Churchill. At 8 A.M. he called Knox to say that the Prime Minister had given his assent in principle. That afternoon the Ambassador was at the White House, instructed to sound the President more fully on the touchy question of sovereignty, to make certain that Knox's assurances faithfully reflected Mr. Roosevelt's attitude.

The Presidential office was air-conditioned, the Presidential mood serene. Just a week before to the day Mr. Roosevelt had been renominated for the third term at Chicago, and the strain of his protracted preconvention silence was therefore broken.

The long cigarette holder twinkled about, and the President beamed on his friend, the Ambassador, as he disavowed any secret desire to annex the islands. Although the Ambassador seemed content with the President's assurances, Mr. Roosevelt thought he detected a shade of misgiving in Lothian's normally forthright manner.

"See here, Philip," * the President said decisively, "you may as well get this straight once and for all: I'm not purchasing any headaches for the United States. We don't want your colonies." Whereupon the President took the Ambassador on a swift, personally conducted tour of Britain's American possessions.

"Why should we want Newfoundland: that's a bankrupt colony? If you're thinking of giving it away, give it to Canada —not us. And Bermuda—we don't want it. We think too much of Bermuda! Bermuda is an American resort; Americans go there because they like to be under another flag when they travel. They wouldn't enjoy Bermuda half so much if it was under our flag. It would lose its quaintness.

"Trinidad? No, thanks. What a problem you have there! What a scrambled population! Just consider what has happened to Trinidad! The original Caribs, peaceful souls, were overrun, just before Columbus came, by warlike savages from what is now Venezuela, who murdered the men and married the women. Then came Columbus with his Spaniards; then the conquistadors and buccaneers from all the Mediterranean world. Then the English took Trinidad, and with them came a lot of Scotch and Welsh—and you will agree that they are *strange* people." (Kerr was a Scot.) "Meanwhile, a lot of slaves were being imported from Africa. Just to add to the mixture, four thousand French and Creole refugees from Haiti fled the wrath of Toussaint l'Ouverture. And, as if that weren't enough, you people brought in fifty thousand Hindus in 1860.

* Before two uncles died, bequeathing him almost a dozen English, Scottish, and United Kingdom titles, Lothian was plain Philip Kerr.

What an ethnic potpourri you have there! No, thank you, Philip: you people just go on ruling Trinidad."

The President has a theory that British statesmen usually find it almost unbelievable that another nation does not wish land. It has been the President's experience that they will say, "Yes, of course," and "Naturally," while still distrusting self-denying utterances by American statesmen. The acquisitive habits of centuries have left a certain mental groove in British statesmanship. Although the destroyers-bases trade was fifteen months old when Mr. Churchill came to Washington around Christmas, 1941, he still seemed a little uneasy about the question of sovereignty. He asked the President if he would mind issuing a reassuring statement at his convenience. The President was good-humoredly obliging.

"Well, Winston," he said, "I've been saying that for a year and a half, but if it will make you feel any better I'll say it again." The President, whose buoyant nature dislikes the formality of titles and last names, has called the Prime Minister, his senior by several years, by his first name from early in their close, personal association, which began by transatlantic telephone, being subsequently strengthened by their conferences at sea and in the White House. Mr. Churchill, whether out of consideration for the President's superior rank, or from a reserve either personal or just plain British, uniformly addressed Mr. Roosevelt as "Mister President." *

Mr. Roosevelt's lecture to Lord Lothian, while superficially jocular, was serious in intent. The President wished to remove any barrier to mutual trust. Although the British desperately needed naval re-enforcements, and the Ministry welcomed the establishment of American military strength in the colonies, the method used in effecting that establishment was to

---

* As chief of the American state, Mr. Roosevelt, of course, takes precedence over the Prime Minister, who is only chief of government, King George being the President's opposite number. Since the death of Louis McHenry Howe no one associated officially with the President addresses him by his first name.

them a matter of the gravest concern. The British public never has condoned the alienation of territory once under the flag. There were, in addition, the sentiments of the colonials to consider. Loyal to the crown, these people were not lightly to be shifted to the care of another power. Moreover, Churchill must have given thought to the storm raised by Lord Salisbury when, in 1890, he traded Helgoland, "a sandspit" wasting under the sea's poundings, to Germany for a vast empire in eastern Africa. Victoria grumbled about entrusting the poor Helgolanders to the rule of her uncertain nephew, Wilhelm, and the Ministry for a time faced repudiation in the Commons. The times had changed, Britain was approaching her "darkest hour," but British statesmanship, even in crisis, is seldom less than traditional.

—2—

To understand the destroyers-bases transaction, with all its significance for the defense of the Atlantic world, we must recapture both the plight and the mood of Britain and America in the summer of 1940. The rout in Belgium came nearer than anyone liked to think to beating England to her knees. At the time of Dunkirk, when 335,000 troops were evacuated across the Channel through British skill on the sea and in the air, there was in all England only one brigade of soldiers equipped for modern battle, apart from special branches such as coast and antiaircraft artillery.

The evacuated troops escaped with no more than small arms and not always those, leaving behind big guns, fifty thousand motorized vehicles, and huge stores. After Dunkirk half the British destroyer fleet was laid up for repairs. The air struggle over the Channel had also taken an immense toll. Nor was that the end of it. In France, at base depots near the coast, the British had stored most of their arms and munitions production for the last several months as reserve supplies for forces they intended shipping later to the Continent. Those were, of course, also lost.

The cupboard was all but bare, and it is no wonder that, as Lord Halifax has observed, the Ministry followed the convoy bearing surplus World War I arms to Britain in June with the anxiety of "a mother watching her two-year-old child toddle across the traffic of Fifth Avenue." Although this country could dig up only a hundred rounds of ammunition for each of the 500,000 Lee-Enfield rifles, and British cartridges didn't fit (thus even retarding target practice), Mr. Roosevelt's gamble did hearten the British, the public as well as the Ministry.

Those were truly dark days, with the test of the RAF's ability to hurl back the *Luftwaffe* still to come and the danger at sea growing daily more frightening. Although the air menace monopolized popular dread in this country, the British Ministry was gravely beset by the threat to the United Kingdom's life lines of supply. Without food and other provisions from overseas, England would perish; and doubly was this apparent when the rape of Denmark and Norway and the conquest of the Low Countries and France shut off her normal short-haul intercourse with the Continent. Not since the rigorous days of Napoleon's Continental System had the United Kingdom been so excluded from Europe. Only by sea, moreover, could munitions, aircraft, and the other weapons needed to supplement her own production arrive from the Dominions, from South America, and from the United States.

The events of May and June had opened the ports of Holland, Belgium, and France to the Nazis, giving them a wide window on the Atlantic itself. With Norway in German hands, land-based aircraft and submarines were able to flank the British Isles, Hitler's "clutching fingers" being enabled now, in Churchill's words, "to reach out on both sides of us into the ocean." That had not been true in World War I. At that time, moreover, the French and Italian Fleets stood with the British; after April, 1917, the United States Fleet joined in convoy and patrol and in the far Pacific, Japan had the status of an ally. Since that war, too, the airplane had become a more effectual weapon.

A casting up of the factors in June, 1940, showed a Britain weaker at sea than in 1914-18, with Nazi sea power so improved that it began soon to reflect itself in the toll of merchant shipping. Whereas in May only 75,000 tons of British shipping went to the bottom, the figure mounted steeply to 269,000 tons in June and to 290,000 tons in July. In addition, 115,000 tons of Allied commerce were sunk in July. While this loss failed to reach the horrible ravages of the late winter and spring of 1917, the British Government had no assurance that, unaided, it could stem the tide and stabilize its losses. Nor did the gross tonnage sunk at sea represent the whole story, which was told otherwise in longer, time-consuming voyages, in the necessity of repairing damaged vessels in shipyards and drydocks already overburdened with new work and naval repairs, the works being at the same time subject to bombardment that also entailed destruction and lost time.

Out of those dire straits arose the British desire for naval assistance from the United States. As early as May, Lord Lothian, calling on the President and State Department with Count Saint-Quentin, the last Ambassador of Republican France, had begun to mention the possible purchase of American men-of-war. The British Admiralty was aware that we had more than one hundred World War I destroyers tied up in port. After the invasion of Poland the Navy had gone to work on these vessels, modernizing and recommissioning some. Useful little craft of from 1000 to 1200 tons, known as "four-stackers," they were superfluous to our defense so long as the British Navy held the exits from Europe into the Atlantic. Otherwise, they were worth their weight in gold. That was the dilemma facing the Administration when confronted with the first British requests for some of these ships. Would Britain hold?

In June, with France demonstrably out of the war and her fleet immobilized, Lothian renewed his solicitation. At the same time, voices began to be heard in this country advocating naval aid for the British. On June 12, for example, one of the present authors, writing in his column for *The Washington Post* and other newspapers, suggested that we run the risk of violating international law and convoy ships to England or, failing that, "sell a flock of our old destroyers to the British." Soon that expedient would be urged by pro-Allied journalists and newspapers throughout the country, and early in July the William Allen White Committee to Defend America by Aiding the Allies jumped into the breach.

By August 4, when General John J. Pershing, that oaklike survivor of World War I, appealed on a nationwide radio broadcast for getting destroyers to the British, the matter had become a major issue of American policy. A group of Washington columnists and newspaper editors were promoting the cause in print and by the use of their personal influence. These included Walter Lippmann, and Geoffrey Parsons, chief editorial writer of the *New York Herald Tribune*; Barry Bingham, publisher, and Herbert Agar, editor of the *Louisville Courier-Journal*; Joseph Alsop and Robert Allen, columnists; Frank R. Kent of the *Baltimore Sun*; and Russell Davenport, an editor, who had detached himself from the magazine *Fortune,* to lend his personal services to the Republican Presidential campaign of Wendell Willkie. Also active in this camp was Archibald MacLeish, poet, Librarian of Congress, and member of the White House circle.

MacLeish and Davenport popularly were supposed to have entered into a benevolent conspiracy to win Mr. Willkie's adherence in advance to the alienation of the ships; but the Republican candidate declined to give the Administration a blank check, although he approved of the objective. In his address, General Pershing put his support on the ground that by bulwarking the British Navy "we can still hope with confidence to keep the war on the other side of the Atlantic Ocean." Pershing's appeal was echoed by similar statements from Rear Admiral William H. Standley, later to be Ambassador to Russia, Real Admiral Harry E. Yarnell, and Rear Admiral Yates Stirling.

A few hours before General Pershing spoke, Colonel Charles A. Lindbergh uttered his views on strategy before a Keep America Out of War mass meeting in Chicago. Lindbergh asserted that we could get along as well with Germany as with England as our nearest neighbor across the Atlantic, urged the Government to intervene in Europe in the interest of a negotiated peace, and called for "guarding the independence that the soldiers of our Revolution won," adding:

> What, I ask you, would those soldiers say if they could hear this nation . . . being told that only the British fleet protects us from invasion?

The implied preference of Lindbergh for a Nazi Europe, as well as his ignorance of the collateral role of Anglo-American sea power in the Atlantic, ill accorded with the national policy as expressed that summer by the Administration and by Congress. On June 17, the day Pétain sued for an armistice, Admiral Harold R. Stark, Chief of Naval Operations, asked the House Committee on Naval Affairs to authorize an additional four billion dollars for a "two-ocean navy." After only a few hours' deliberation the committee unanimously approved provisions for the largest Navy ever conceived, and on July 19 the bill became law.

Only once before had this Government adopted a policy of naval aggrandizement on anything like that scale. Then it was known as "a navy second to none." The earlier expansion came in 1916, when it appeared that Britain might be reduced by Germany and that the eastern shore of the Atlantic might pass into the control of a power other than England. Thus it was that twice within twenty-five years our national policy clearly had recognized that "the British fleet protects us from invasion." Only those who, like Lindbergh, presumed to advise the nation out of insufficient knowledge and a bottomless conceit failed to understand that our policy for well over a century had been based on that recognition.

A few weeks later Mr. Willkie, accepting the Republican nomination at Elwood, Indiana, advocated all-out aid and conscription of American youth, declaring that "the loss of the British Fleet would be a calamity for us."

—3—

Under the forensic drumfire of this debate, the President and certain of his advisors patiently were seeking means whereby the destroyers could be made available to the British. The President's understanding of sea power needed no reminder of the urgency of Britain's plight. Nor did he need to be advised that defense of the hemisphere depended upon command of the Atlantic by the United States in tacit league with a friendly European power, in this case England. But there were hindrances: "We couldn't," as the President was to explain to a sympathetic caller, "just up and give 'em to 'em." There had to be a formula that took account of American defense once the legal obstacle could be cleared away, a feat presently to be accomplished in a ruling by the Attorney General.

The mood of official Washington in the summer of 1940 was pessimistic. Except for the White House and the State Department, officialdom, "downtown" and "on the Hill," held at a discount England's chances of surviving. In the services this skepticism was especially marked. The cult of Nazi invincibility had numerous adherents in the Army and Navy, partly because of the air arm's professional enthusiasm for the

Luftwaffe and in part because of insufficient weight given by
military men to such political factors as civilian spirit and
determination. Four fifths of the General Staff regarded England's prospects as desperate.*

A great many plain Americans, impressed by the demonstrated might of the *Luftwaffe* and the *Reichswehr*, likewise
despaired of England. Hitler repeatedly had pronounced the
doom of western Europe by July, and the belief that nothing
could withstand Nazi power amounted in the summer of 1940
to an illusion—one of the series of great illusions which have
contributed to the bewilderment of the Western World since
World War II opened.

In no previous modern war has public opinion been so be-
fuddled. There was the almost universal belief that France
stood rocklike across the Nazi path, her army the "greatest in
Europe," her Maginot Line impregnable. Until put to the test,
Italy bore the general reputation of a first-class military and
naval power. The German opinion that Russia could be conquered within six weeks to three months was widely accepted.
Who thought in the critical months before December 7, 1941,
that Japan, a second-rate power, would dare attack the United
States and Great Britain head on? Nor can the greatest illusion
of all, cherished by a minority of Americans and waning as the
war went on, be overlooked. That illusion was that war would
not touch the United States if our Government minded its
own business and refrained from antagonizing the dictators
of Europe and Asia. Nothing could have been more fatuous
and more pusillanimous. Certain of these illusions derived
from propaganda; others represented the wishes of those who
entertained them, and some came from sheer inability to understand the power and purpose of the forces arrayed against
Western civilization.

In general, military opinion in Washington conformed to

* A like proportion, in June, 1941, underestimated the Soviet Union's power
of resistance.

the reports of professional observers abroad. At the top, political opinion did not. Mr. Roosevelt and Mr. Hull managed to keep cheerful by disregarding the gloom of their No. 1 observer in England, Ambassador Joseph P. Kennedy, who had steadily foreseen the downfall of Britain since the Nazis marched into Poland.

A businessman originally from Boston, who had done well in Wall Street and as chief of the Securities and Exchange Commission and the Maritime Commission, Kennedy was bearish on the British Empire. As long as Neville Chamberlain, Sir Samuel Hoare, and Sir John Simon remained in power, with Sir Horace Wilson, the eminent civil servant and Chamberlain's "gray eminence" at their elbow, Kennedy enjoyed his post. The advent of Churchill disturbed his relations with the Government, Churchill making no bones about his aversion to the American defeatist. In his turn, Kennedy did not mask his distrust of Churchill. Although he had lost his usefulness and strongly urged his own return, Kennedy was kept on, partly because the President did not wish to choose his successor until after the election.

The Kennedy dispatches from May, 1940, until his return in October were an unrelieved study in indigo. He had no faith that England could resist an invasion, believing that the Nazi bombers would knock out their ports and starve the English even if an actual physical invasion could not be accomplished at once. He had, moreover, a suspicion that the English would quit if pounded too hard and suspected that the Nazis, after winning England, would hold the island as hostage for the good behavior of the fleet and the Dominions. He was sure the fleet would not survive the mass invasion he anticipated.

But neither the President nor Mr. Hull lost heart. Mr. Roosevelt based his confidence in England on two observable factors and one less tangible. His study of the reports of Dunkirk convinced him that the RAF had qualitative superiority

over the *Luftwaffe*. He knew something about the advantages
of a defense in depth and was assured that the British command, husbanding their numerical inferiority in the air, would
take full advantage of that. Secondly, he found no evidence
that the Nazis had accumulated the multitude of small craft
necessary to transport sufficient men and equipment across
the English Channel against formidable air and sea power. A
navy man, Mr. Roosevelt also reposed considerable confidence
in English seamanship—a confidence justified at Dunkirk. On
the political side, he had faith in the tenacity and coolheaded-
ness of the British. That faith was yet to be justified, it should
be remembered, when the President announced the policy of
all aid to the Allies and determined to put the destroyers in
their hands.

Subsequently, White House optimism was re-enforced by
the judgment of Colonel William J. Donovan, commander of
the old 69th Regiment, New York, in World War I, a leading
New York lawyer by profession and an amateur of war, whose
hobby is military history, tactics, and soldiering in general.
Donovan goes to all the wars much as an amateur explorer
goes to all the continents. He was the first expert visitor in the
summer of 1940 to give the English more than a fifty-fifty
chance, reporting to the President that they could hold out.
Thereupon Mr. Roosevelt advised the General Staff that a
new survey made on the ground by a competent professional
observer would be helpful. Accordingly, Brigadier General
George V. Strong, chief of war plans for the General Staff,
was flown to London. The British afforded Strong ample op-
portunities to examine the whole difficult scene—military and
supply effort and civilian morale—and he reported to the
President that England could resist invasion that fall unless
Hitler was willing to pay a staggering and incomputable toll.
This was before the RAF had clinched victory in the air battle
of Britain.

—4—

The Yankee horse trade by which Mr. Roosevelt proposed getting the destroyers to England gratified his highly developed sense of political finesse. It was a fair swap with nothing against it, neatly answering all domestic objections. The admirals, some of whom had opposed losing the destroyers, could not dispute that these bases, extending American power hundreds of miles offshore, were a satisfactory *quid pro quo*. Nor were the generals unaware of the advantage of these bases. On May 6, General Strong, addressing the Society of Military Engineers, had depicted in the gravest terms the harm that could be wrought upon North America by an inimical power should it establish air bases on Newfoundland, in the Bahamas, or on Jamaica or Trinidad. Strong declared that the development of air power since World War I had greatly enhanced the desirability to us of these islands.

From the huge country-wide majority favoring aid to England the President could look for the warmest sanction. By August 18, when a Gallup poll on the destroyer issue came out, there was even more specific approval. That test showed 61 per cent favoring the transference of the ships to England. Dr. Gallup also probed the public reaction on several questions dealing with acquisition by this country of islands strategically useful, in the Atlantic and Caribbean, either by purchase, in exchange for unpaid war debts, or by occupation in the event of a Nazi victory in Europe. In June, a poll disclosed that 84 per cent would fight to keep the Nazis out of the Caribbean; on July 20 a sampling gave 87 per cent in favor of immediate occupation of those islands and areas should England go down; 81 per cent expressed their willingness to buy the British, French, and Dutch possessions in the Caribbean, and 64 per cent would trade England's unpaid war-debt balance for certain unspecified islands or lands near the Panama Canal.

There was no doubt that Americans considered these various territories vital to our security and prestige.

This being a Presidential election year, when candidates reduce their smallest words and deeds to political analysis, the President also observed, with some amusement, that those groups most opposed to his foreign policy were on record for the extension of American power offshore. *The Chicago Tribune,* which automatically placed itself in opposition to each development in the Administration's national policy, had been demanding such bases for eighteen years. The isolationists, in the Senate and out, were committed to an impossible policy of making the United States so strong it could not be placed in jeopardy. Manifestly, the bases contributed to such an ideal. And in the suspect fringes of the antiwar movement there existed, as typical of the Anglophobia motivating such groups, an organization known as the Islands for War Debts Committee, established in Washington and supported (as it turned out) by George Sylvester Viereck, chief of the acknowledged Nazi propagandists in this country.

A ground swell was running in favor of both the objectives toward which the President was steering. For Candidate Roosevelt only a net good could accrue from trading destroyers for bases. That was not the case with Churchill, compelled, under the British system, to maintain himself in power on a day-to-day basis. Both men wished the exchange made. Mr. Churchill regarded the idle destroyers in American harbors with the ardor of a hungry man approaching a beefsteak. It was also his desire, as he was to say presently in a disconcerting speech, that "the United States should have facilities for the naval and air defense of the Western Hemisphere against the attack of a Nazi power, which might have acquired temporary but lengthy control of a large part of western Europe and its formidable resources." In this address of August 20, which temporarily was to derail the negotiations, Mr. Churchill declared that he had "decided spontaneously and without being asked or offered any inducement" to offer such facilities.

The Prime Minister's decision may have coincided with his utterance of June 4. In that report on Dunkirk, it will be recalled, he announced a final determination to carry on the war from the Dominions behind the screen of the British Fleet. At the moment, the British Government had that eventuality in mind. Under such distressing circumstances, it is apparent, the interests of Britain and its Empire would be served by a ring of Atlantic and Caribbean bases fortified, manned, and supplied by the United States. The identity of British and American advantage was at that moment abundantly clear.

Mr. Churchill's immediate problem turned on domestic and imperial politics. The English-speaking Powers ultimately are governed, as none know better than Mr. Roosevelt and Mr. Churchill, by public opinion. The Prime Minister had not only to satisfy the governments and peoples of the colonies involved that neither Britain nor America wished a change in sovereignty, he had also to win the approval of important blocs of public sentiment at home. This complicated his acquiescence in the President's solution. Mr. Churchill shrank from trading leases for destroyers, fearing that the exchange stated in bald terms would seem inequitable to large sections of his Tory following, the die-hard imperialists thinking still in terms of Drake and Clive. In such seawise quarters, the alienation of pieces of British territory, even though safeguarded by all sorts of legal phrases, represented, as Churchill understood, too high a price for fifty overage destroyers.

The Prime Minister ran the risk of being held up to attack as soft, as having been outwitted and outtraded by the Yankees. No politician in either English-speaking Power relishes the imputation of having been "used" by the statesmen of the other. For generations Anglophobes have so earnestly nourished a belief that the British constantly hoodwink this Gov-

ernment that it has become a hoary cliché. Although the idea
is, no doubt, novel to our Anglophobes, their opposite numbers have bedeviled successive British Governments by identical cries that the Empire was being sold down the river to the
ingenious Americans.

Mr. Churchill's political judgment apprehended that the
exchange would be vastly more palatable, hence more defensible, if put into terms of gratuity. He wished to make a
free gift of bases, receiving in return a free gift of the destroyers. But he did not wish to give as many bases as the United
States desired. The consequent preoccupation over the transaction's form and scope delayed action during the crowded
month of August, and so closely veiled were the negotiations
that numerous commentators in this country blamed the President for protracting England's naval extremity. Although the
President good-humoredly regarded the Prime Minister's objections as "trivial," when measured against the urgency of his
situation, we have no record of the Prime Minister's judgment
of the President's equally firm position.

So it was that the negotiations dragged. Mr. Hull left Washington on August 2 for an eighteen-day holiday at Virginia
Hot Springs. Thereafter parleys began between Lord Lothian
and Mr. Welles. Meanwhile, early in August, the President
plunged into U. S.-Canadian defense in matters wider than
the offshore bases. The Canadian situation reached a head on
August 16, when, after conferences with Lothian, Loring
Christie, the Canadian Minister, and Welles, the President telephoned Churchill. All hands agreed on a joint pact between
the Dominion and the United States, establishing a Permanent
Joint Board on Defense.

After talking with Churchill, the President telegraphed W.
L. Mackenzie King, the Canadian Prime Minister, inviting
him to a face-to-face conference the next day, August 17, at
Odgensburg, New York—a locality where American and Canadian forces had met twice in battle in the War of 1812.

King had, of course, adhered to the project in advance. The President gave these matters to the press at his biweekly conference of the 16th, authorizing for direct quotation:

> The United States Government is holding conversations with the Government of the British Empire with regard to the acquisition of naval and air bases for the defense of the Western Hemisphere and especially the Panama Canal. The United States Government is carrying on conversations with the Canadian Government on the defense of the Western Hemisphere.

The President, it will be noted, made no reference to a swap, likewise omitting reference to the destroyers. His disclosure on the bases, however, implied confidence in the outcome.

Mr. Roosevelt and Mr. King met the next evening on the President's train near Ogdensburg, where the President, with Secretary Stimson, had passed the day inspecting the First Army at maneuvers. Roosevelt and King dined alone and conferred until late, agreeing on the text of a mutual defense statement, which was released the next day, the 18th.

Two days later Mr. Churchill momentarily upset the apple-cart. In his speech of the 20th, a report to the public on the war situation to date, the Prime Minister not only omitted any reference to the destroyers but clearly asserted that the idea of granting bases to the United States was his own inspiration. We have already noted his language, which pointedly dissociated the bases question from any other consideration. It had been hoped that the Prime Minister would prepare his public for acceptance of the American proposal. What he did was the reverse.

Mr. Churchill, it was plain, had not abandoned his position. There was only one hint in the speech, and that remote, of reciprocal arrangement; plainer was a confident assumption of closer Anglo-American relations that irked, although it did not fail to convince, the traditional enemies of England in this

country. Emphasizing his desire to give ninety-nine-year leaseholds to the United States, the Prime Minister concluded that

> . . . these two great organizations of the English-speaking
> democracies, the British Empire and the United States, will
> have to be somewhat mixed up together in some of their
> affairs for mutual and general advantage. For my own part,
> looking out upon the future, I do not view the process with
> any misgivings. I could not stop it if I wished; no one can stop
> it. Like the Mississippi, it just keeps rolling along. Let it roll.
> Let it roll on full flood, inexorable, irresistible, benignant, to
> broader lands and better days.

—5—

Behind the scenes in Washington the relationship between
the Governments was indeed "mixed up," but in another
sense. Mr. Hull returned to find that Lord Lothian showed no
signs of yielding the British desire for gifts rather than a trade.
Representations to London failed to move Churchill, and the
President remained likewise immovable. By the 25th the
negotiations seemed definitely at checkmate. It was then that
the President sent for Mr. Hull and Lord Lothian and, in
somewhat direct language, called upon them to break the
deadlock.

The President's relations with the Prime Minister had not
at that time attained the plain-spokenness that was to char-
acterize them after the Atlantic conference, or Roosevelt might
himself have undertaken the task. From August, 1941, the
President and Prime Minister were to employ frankness in
man-to-man dealings; and upon his return from America early
in 1942, Mr. Churchill assured the House of Commons that
he and the President were on such a footing that they could
"say anything to each other."

Among Hull's aptitudes is one for the patient exploration
of difficulties and the unhurried elaboration of compromise.
Set to the task of resolving the difference, he impartially re-

viewed the case for each side. In one of the conversations of the period, with the State Department's Legal Advisor, Green H. Hackworth, a plausible formula was evolved. Churchill wished to give some bases; Roosevelt insisted on a trade and wanted more bases than Churchill had offered. Very well, why not satisfy both? Allow Churchill to donate bases on Newfoundland and Bermuda, which, presumably, would serve Canada as well as the United States; then trade the bases in the Caribbean area, more specifically valuable to this country because of the Panama Canal than to the Empire, for the destroyers. The Secretary crossed the street to the White House, where his formula delighted the President. There remained the job of gaining Churchill's compliance.

As it happened Lord Lothian was again dining with Secretary Knox that night on the *Sequoia*. Neither had heard of the Hull compromise. The stalemate seemed hard to get around as they steamed down the river. The wills of two strong men had collided across the Atlantic. As Lord Lothian prepared to go ashore, Knox suggested that they lay their burden on Secretary Hull. "Let's see," he said, "if Cordell's fertile mind has worked out anything." Knox telephoned from the yacht, finding that Hull had already retired but was not asleep and would be willing to receive two perplexed visitors.

Knox and Lothian motored through a sweltering August midnight to the Carlton Hotel, where Hull greeted them in pajamas and summer dressing gown. As he outlined his compromise, Lothian's spirits rose.

"That does it," said the Ambassador.

The next day Churchill's assent came by telephone. A series of conferences at the White House settled on the outline of the agreement to be drawn. Attorney General Robert H. Jackson already had armed the President with an ingenious opinion enabling him to trade the destroyers for certain leaseholds in his capacity of commander in chief of the United States armed forces and under his Constitutional power to conduct foreign affairs. Jackson ruled that the transaction need not be embodied in treaty form and hence was not subject to ratification by the Senate.

The agreements promptly were drafted at the State and Justice Departments, being ready for signature on Saturday, August 31. Lothian found it necessary to be in New York over that week end, returning Monday evening, Labor Day. Mr. Hull was at his apartment. The Ambassador, therefore, hurried from the station to the Carlton, where the documents were signed by the Secretary and himself.

As an added safeguard and to meet opposition arguments in advance, Mr. Hull on the preceding Thursday, the 29th, had asked Lothian for a formal reaffirmation of the Prime Minister's declaration of June 4. In a note, Mr. Hull inquired if this were "the settled policy" of the British Government, an inquiry answered with sardonic humor. Lothian replied that the June 4 statement "certainly does represent the settled policy of His Majesty's Government," adding that "Mr. Churchill must, however, observe that these hypothetical contingencies seem more likely to concern the German Fleet, or what is left of it, than the British."

Mr. Roosevelt was absent from Washington when the trade reached its conclusion in the Secretary's apartment. On Labor Day, the President dedicated Chickamauga Dam, motoring from there to Newfound Gap on the Tennessee-North Carolina border for another speech, in which he said with a certain pertinence to the development being consummated at about that moment in Washington:

> The greatest attack that has ever been launched against the liberty of the individual is nearer the Americas than ever before. To meet that attack, we must prepare beforehand, for preparing later may and probably will be too late.

On the next day the news of the exchange was to be given out in Washington, and the President, riding by train from

Charleston, West Virginia, toward the capital, was able to extract a joke to his own liking out of a situation contrived by himself. When the train was well out of the Charleston station, Steve Early called the twenty-three correspondents aboard into the President's car, the *Roald Amundsen*. The correspondents crowded into the large salon; five of them squeezed on a couch, three squatted on the floor, and the rest sat on chairs or stood, except for two unable to move farther than the corridor. When they were settled, the President announced that he had a big story to impart—but, and he grinned delightedly, one that the correspondents needn't write. The story was to "break" in Washington within a quarter of an hour, but, as there was no stop scheduled for much longer ahead than that, the story couldn't be put off the train until after it had reached the country from Washington. He then outlined the destroyers-bases trade, comparing it to the Louisiana Purchase, both because it added greatly to the country's strategical resources and because he, like Jefferson, had concluded it under stress of emergency before informing Congress.

So it was that a "protective girdle of steel" was flung, in Mr. Hull's words, along the Atlantic and Caribbean coasts. To the Prime Minister, reporting in the House of Commons, the frontiers of the United States had been "advanced along a wide arc into the Atlantic Ocean," a move enabling this country "to take danger by the throat while it is still hundreds of miles from their homeland." And, by what Mr. Churchill ironically called "the long arm of coincidence," British crews already were in Canadian ports awaiting the prompt arrival of fifty "four-stackers," their tanks filled with oil, their tubes with torpedoes, their larders abundantly stocked with food and other provisions by order of Secretary Knox.

Under the Hull formula, the bases on the Avalon Peninsula and the southern coast of Newfoundland and on the Great Bay and east coast of Bermuda came to the United States "freely and without consideration." "These were . . . gifts generously given and gladly received," in the President's words. Exchanged for the destroyers were rights to bases on the "eastern side of the Bahamas, the southern coast of Jamaica, the western coast of St. Lucia, the west coast of Trinidad in the Gulf of Paria, in the island of Antigua, and in British Guiana within fifty miles of Georgetown. . . ." All these bases were to be leased for ninety-nine years, "free from all rent and charges other than such compensation to be mutually agreed on" to private property owners. "This is," said the President, in transmitting the agreements to Congress on September 3, "the most important action in the re-enforcement of our national defense that has been taken since the Louisiana Purchase. Then as now, considerations of safety from overseas attack were fundamental."

Mr. Roosevelt might have added that the agreements represented the final withdrawal in force of Great Britain from waters that she had dominated for most of three centuries. The American flag had been senior in the Caribbean for a generation, it is true, and the realities of the situation in 1940 conformed to the new arrangements; yet it should not be overlooked that the British, in ceding the leaseholds as in the preceding steps of their retirement dating back to 1898, had done so peacefully and, on the whole, gracefully. The supremacy of the United States in its own eastern and southern waters was now completely recognized, and never during the process had either country seriously considered resorting to war.

A wave of approval for Mr. Roosevelt's results, if not his method, swept the country. The Presidential campaign had begun to warm up, as usual, after Labor Day, and the Yankee horse trade was therefore examined in the light of political advantage as well as national interest. Mr. Willkie endorsed the acquisition of bases but stigmatized the President's exercise of his powers without reference to Congress as the "most dictatorial action ever taken by any President." Allowance has, of course, to be made for the superlative character of campaign utterances.

On the whole, the country probably agreed with the anti-New Deal but strongly patriotic *New York Herald Tribune,* when it acclaimed the exchange as "admirable and long over-due," hoping that the President's "uniting them in one sensational bargain will not blind the country to the vital national importance of the agreement as to bases and the high desirability of the sale of the destroyers."

No one could doubt that the transfer of fifty naval vessels from a country at peace to a belligerent cracked, if it did not wholly fracture, our neutrality. Within two weeks, with the Canadian and bases-destroyers commitments, this country had witnessed a sweeping change in status. Toward Canada we now stood as an ally, a link approved, according to Dr. Gallup's findings, by nine out of every ten Americans. Toward Great Britain we were something more than neutral, though few persons regretted that and fewer worried over the legal definition of the relationship. There was a general disposition to share the London *Times'* conclusion that, though our intervention on England's behalf represented an innovation in international law, the old concepts of that law itself had "become an anachronism in a world containing Hitler and Mussolini."

The despot countries themselves ignored this aspect of the deal. It did not suit them to make an issue of American un-neutrality. The Rome and Berlin press uniformly took the line that a soon-to-be-defeated England already was dismembering her Empire and that a greedy, imperialistic Uncle Sam had not been above preying on a friend in need. The enormous utility of the destroyers to Britain naturally was minimized in that servile press.

—6—

The United States, one could not doubt, was now set on a course of open collaboration with wartime England. A far closer association, as Churchill had hinted on August 20, already was in the making. A further inkling had been dropped by *The Times* of London in its comment on the destroyers-bases matter when it placed the trade in "a larger strategic plan for mutual assistance in self-defense which is now being worked out between the British Empire and the United States." The first vague shadowings of lend-lease could be discerned in Washington and London even before the announcement of September 2. England, taking the pummelings of the enemy alone in the air and at sea, could not go it alone industrially and, if she were to survive for long, she would lack the means to purchase assistance. The bottom of the barrel was constructively in sight before the battle of Britain burst in its full fury in September.

Two days after announcement of the destroyers-bases trade, Hitler, speaking in the Berlin Sportpalast, promised his infatuated minions the immediate destruction of England from the air. The all-out *Blitz* began on September 7, a Saturday preceding a Sunday set aside in Britain as a day of prayer for victory and in the United States for prayer for peace. But Hitler was not to gain control of the daylight skies over England and, during the height of the air *Blitz,* Gallup announced that, whereas in October, 1939, only 34 per cent of Americans were willing to aid the Allies at the risk of going to war, by September, 1940, a clear majority of 52 per cent would now assume that chance.

Scarcely had the ink dried on the destroyers-bases agreement when Secretary Hull offered the use of the bases "on the fullest co-operative basis" to all other American republics. Mr. Hull instructed our Embassies and Legations to assure the Latin Governments that the United States had

> ... taken this step to strengthen its ability not only to defend the United States, but in order the more effectively to co-operate with the other American republics in the common defense of the hemisphere.

The British, it should be noted, executed the broad provisions of the agreement in entire good faith. In London, where groups of experts representing the United States, Great Britain, and the colonial governments met early in 1941 to agree on details, no real difficulties arose.

The United States obtained complete rights to the use of the waters around the bases, the air overhead, all harbor facilities, the use of highways, etc., without payment. United States military law was to apply in the leased areas. No taxes were to be paid, either customs, local land, income, or inheritance, by the United States or its personnel. To guard against extortionate prices being set on the land by private owners, the colonial governments agreed to use their right of eminent domain to obtain private lands for the use of the United States. Moreover, the bases themselves were to be exempt from the intrusion of local peace officers and process servers in exactly the same fashion as Federal establishments are so exempt within the United States.

—7—

Soon after Mr. Roosevelt's re-election, he departed, with Harry Hopkins, on the cruiser *Tuscaloosa* for a holiday, which was to include a personal inspection of the new base sites. Throughout the negotiations the President's precise knowledge of these islands, their harbors, currents, climate, and economic status, astonished the other negotiators. He wished now to refresh his recollections, and, as the *Tuscaloosa* poked in and out of the islands, from the Bahamas south, the President explored harbors with the enthusiasm of a sea scout. In small boats, he ran alongside breakwaters, studied harbor facilities, and had soundings taken.

Lying off the Bahaman group, the President took aboard their Governor, the Duke of Windsor, for a conference at which they arranged for a second base in the Bahamas. Although Martinique was off his beat, he put in for a quick look at that French port, finding the harbor unsuitable for a naval base. It wasn't, he observed, a harbor: merely a roadstead, unsheltered from the sea, its mouth too wide to be successfully netted and the inner harbor too small for anything more than a squadron or so.

At St. Lucia, which possessed a "sweet little harbor," his small boat attracted a throng of cheering Negro islanders. One among them, a girl, clad in city finery including a flopping red hat, danced out on a stringpiece hailing the President: "Mr. President, I'se from Harlem; I'se the only American here!" The President recognized her claim with a friendly wave. In the mouth of the harbor on an islet stood the fort of the great English Admiral, Rodney, who based on St. Lucia. The islet, the President found, had been purchased and restored by "an English widow," who lived there with a staff of servants. Observing from the water that she had furbished up the old fort with its guns, and made of it an attractive residence, Mr. Roosevelt lightly suggested that she might be induced to stay on as "our caretaker."

The cruise produced more, however, than entertaining impressions of the islands. The support of England, still enduring a nightly strafing, was this Administration's topmost concern, and the President had brought the problem to sea with him. It was apparent that the British, if they were to survive, would need an immense volume of munitions. On November 8, three days after election, Mr. Roosevelt, by announcing that henceforth American war production would be divided in two equal parts, half to go to the British, had taken a step toward accelerating the flow. On that day also the British received from the National Defense Advisory Commission, forerunner of OPM and WPB, authority to order 12,000 airplanes, in addition to the 14,300 already on order. Moreover, while the President was in the Caribbean, twenty-six "flying fortresses" were released to the British.

There remained, however, even if the problem of industrial production could be solved, two other gaps in the British supply lines: (1) the money or means to pay for munitions here and (2) sufficient ships in which to carry them. The first would promptly be closed. Not so with the second, a more baffling problem.

This Government stood committed to all-out assistance. In mid-October, the President had defied the Axis dictators to "stop the help we are giving to almost the last people now holding them at bay." In every test of opinion, the people overwhelmingly had supported that policy. But who was to pay for the materials?

Since August, the problem of financing British purchases had been under lively discussion in the Treasury. Lord Lothian, who tactfully had absented himself from the United States during the last weeks of the Presidential campaign, publicly raised the question of financial assistance on his return to New York after the election. This direct approach to the American public, through an interview with ship news reporters, annoyed the President, who reproved Lothian when he called at the White House. The President also reminded the Ambassador of the immense financial assets that Great Britain had scattered over the world—assets sufficient to pay for British purchases abroad for a long time to come.

By clever management, Great Britain had managed to come through World War I with scarcely any diminution of her overseas financial empire and had begun this one with the equivalent of between fifteen and eighteen billion dollars in overseas investments. Actually, British investments and bank balances in the United States had been greater in 1939 than in 1914, when the United States was generally recognized as a "debtor" nation. What the British were beginning to run short of was cash and American securities which could readily be converted into cash by direct sale to American investors. Even these had not been exhausted, but commitments already made brought their end in sight. There remained valuable properties, ranging from cotton plantations to wholly British owned factories, in this country. There were also securities and property holdings in Africa, Canada, South and Central America and the West Indies, Malaya, and the East Indies. In addition, there were large investments abroad owned by citizens of Canada, Australia, and other portions of the British Empire, as well as by the British allies, including the immensely wealthy Dutch. Add the gold output of South Africa and Canada, accepted by the American Treasury in unlimited quantities, and exports to the United States from all parts of the British Empire, and the British were very far from impoverished. Indeed, their financial empire had not yet been seriously impaired.

But most of these assets could not readily be sold to American private investors, except perhaps at sacrifice prices. At the minimum, the British needed American banking aid in converting these assets, or some of them, into dollars.

On our statute books stood two laws effectually stopping financial aid—even loans well secured with collateral—to Britain. One was the Johnson Act of 1934 forbidding loans to countries in default on their World War I debts, and the other was the Neutrality Act of 1939, forbidding money advances to belligerents.

In a democracy a large part of Governmental energy at the top is expended in looking for justifiable formulas by means of which to accomplish categorically imperative results. So, the search in Washington, as the President put to sea, was for a formula. In his circle there was general agreement on one point: Britain's plight should not be permitted to become a bonanza for private banking interests.*

In the cold light of finance, the British needed, for a long time to come, no more than credit—for which they could post many billion dollars' worth of collateral. But other, deeper aspects were to be considered. First was the effect on British morale of a hardheaded bankers' attitude on the part of this Government. The RAF had beaten back the *Luftwaffe* in the great battle of August to October for control of the daylight air over Great Britain. But the British were beginning to suffer heavily from night bombing raids. Although the British public did not realize it, their military strategists knew that without aid from one or more powerful new allies Great Britain could never win the war: that the most it could hope for was a negotiated peace. Such a peace obviously could never be negotiated by Churchill.

The President always was mindful of the possibility that the magnificent resolution of the British people, fired by the spirit of Churchill, might begin to sag beneath the sheer weight of Nazi power. There could be no guarantee that appeasement would not be revived by the spread of a fatalistic feeling that the only hope lay in trying to reach a bargain with Hitler. Such a feeling might easily be promoted if the price of American help were to be the gradual transfer of the British financial empire overseas into American hands. And the conservative financial and industrial leaders and penny-counting civil servants, who had appeased Hitler until the attack on Poland, and

* Later, during the lend-lease debate, Secretary Morgenthau insisted that the British begin to sell some of their direct American investments as an earnest of their intention to exhaust their own resources before accepting American aid. The first sale, of a choice manufacturing establishment, brought a low price, but a fee to private bankers which seemed to the Treasury so excessive that it unsuccessfully demanded a rebate to the British. After that, with the passage of lend-lease, similar British properties were assigned to the Reconstruction Finance Corporation as security for a loan.

had then tried to fight a cheap war, were the very men who had the most tenacious interest in the British financial empire overseas.

The great question posed at Dunkirk, and still not finally answered, was whether Great Britain was to move in the orbit of Germany or was to continue to serve as the powerful eastern bastion of the defense of North America. The British, almost miraculously it seemed, had survived the summer and fall without invasion. In the vital interest of the security of the United States, the President could not risk a policy which might sap the British will to resist and so open the way for negotiated peace, if not for a Nazi invasion. For a peace would, and could, have been negotiated only by a government acceptable to Hitler, composed of men who believed they could "do business" with him. This meant the end of Churchill and the decline and probably the erasure of American influence on British policy.

Without question, this country overwhelmingly was ready to give the British financial aid when they needed it. But to plan ahead, to pursue the war, the British needed at once a firm long-range commitment.

Henry Morgenthau, Jr., humorless and intensely anti-Nazi, early supported the view that England was carrying the ball for the democratic Western World and must therefore have our financial assistance. Morgenthau and Hopkins collaborated in pressing that case in the oval room. There were few dissenters. The President felt it necessary to bolster, by a generous underwriting, the British determination to fight on—but in such a way as to keep in our hands a measure of influence over British policy throughout and after the war.

By early November a number of formulas had been discussed at sessions in the White House, in Morgenthau's office, and in Mr. Hull's leisurely sanctum, including repeal of the Johnson Act and of the loan provisions of the Neutrality Act. Talk of repeal quickly went into the discard, because of an anticipated reluctance in Congress to tamper with the complex of well-meaning neutrality legislation. Furthermore, all hands agreed that aid this time should not take the form of dollar loans. The chaffering, disillusioning aftermath of the last war, when intergovernmental debts roiled diplomatic and financial relationships alike, put a firm quietus on that materialistic and ungenerous method.

Hopkins, convinced that the British were also fighting our war and a little shamefaced at our unwillingness to extend more than material help, advocated giving them whatever they needed without cost. From outside the Administration and usually from sources hostile to the British came proposals that we exact payment in title to the West Indies islands, which the Government would not have had as a gift.

As the President and Hopkins fished and loafed, they reviewed the alternatives, together with additional suggestions arriving by wireless from Morgenthau and the other conferees in Washington. Mr. Roosevelt thought the proposal of an outright gift too sweeping to be sound and, besides, he suspected British pride might react adversely. Dollar loans were out, but, the President felt, there must be a middle way open to fewer objections than either extreme.

Out of the talks on the *Tuscaloosa* came a formula which would provide a steady flow of goods for Britain and the other nations "resisting aggression." This formula, when adopted by Congress in March, 1941, would once and for all place this country in the war as a nonbelligerent ally of the anti-Axis Powers.

Mr. Roosevelt, who has a sophisticated taste for parable, saw our situation in terms of a homely simile. There was, as he phrased it to Hopkins, a conflagration raging, a fierce fire which might spread to other parts of the world, even to America. The English, the Greeks, the Chinese, and the Governments in exile were fighting the fire. Reducing this vast catastrophe to domestic terms, what does a householder do when a neighbor's house is being attacked by flames? Why, he helps of course! He lends the neighbor his garden hose to play water on the fire. He does this, first, out of a neighborly impulse, and, secondly, for selfish reasons. The wind might carry sparks from the neighbor's house to his own. Once the fire was extinguished, the neighbor would, of course, return the hose or, if it had been destroyed, replace it.

The President failed to pursue his simile to its obvious and inexorable end. A good neighbor lends his hose, but he also lends himself with it. A valid criticism of the President's prewar course may be recorded by history. It may be said that, just as Mr. Roosevelt failed to carry through his garden-hose simile, he failed sufficiently to prepare the country by refusing to accept in advance the war that many of his countrymen saw as inescapable. It seems clear that, during this entire crisis, the President lagged behind public opinion, reflecting rather than creating trends. His position on participation in the war was nevertheless far ahead of the voluble Congressional minority, which misunderstood the public temper as it misread conditions in the world outside America.

—8—

The *Tuscaloosa* talks between the President and his closest advisor ranged the whole field of world problems. Mr. Roosevelt, re-elected, would be at the helm for another four years. Across the Atlantic, Churchill seemed also entrenched in public favor. Upon the shoulders of these leaders, one fighting an uphill battle, the other carefully nonbelligerent, would, in all likelihood, rest the burden of opposing the Axis. It seemed to the President that he and Churchill should have a clearer insight into each other's minds, motives, and character.

There was no uninterrupted line between the White House and No. 10 Downing Street. The Prime Minister might rely upon Lord Lothian, but the President lacked even an Ambassador in London. Kennedy had come home and was not returning. Already out of sympathy with the British Government, he had given an interview, unconvincingly repudiated, which aroused British sentiment against him and even created mistrust of the Administration's good will toward them. Kennedy was quoted as expressing doubt that England could win and certainty that democracy was now finished in the United Kingdom. Voices in England were asking how an Ambassador (Kennedy still had not been relieved) could speak so indiscreetly without at least the tacit approval of the President. Although unconsulted, Mr. Roosevelt had no doubt that the Ambassador had been quoted accurately, the interview according with Kennedy's diplomatic reports and his personal advices to the White House.

The President had not yet settled upon Kennedy's successor and, because of the extreme importance of the job, he intended to take his time about it. Furthermore, he wished to establish even a more personal link than that normally afforded by diplomacy. The thought that he should organize his own liaison with the Prime Minister recurred in the conversations. Once the President casually remarked: "Harry, I think maybe you ought to go over and see Churchill." Nothing more was said for the time being.

Mr. Roosevelt prolonged his postelection vacation by stopping off at Warm Springs, Georgia. While there, on December 12, he had word of Lord Lothian's tragic death that morning after what was to be his final appeal for assistance had been read for him the evening before in Baltimore. The British Ambassador's death fortified Mr. Roosevelt's determination to run a direct line to Churchill. He departed Warm Springs on the 15th, his leavetaking grim as he announced his return in March "if the world survives."

Back in Washington on the 17th, the President found a leaderless, bewildered capital and a country sinking in spirit. Since election, there had been a long hiatus during which it seemed to anxious Americans that this country was standing still while the European catastrophe whirled ever faster. Mr. Roosevelt caught up the slack at a press conference on the 17th, where, renewed by his holiday and in fine fettle, he propounded the lend-lease plan for assisting the anti-Axis forces, making effective use of the garden-hose simile.

Dismissing the repeal of obstructive legislation or a direct gift to the Allies as the product of "traditional or banal minds," the President offered what he termed a brand-new plan which would eliminate the "silly-fool dollar sign" and get down to realities. He proposed that the Government take over all production for war and then lend or sell, under mortgage, whatever could be spared to Britain and the other countries. At the war's end, they could return unharmed ships, guns, airplanes, etc., and replace in kind what had been destroyed.

In mid-December the formula had not advanced beyond repayment in kind. Before the proposal went to Congress in January it had evolved further, though the formula remained fluid during the protracted Congressional debate. As the men charged with the problem considered it further, they came to the conclusion that the program should be kept as elastic as possible, having realized that repayment in kind also was open to many objections.

At the State Department, during one of the Sunday-morning sessions, the conferees canvassed the possibilities of a postwar world in which a stringent demand by this Government for so many ships, tanks, planes, and guns from England, from China, or from other assisted powers might be wholly inadvisable and unnecessary from our point of view, from theirs, and from that of humanity in general. We might easily prefer not to have delivery in kind. Such delivery might, for example, injure our interest by requiring that other nations maintain war industries in order to produce munitions for us.

The eventualities opening before the conferees staggered them. Suppose a domestic political upheaval following the

war brought to the Presidency a xenophobic, narrow isolationist? Under such circumstances, a rigid contract for repayment might be used as a weapon against our late bene-
ficiaries and friends, frustrating efforts toward international
co-operation and sowing the seeds of new bitterness. In the
minds of the President and those about him the terms of repayment gradually were broadened to include other considerations of value—new leaseholds, perhaps, raw materials, and
trade agreements—as well as articles in kind. Or, as the President said to a friend: "If everything turns out all right, we can
forget all about it."

So it was that the lend-lease legislation relegated the terms
of payment to the future, investing their negotiation with the
Executive. And when the first preliminary agreement between
the United States and Great Britain was signed in Washington on February 23, 1942, it covered the question of reimburse-
ment in generalized form, stipulating only that the final determination should not

> . . . burden commerce between the two countries, but . . .
> promote mutually advantageous economic relations between
> them and the betterment of world-wide economic relations.

Other countries accepting lend-lease aid were to be included
in the final settlement, which was to have for its aim the "economic objectives" set forth in the Atlantic Charter. For some
reason this agreement, signed by Acting Secretary Welles and
Lord Halifax, Lothian's successor, failed to revive the public's
memories of the anxious discussions of 1940 over the form of
financial aid to the British. At that moment in history the
point uppermost was how to make and ship sufficient weapons
to a beleaguered Britain so that it might survive as a fortress
off the shores of a Nazi Europe.

On December 17, Secretary Morgenthau testified before a
subcommittee of the House Appropriations Committee that
the British were scraping the bottom of the barrel. Future or-

ders could only be placed on credit. It was, said Morgenthau, "for Congress to decide how . . . financial assistance should be given." A few days earlier Sir Frederick Phillips, Under Secretary of the British Treasury, had arrived in Washington to submit a balance sheet of his country's assets and commitments, a report satisfying Congress that, without credit, Britain could not continue indefinitely to receive our material support.

The credit policy had been initiated on the *Tuscaloosa*. Its authorization rested with Congress. Few persons doubted that Congress would approve. On December 18, the British Purchasing Commission was advised to place new orders for $3,000,000,000 in war materials without delay, and the orders, for which no British cash was available, were so placed.

CHAPTER IV

Diplomacy in a "World-Wide Arena"

AN UNEXPECTED telephone call from Montevideo, Uruguay, on June 17, 1940, ruffled the pool of rigorous calm that normally surrounds Sumner Welles. It had, as the Under Secretary now reflects, a premonitory ring. At the Montevideo end was Edwin C. Wilson, the American Minister, reporting that a *Putsch*, timed for the fall of Britain and calculated to signal the Nazi *Tag* in that region of South America, had been exploded prematurely with the arrest of a dozen leading conspirators. Pro-Nazi Uruguayans, re-enforced by adventurers from Argentina across the Rio de la Plata estuary, were congregating in Montevideo. There were mutterings of an uprising, and Alfredo Baldomir, the bluffly liberal, pro-North American President, considered that his people needed the tonic reassurance of a Yankee man-of-war.

Wilson was recommending that a cruiser be sent at once to Montevideo.

The Montevideo call was only a foretaste. Thereafter, until Pearl Harbor, the makers of American policy increasingly were to be subjected to abrupt dislocation of their schedules caused by Axis stratagems in all corners of the earth. It was on June 17—as nearly as these matters may be reckoned on the calendar—that this country's world relationships entered a new order of magnitude. Only a week before, at Charlottesville, Mr. Roosevelt, confronted by Italy's entrance into the war and the French Government's flight from Paris, had observed that America now "perceived peril in a world-wide arena."

On the 17th the President's forebodings were convincingly confirmed. The surrender of France suddenly opened two new diplomatic fronts. France's fall orphaned distant parts of her empire. The outlying possessions in America and Asia had relied for their protection on the Anglo-French naval supremacy in European waters. That day the frailty of French rule became patent.

Tokyo, with the prompt and unerring instinct of the buzzard, pounced on the Pétain regime tarrying at Bordeaux, demanding that the last remaining railway line into free China—from Haiphong, Indo-China, to Kunming—be closed to shipments of motor equipment, fuel, and other goods useful to Chungking's war effort.* Pétain yielded on the 20th. Having just surrendered France, he was not likely to stickle over a fragment of her empire.

The Japanese also gained the right to police the railway line with military inspectors. That placed their steadily pushing foot in the door of Indo-China. Ten weeks later, Major General Issaku Nisihara, commanding the railroad inspectors, served the ultimatum on the French authorities in Indo-China and at Vichy that brought about occupation of the northern provinces. A glance at a map will show how essentially Indo-China bridged the gap for the Japanese between southern China and Malaya and Singapore, and the demand of June 17 may be put down as a long link in the chain of events leading to Pearl Harbor and war in the Pacific.

That day also this Government took swift cognizance of the changed status of the French (and Dutch) possessions in this hemisphere. A call went out from Washington to the twenty sister republics for a conference at Havana on July 21 for the purpose of fixing the lot of these colonies. That day the Senate unanimously adopted a resolution, offered by Key Pittman, chairman of the Foreign Relations Committee, warning Ger-

---

* Since 1939 it had been closed to munitions by the acquiescent French.

many away from transatlantic fruits of conquest. Likewise on the 17th, Secretary Hull presided over a conference of the Secretaries of State, Treasury, Agriculture, and Commerce, appointed by the President to wrestle with the dislocations of the raw-material economies of the Latin Republics brought on by the fall of France and the Low Countries, the entrance of Italy into the war, and the consequent enlargement of the British blockade.

On that crowded day Washington became, in a very real sense, the capital of the Americas.

Thus, on the day France withdrew from World War II, this Government found itself obliged to face both South and West toward new areas of possible disturbance. Among our external interests, defense of the Atlantic line remained, and would continue to remain, our first consideration. That meant seeking to forestall disadvantageous developments in the harbors of France and in the French African colonies. It also meant safeguarding the southern flank, below the Rio Grande, and strengthening the democratic will to resist in the Latin Republics.

Soon American diplomacy would be hard at work building a dike around French Africa against the Axis and in behalf of the Atlantic cause. Soon also, with the growth of apprehension over Japan's incursions southward in Asia, it would turn to the northern flank, feeling out the ground for *rapprochement* with the Kremlin. These were positive efforts, which could, in the sad state of American preparedness, be conducted solely with the weapons of diplomacy.

In the Pacific, the United States would stand for the time being on the defensive, seeking to contain the potential enemy in its rear. In view of the world in June, 1940, with the superior day-to-day insight of the White House and the State Department, Mahan's truism about America's island status came more and more to mind. The job of assuring American security and vindicating American principles was, as Adolf

Berle would recapitulate the problem in an address at Des Moines in February, 1942, immense and unprecedented. Berle said:

> In the summer of 1940 there was laid on the shoulders of two men, President Roosevelt and Mr. Cordell Hull, one of the greatest burdens of which history has record. . . . Specifically, there was assigned to Mr. Hull the task of holding, in time of peace, not merely the American hemisphere, but also all that was left of France and of French Africa; to hold at bay the Japanese ambition and to provide uninterrupted supply lines for Great Britain.

Fortunately, Mr. Roosevelt, Mr. Hull, and their subordinates in the definition and execution of foreign policy were Pan-Western men, committed without reservation to the cause of democratic self-government. To Mr. Roosevelt, speaking on Armistice Day, 1940, the democracy which grew out of the experiments in human association in the seaboard colonies of North America was "truly and fundamentally" new and, under changing modes and patterns of government, he had faith that it would continue to afford mankind the surest path to developing well-being.

—2—

In his telephone talk with Minister Wilson, Welles wanted assurances that President Baldomir understood the implications of his request and that, moreover, the Uruguayan public would welcome the showing of the flag and not regard it as an interference in their affairs. Wilson satisfied him on these points. The Under Secretary thereupon telephoned Admiral Stark, who, calling at the State Department, could not at first see his way clear to detach a cruiser for this diplomatic errand.

Finally, however, the cruiser *Quincy,* which had been somewhere on the South Atlantic patrol, dropped her hook off the quay at Montevideo on June 20. Wilson's estimate of the situation had been accurate. The streets of Montevideo blossomed with American colors overnight, and a hundred thousand of Uruguay's two million souls packed the water front, cheering the flag. Captain Williams C. Wickham, the *Quincy*'s skipper, became Montevideo's hero for a day.

The pro-Axis minority dwindled from sight and, at a state luncheon given by the Government in Wickham's honor, the American Minister re-enforced the cruiser's presence by a blunt declaration aimed at a continent-wide audience. He was "authorized to state," said Wilson, "that it is the intention and avowed policy of my Government to co-operate fully, whenever such co-operation is desired, with the other American Governments in crushing all activities which arise from non-American sources and which imperil our political and economic freedom."

The frustrated *Putsch* in Uruguay alarmed Washington, disclosing, from evidence found on the plotters, the infamous detail with which the Uruguayan Nazi party had planned to overthrow the democratic regime. A prospectus seized in the police raids outlined the so-called Fuhrmann Plan for Uruguay's allotted role as a disciplined, subservient raw-materials *Gau,* or province, under the Third Reich.* Here, the State Department concluded, might be observed the pattern to which all of South America would be reduced should Hitler subdue England and gain command of the South Atlantic.

Scarcely less disturbing to Welles, who, having served in Buenos Aires during World War I, had maintained his understanding of the Plata River region in the years intervening, were broad intimations from Montevideo that pro-Nazi army officers from Argentina were implicated. That implied a wider base for the Nazi enterprise than Uruguay, suggesting that the encroachments of the Germans must be met on a continental

* Arnulf Fuhrmann, director of anti-Semitic activities and propaganda for South America, was the theoretician, the Dr. Rosenberg, of the conspiracy. Arrested, he called the plot a "joke," was freed, and fled to Argentina.

front. The plot had included many, although by no means all, of the supporters of Dr. Luis Alberto de Herrera, the leader of the official *Blanco* (white) party, the organ of agrarian reactionaries. Herrera, an unreconstructed agitator against "*Yanqui* imperialism," made no secret of his fondness for the Nazi-Fascist political theory and practice and, upon a visit to Europe, had been marked for special honors by both Hitler and Mussolini. Apart from revealing the copious organization of German preparations for colonizing Latin America by insurrection, the thwarted *Putsch* likewise clearly had unearthed the existence of a potential fifth column in the Plata River basin.

A ringleader in the Uruguayan plot was Julius Dalldorf, a wool exporter who enjoyed diplomatic immunity as press attaché of the German Legation and was known to his fellow conspirators as the "little *Führer*." The practice, introduced into modern diplomacy by the Nazis, of perverting the foreign service into an agency for espionage, sabotage, and the political corruption of countries whose hospitality it enjoyed, aggravated the situation in all the western countries. This phase of Nazi infiltration south of the United States, as well as in this country, went on the agenda for action at Havana largely as the result of the Montevideo disclosures.

Intertwined with the political problem was the economic. Total war in the Nazi manner advances on economic fronts along with the political and military. The southern hemisphere had to be defended economically as well as politically. That, too, was a complex problem. Normally, 55 per cent of South American exports went to western Europe. With France, Italy, and the Low Countries withdrawn into the Axis orbit and Britain intensifying its blockade, that market was all but destroyed. Failing intelligent action on a vast scale, the Latin Republics faced the sort of distress which might provoke internal disorder and fertilize the soil for Axis intrigue.

All this was assuming that Britain would hold the fort. Should England go down, a Hitler-organized Europe would be in a position to apply enormous pressure on the raw-materials-producing economies of all South America. A Nazi cartel purchasing for all of Europe would have infinite capacity to reward and punish. Much of South America might then be absorbed bloodlessly into the Nazi scheme from a central purchasing bureau in Berlin.

Both contingencies, the second bleakly terrifying, confronted the President's Cabinet committee when, on June 17, it first sat in Mr. Hull's office charged with mapping the "most effective manner of disposing profitably of export surpluses in the Western Hemisphere." Uppermost in the consideration of that first session was a so-called cartel plan for the lump purchase of South America's export surpluses or raw materials. Presupposing or at least contemplating the fall of Britain, it projected a gigantic hemispheric selling agency which might match itself against a Nazi buying agency on something like even terms. A breath-taking formula, the cartel of the Americas would, as outlined, underwrite and store the wheat, flaxseed, and beef of the Argentine, the wool and beef of Uruguay, the copper and nitrates of Chile, the coffee, meat, and metals of Brazil, and various products of other Latin American countries for trade with all nonhemisphere customers.

Although the cartel proposal was publicly associated with Assistant Secretary Berle more than with any other individual, it came in fact from several minds all seeking to anticipate the devastating effects on hemispheric solidarity of a Nazi triumph across the Atlantic. Mr. Berle, author of a definite work on the history of corporations, has made the field of Government finance his own, and he worked, as did Leo Pasvolsky, an economic advisor to the State Department, on all phases of the problem. It was Harry Hopkins who christened the plan, which took its rise in the State Department, the

"inter-American cartel," and in his White House press conferences Stephen Early, with the President's approval, familiar-
ized first the press, and then the public, with its general
nature.

The cartel idea grew out of the grim realities of German
intentions as of June, 1940. Anticipating the fall of Britain
and command of the Atlantic, the Germans already had prepared for the commercial penetration and domination of
South America. Specifically, the Nazis had undertaken to sell
a large proportion of South America's needs for manufactured
goods and especially for machinery, railway supplies, and agricultural machinery. Firm contracts had been entered into with
delivery guaranteed on or after October 1, the Nazis' professed day of certain victory. They had likewise opened negotiations to buy large quantities of South American commodities.

It thus became plain that, in the event of Britain's defeat
or surrender, the United States would be confronted not only
with a military threat to the south, but also with an immediate
economic penetration of all of South and Central America
and Mexico, bringing in its train spies, fifth columnists, *sabo-
teurs,* and political warfare agents.

Berle, who had been assigned the task of studying the
situation, proposed that the Department explore the possibilities and implications of a countermarch, involving the
purchase of all South America's exportable products, for dollars, at favorable prices. This formidable plan soon had the
approval of, among others, Bernard M. Baruch. The South
American export aggregate ran to approximately nine hundred millions a year, but it was reckoned that, with judicious
trimming and the subtraction of that portion which normally
went into inter-American trade and to Britain, Asia, and
Africa, the sum to be advanced yearly would not exceed five
hundred millions. With this proposal was bracketed an undertaking to resell these goods to Europe on a basis that would

divide any profits accruing between the cartel and the South American producers. A part, or all, of the credit investment would be returned each year to the cartel.

The plan had considerable elasticity. In the case of certain commodities, it was supposed that the cartel would need only to establish itself as sole selling agent, with a guaranty to purchase any unsold goods. The combination of immediate and ready cash and an offer to defend against oppressive price policies would, it was believed, build a first line of economic defense against a Nazi-controlled Europe. If it were necessary to accept European goods in exchange, the cartel would at least be standing by to assure a fair exchange. It was felt that, even if a complete buying and selling arrangement were not necessary, or feasible, the very fact that the United States stood by as a willing and generous bidder in the open South American market would make it impossible for the Nazis to dominate South American economies and, hence, political life as well.

A preliminary sketch of this project reached Hopkins, then Secretary of Commerce. Hopkins joined in making representations to the President, endorsing the plan and urging its early adoption to forestall the penetration which already was assuming form. Mr. Roosevelt indicated that he would back Hopkins the whole way. Talks then were had with Jesse Jones, head of the Reconstruction Finance Corporation, about finding the credits necessary to launch a cartel. Mr. Jones foresaw difficulties in obtaining from Congress appropriations of the huge sums envisaged until the emergency took on bolder and more menacing outlines. In point of fact, as the totality of French disaster grew apparent and England's plight aroused this country's urgent concern, public sentiment in favor of a bold policy in South America increased so that by midsummer Congress readily granted a huge appropriation for the purpose of bolstering Latin American economies.

The State Department building is not air-conditioned. Mr.

Hull's office faces south. On late afternoons in June and July it can scarcely be recommended as a comfortable gathering place. At several conferences, in that office, the Cabinet committee, flanked by its experts, threshed out the economic defense of the hemisphere.

A less ambitious formula finally emerged, to be embodied, on July 22, in a special message to Congress, proposing the enlargement of the Export-Import Bank's capital by half a billion dollars. That sum, the President advised Congress, would be earmarked for the assistance of "our neighbors south of the Rio Grande," in large part to finance the "handling and orderly marketing of some part of their surpluses." Congress would in time agree, and thus a bottom was to be placed under the export markets of our neighbors, whatever happened. The umbrellalike cartel formula had been cast aside, temporarily at least, partly on economic grounds but in part also because England still stood.

In practice, and as defense needs and wartime requirements of the democracies grew, the plan was to be implemented along lines not foreseen in June, 1940. The five hundred millions placed in the Export-Import Bank treasury by Congress were used to stabilize the Latin-American economy during 1940 and 1941, but meanwhile other large appropriations were made for the purchase of Army and Navy materials in those countries. Gradually it became plain that the Defense Materials Corporation could buy virtually every South American exportable product to advantage, for the use of ourselves and our allies and not for resale.

The State Department thereupon co-ordinated that effort with the political situation and entered into agreements with the various countries to the south by which they consigned substantially all their production to this country's account. Such agreements are now in force over almost all of South America.

—3—

The problem of the orphaned French colonies—French Guiana, the Caribbean islands of Martinique and Guadeloupe, and the islets of St. Pierre and Miquelon off the coast of New-foundland—was, of course, even more imminent than that of the South American surpluses. In the same category fell the Netherlands possessions, Dutch Guiana, and the Curaçao group off Venezuela, which included the important oil-refining island of Aruba. British command of the Atlantic, together with our own naval force, might be counted upon to prevent actual physical possession of these small dependencies by the Nazis. Yet there was no warrant that Quisling governments in France and Holland, if such came to power, might not turn over the islands and territories by subterfuge, installing colonial governors taking orders from Berlin. In that case, these possessions would become spearheads of Nazi penetration in the heart of the Caribbean and off our Atlantic coast.

On June 15, for whatever purposes of his own, Hitler had disavowed interest in the American colonies of France and Holland. In an interview with a Hearst correspondent, Karl H. von Wiegand, the *Führer* coupled, however, a warning with his disavowal. Not only, said Hitler, had the Nazis planned no incursion into the Americas, but "the manner in which the American continent shapes its life" was "of no interest to us." There could, he admonished, however, be "no one-sided claim to freedom from intervention." His policy, he volunteered, was "America for the Americans, Europe for the Europeans." This was, of course, merely a restatement of a traditional German attitude. Germany, in truth, never had acknowledged the Monroe Doctrine either under the Empire or the Third Reich.

Three days later, Mr. Hull dispatched a note to Berlin and Rome, warning those Governments that the United States, in accordance with its "traditional policy," would recognize no transfer of sovereignty in this hemisphere from one European state to another. The Secretary was paraphrasing the Senate resolution, which he had helped to shape, as well as a similar declaration adopted by the House on that same day by a vote of 380 to 8. Sol Bloom, chairman of the House Foreign Affairs Committee, had fathered the House pronouncement, which had been based on the Monroe Doctrine.

Of the Axis powers, only Germany replied definitely to the Hull note. Von Ribbentrop's attitude was spirited. Inasmuch as Germany had no possessions on this side of the water and had shown no disposition to acquire any, the American representation was, as regards Germany, "without object." Furthermore, he held the American position basically discriminatory, in effect denying, as it did, the right of powers other than France, Britain, and Holland to fly their flag in the hemisphere. He challenged also the legal right of this country to draw a line around the Americas unless it abstained from interference in the "affairs of the European continent." *

It suited Ribbentrop, as it had imperial foreign ministers, to assume that the Monroe Doctrine was a mere imperialistic shield behind which the United States exerted dominance over the hemisphere. In his answer, the Secretary, not unnaturally finding Herr von Ribbentrop's view a twisting of basic principles, redefined the Monroe Doctrine as a "policy of self-defense" for the whole hemisphere, containing "within it not the slightest vestige of any implication . . . of hegemony on the part of the United States."

In Tokyo, Japanese apologists for the "East Asia Co-Prosperity Sphere" had been seeking to approximate it to the Monroe Doctrine. Mr. Hull emphatically rejected the Japanese attempt to borrow the Doctrine, which, he said, with a sharp glance toward Tokyo, had no correspondence with "pol-

* Von Ribbentrop's arguments were a recapitulation of views he expressed to Sumner Welles during the latter's visit to Berlin in March of 1940.

icies which appear to be rising in other geographical areas of the world." Such policies, it seemed to him, were merely a "pretext for carrying out of conquest by the sword, for military occupation, and of complete economic and political domination by certain powers of other free and independent peoples."

In response to the warnings of Hitler and Ribbentrop, the Secretary affirmed the right of the United States to co-operate with "all other nations," whenever and wherever it chose, solely in its own interest or "for the purpose of promoting economic, commercial, and social rehabilitation, and of advancing the cause of international law and order, of which the entire world stands so tragically in need today."

With the call for the Havana Conference, which provided automatically for the assembling of the American republics, a start was made toward the more active defense of the hemisphere. Under terms of a resolution adopted at the Inter-American Conference for the Maintenance of Peace at Buenos Aires, and later implemented at the Lima Conference, presence at a meeting of foreign ministers whenever any one of them judges the peace of the hemisphere imperiled is obligatory. There remained the job of fitting such defense into the mold of hemispheric co-operation formed at the successive inter-American conferences under the Good Neighbor policy at Montevideo, Buenos Aires, Lima, and Panama. As a result of these consultations, the Monroe Doctrine had undergone another of its numerous transformations, this time emerging as a multilateral policy founded on the consent of all the American republics.

—4—

Mr. Hull led the United States delegation to Havana, with Mr. Berle as his chief coadjutor. It has become an asset to this Government in the continuing inter-American relationships that the Secretary and the Department's two principal officers have a full inter-American experience. Thus, the auspices at Havana were favorable, though outwardly Axis propaganda made an impressive showing.

In casting doubt on British survival and suspicion on American motives, the German and Italian diplomats and other agents on the ground had support from a new quarter—the Spanish Falange. An Axis subsidiary, the Falange, directed from Madrid by Foreign Minister Serrano Suñer, Franco's brother-in-law, professes aspirations toward Spanish-speaking solidarity in the "new order." Violently anti-American and anti-British, it enlisted support at Havana from Spanish nationals and nostalgic elements among the reactionary forces in Cuba. Fortunately, however, because of its high-flown talk about a new Spanish-American empire, undoing the work of the nineteenth-century revolutions, it fared ill in political, labor, and other more realistic circles. But the Falange was to serve as a not inconsiderable channel of Axis propaganda in Latin American quarters into which the Nazis themselves could not penetrate because of language or antipathy.

The Nazi agents played on the uncertainty of Anglo-American command of the Atlantic—the battle of that ocean having only just begun—pointedly suggesting that Latin America might have to do business with Hitler. Ostentatiously, German commercial agents at Havana, as elsewhere in the United States, offered the October 1 contracts for deliveries of chemicals, heavy machinery, and other representative German products. In one pre-Havana case, the Nazis had resorted to political blackmail: Otto Reinebeck, German Minister to the Central American states, openly warning those Governments against collaboration on penalty of punishment after the German victory. When Costa Rica threatened to air the threat, Reinebeck withdrew his notes to the Government.

The conference met in Cuba's splendid Capitol in the busy Prado. On the opening day Mr. Hull smiled with grave satisfaction as the name of republic after republic was announced by a trilingual functionary. The United States came last. To Mr. Hull that was a good augury. One of the Secretary's aptitudes is for the successful concealment at inter-American gatherings of the disproportionate power, wealth, population, and other potentially discomforting attributes of the United States.

As the Captain of Company H, Fourth Tennessee Volunteers, Cordell Hull had shown a willingness to help with the freeing of Cuba in '98. The service in Cuba sharpened his facility at poker, as well as his administrative talents when Inspector General of the city of Trinidad, near the south coast. That link to Cuba's heroic past now stood him in good stead, being enthusiastically publicized in Havana, with sometimes surprising results. On the evening of Hull's arrival a street gamin accosted a saber-scarred German outside the American Club, begging a coin. The German took no notice, whereupon the boy shrilled: "German dog! Colonel Batista will get you, and if he doesn't, Cordell Hool will!" The Secretary's smile always has a tinge of sadness. When repeated to him, this story only deepened the tinge.

Hull keynoted the session on the second day. Before he spoke the President strengthened his hand by sending his special message to Congress on Latin American surpluses. Berle had been among the first to suggest this opportune timing. The President's message was accepted at Havana as an earnest of good faith in the solution of common problems. In his address, Mr. Hull came to the heart of the matter of the semiorphaned colonies by proposing a "collective trusteeship," with which to expropriate and administer a colony or colonies, should that become necessary. The principle of a trusteeship for European colonies dated back to 1811; the collective feature alone was novel. Since 1811, and more especially since 1933, the United States had advanced into a state of grace by which it preferred multilateral to unilateral sanctions in hemispheric matters. The United States did not, however, carry quixotism to the point of leaving action to a committee. Mr. Hull suggested that, in case of emergency, one nation could act for all; and that was to be agreed upon.

A scattering of other proposals reached the conference floor, including a revival of the League of Nations mandate formula. Brazil and Colombia backed the mandate alternative, under which an individual republic might be charged with administering a pre-empted colony. Dr. Leopoldo Melo, veteran of inter-American gatherings, represented Argentina.

A week after the conference opened only Argentina was holding out, and Dr. Melo, finding himself in the customary Argentine minority of one, yielded on the vital points.

The conference disposed of two other major topics. In his address, Mr. Hull dealt sternly with the abuse of diplomatic hospitality by Nazi agents—"termites of alien propaganda"—in the guise of legation attachés, calling for "decisive remedial action" against the Axis' "new and evil technique." As one remedy, the conference arranged for the exchange of information regarding improper activities by Axis diplomats. The second major consideration was economic, and there the conferees authorized enlargement of the Inter-American Financial and Economic Advisory Committee, created at Panama, and reference to it of the problems of surplus marketing, commodity loans, currency stabilization, and the stimulation of inter-American trade. In the economic nature of things, the load of adjusting the Latin States to wartime conditions would have to be borne primarily by the power most able to bear it, the United States. This Government gladly shouldered the burden.

Out of the conference came the Act of Havana, which, giving multilateral sanction to Washington's determination not to allow American colonies to fall to the Axis, also knit the hemisphere closer for its own military and moral defense. Out of the collaborative spirit manifested at Havana issued the gradual enfeeblement of Axis influence. Axis propaganda, seeking to rekindle animosities against the "colossus of the North," prevailed only sporadically. The Good Neighbor policy, patiently pursued, was proof against such cynical falsification.

The Vargas incident dramatically tested the policy of forbearance. Only one day after the President's Charlottesville speech, President Vargas, speaking on the battleship *Minas Geraes* in Rio harbor, uttered sentiments that seemed imitative of the ideological pronouncements of Rome and Berlin. Already suspect because he had dispensed with Congress and set up a personal rule, Senhor Vargas declared that "the era of improvident liberalism, sterile demagoguery, and useless individualism has passed. Vigorous peoples fit for life must follow the route of their aspirations. . . ." Elsewhere in the address, he announced that Brazil was "united by ties of strict solidarity with all American countries around the ideas, aspirations, and common interests of our defense." That avowal was overlooked in the storm of criticism which arose throughout the Americas. In Axis circles the Vargas speech was interpreted as a repudiation of the democratic solidarity championed by Roosevelt.

A wave of indignant protests rolled into the White House and State Department. Some Americans who had been among the most outspoken in condemning the Axis for trampling upon smaller States forgot consistency in urging strong measures against Vargas. Although Mr. Roosevelt and Mr. Hull were disturbed that the Brazilian President should have given comfort to the enemy, they declined to be flurried. Ambassador Carlos Martins, taking note of American sentiment, called on Mr. Hull, assuring him that Senhor Vargas had spoken in justification of his regime and without thought of contradicting Mr. Roosevelt's views. Vargas spoke on June 11; on the 13th he dispatched the following cablegram to the Brazilian embassy:

Speech delivered June 11 can in no sense be regarded as contradictory to that of President Roosevelt, whose speech I had not read at the time. My speech is a warning, a call to reality, addressed to Brazilians and which might cause surprise only to persons devoted to routine, not to a farseeing mind like that of Roosevelt, who is liberal-minded, progressive, and forward-looking, crying out as the voice of the whole continent regarding perils which threaten America and who knows that Brazil will not fail him in loyalty.

The message went to the State Department and from there to the White House on the 14th. No representations had been made by this Government. The Vargas cable closed the incident, if it could be called an incident.

Thus, the co-operative policy has produced immense results in the crusade against Nazism: air and sea bases for hemisphere defense, industrial co-ordination, and the suppression of Axis intrigue.

—5—

The lighthouse on the Cape Verde peninsula, which juts into the Atlantic beyond Dakar, is the only such beacon in the nearly five thousand miles of West African coast from Casablanca, Morocco, to Capetown. The lighthouse signifies a good harbor, which Dakar has, as well as commodious land and seaplane bases. Cape Verde peninsula happens to be the westernmost point of Africa. It faces directly across the Atlantic and Caribbean on Tegucigalpa, Nicaragua, but the nearest land point in the Americas, Natal, on the hump of Brazil, is barely seventeen hundred miles away. In the hands of an enemy of the Western Hemisphere, Dakar, a considerable stronghold and a steaming, French colonial peanut port of eighty thousand souls, mostly black, would be the inevitable jumping-off place for invasion. As a submarine and air base, Dakar might disrupt British and American communications with the Near and Far East by way of the Cape of Good Hope, endangering the American lines of communication to South America as well. For many months Dakar would seldom be long out of the consciousness of the American Government.

At the end of July, 1940, the State Department first heard disquieting news about Dakar. A delegation of Nazi technical experts, naval and air-force men and harbor engineers, had arrived for a survey of Dakar's military installations. Meanwhile, a party of Spanish civilians had turned up in Monrovia, Liberia, the Negro republic on the African west coast, sounding the Liberian authorities on the acquisition of air-base facilities for a proposed air line to South America. These hints at projected interventions on this strategic coast forewarned the Department.

The situation called for emergency action. This Government had no one on the ground, the Dakar consulate having been closed ten years earlier during an economy wave that pruned the foreign service under Hoover. The chore of rectifying our lack of eyes and ears in western Africa was referred to Mr. Berle. On August 6, Thomas C. Wasson, a Montanan and a coldly observant consular officer whose wits had been sharpened in Nigeria, Australia, and Mediterranean ports, was assigned to reopen the consulate in Dakar. So urgent did Berle deem the matter that Wasson was shipped off at once, without asking the Vichy Government for an exequatur. The unauthorized consul arrived at Dakar on September 14, showed his credentials to the gendarmes at the pier, called on Pierre Boisson, the Governor General of West Africa, finding him hospitable, and on the 15th ran up the flag on his consulate. Thereafter Wasson, with his large, expert, and realistic staff, was to keep a sharp watch for Nazi activities should they develop.

Eight days after Wasson's arrival he witnessed the ill-fated Anglo-Free French attempt, first to wean Dakar away from Vichy and, failing that, to subdue the port. De Gaulle had been circumvented by Vichy re-enforcements that slipped past Gibraltar on three cruisers and three destroyers "to overawe the population, grip the defenses, and see to the efficient manning of the powerful shore batteries." That was Winston Churchill's reading of the situation in Parliament. The British nursed wounds to a battleship and a cruiser, a formal inquiry produced disciplinary action against those responsible for the lapse at Gibraltar, and Dakar settled down to allegiance to Vichy. It was all the more important after the De Gaulle expedition that the United States keep an eye on Dakar.

August was a month of speculative gossip and strategical stocktaking in Washington. If Hitler overwhelmed the "tight little island," where would he strike next? Mussolini had started General Graziani on what he hoped was the road to Alexandria and Suez. The strategists pretty generally surmised that the next Nazi move would be south: through France and Spain to Gibraltar and then across the Mediterranean, branching southward along the Atlantic coast to Dakar, and eastward on the African coast of the Mediterranean. A successful venture in that direction would at once endanger Britain's grip on the Mediterranean and the South Atlantic. By that road also, Hitler might support the Italian legions in North Africa, the hollowness of whose military prowess had not yet been disclosed.

In the division of labor at the State Department, African affairs, outside Egypt and the Union of South Africa, fell to Berle. On August 27, in a general talk in Mr. Hull's office, Berle introduced a thought that had been running through his mind for several days: "Why not try to protect our South Atlantic flank and assist the British by holding the French African colonies out of the Axis orbit? Being at peace, and having no arms for the task, we shall have to do it with 'our heads,' that is to say, by diplomacy." Mr. Hull had been working over this problem in his mind for some time. In the ensuing conversation there emerged the first dim outlines of what came to be the enormously useful North African policy. But more pressing events supervened, and the policy would not begin to take form for another three months.

In mid-September the first Ambassador from Vichy France, Gaston Henry-Haye, arrived, preposterously likening his mission to that of Franklin's to France in 1776 and assuring the President that the ideal for which France fought "still remains alive in the hearts of Frenchmen." Henry-Haye, a little man wearing unusually high heels, whose ruddy cheeks, bristling mustache, and bristling manner give him the appearance of chronic truculence, was a Senator and Mayor of Versailles. An Americophile, he rejoiced in the *nom du politique* of "the American Senator" and was a familiar of American circles in Paris, where he seemed sociable and politically harmless, although generally regarded as a parliamentary follower of Laval. Notably, he had supported the Hoare-Laval program for the reduction and partition of Ethiopia.

Although Henry-Haye came in the name of Pétain, there manifestly existed some dubiety in the marshal's mind about his Ambassador, for soon thereafter Camille Chautemps arrived also. The former Premier and Radical parliamentarian, who had been brushed by the Stavisky scandal, bore personal credentials from the marshal and established informal relations with the State Department. His dispatches to Pétain went forward through the American diplomatic pouch, and the marshal communicated with Chautemps through the American embassy at Vichy. By Pétain's request, Chautemps received two thousand dollars a month from French funds frozen by the Treasury. The State Department gave a hearing to Chautemps, as Pétain's personal envoy, on matters involving France, and the little emissary steadily avowed his democratic, liberal, pro-Allied sentiments. Unlike many men in the service of Vichy, Chautemps professed to see his future and the future of France bound up in defeat of the Axis. This anomalous situation came to an end in August, 1941, when, for reasons not made clear to Chautemps, the Vichy Government terminated his assignment and pay.

Upon his installation in the handsome French embassy above Rock Creek Park, Henry-Haye initiated agitation at the State Department for food for unoccupied France. His endeavors synchronized with the wider campaign of Herbert Hoover and others aimed at relaxing the British blockade in the interest of all the Nazi-held countries. The Hoover campaign came to nothing, principally because it conflicted with the national policy, which was constantly being confirmed and elaborated, of defending our Atlantic frontier by faithful support of the British.

The case of France fell, however, into a special category. In the general scheme of the Atlantic powers, it grew more and more evident that Vichy France was to be an American responsibility, a development which pleased Lord Lothian and Prime Minister Churchill. At the time of Henry-Haye's arrival it happened that the President and Norman Davis, president of the American Red Cross, had been consulting on the French food problem. Mr. Davis was seeking, as he put it, to balance military necessity and humanitarian considerations as the President examined the political aspects in regard both to England and France.

The last American supplies to France had reached Marseilles on July 14, the *McKeesport,* laden with food, clothing, medicine, and hospital equipment, being the American Red Cross answer to the French refugee problem. Part of the *McKeesport*'s cargo was unloaded in Bilbao, Spain, but by far the larger bulk went on to France. Owing to the Nazi occupation of Bordeaux, the ship went around to Marseilles in the Mediterranean. Richard F. Allen, the able Red Cross Commissioner for France, supervised distribution of clothing and food, largely concentrates, to Belgian, Polish, French, and central European refugees, the hospital equipment going into the nine departments north of Paris which had been ravaged by the invasion forces. Such hospitals as had not been destroyed in the fighting had been appropriated by the Nazis, the civilian population being left to the mercy of makeshifts hastily improvised by French doctors. The Red Cross hospital supplies were a godsend to the people of the war-torn regions. Although the Nazi command in Paris pursued a correct policy toward Commissioner Allen insofar as this distribution was concerned, it sought to impose restrictions on the Red Cross' future activities in the occupied zone. This ended Red Cross operations in that region, Allen being obliged to reject the Nazi conditions.

Mr. Roosevelt had put off nominating an Ambassador to France until after election. The problem, as he saw it after re-election had freed his hands, was to select an envoy to Pétain rather than to the Vichy regime. Already, American policy was being personalized, keyed to the figure of the old marshal. For that purpose, the President first thought of General Pershing. A bond of friendship, based on their comradeship in the last war, existed between the eighty-four-year-old marshal and the eighty-year old American. Bullitt, who considered Pershing ideal for the job, sounded him unofficially. The general, delighted at the prospect of stepping out of virtual retirement to serve his country in a hard post, was at first mildly incredulous.

"Are you sure the President wants me?" he asked. General Edwin M. ("Pa") Watson, a Presidential secretary, carried the formal tender, which Pershing promptly accepted, only to be overruled by physicians at Walter Reed Hospital, who, after a checkup, advised that he forego the appointment. The General, although bearing his years well, had been wintering in Arizona for some time past, and his physicians believed he needed that dry, sunny climate.

With Pershing out, the difficult chore at Vichy fell to a retired admiral, William Daniel Leahy, a native of Iowa, a salty officer, one of the few survivors of the gallant dash around the Horn of the battleship *Oregon* in 1898, a Presidential favorite and, at the time of his appointment to Vichy, Governor of Puerto Rico. Leahy, only sixty-five, had an impressively blunt quarterdeck manner, a reputation for candor, and a rather Spartan devotion to duty. It is a Navy legend that Leahy once stayed on his bridge for six weeks at a stretch during fleet maneuvers, relaxing only in brief naps. When Chief of Naval Operations, he customarily lunched in the Navy Department Building cafeteria, standing in line with junior officers, clerks, and stenographers and carrying his own tray. The President anticipated accurately, as it turned out, that Leahy would get on a sound, realistic, and comradely footing with the marshal. Our urgent concern about the future of the French Fleet and naval bases also made appropriate the choice of a naval man as the new Ambassador.

Mr. Roosevelt selected Admiral Leahy before departing on his West Indies cruise. At first the pro-Nazi press of Paris hailed the appointment as evidence of White House approval of the Vichy policies, which were, at the moment, being spun by Laval as a web around Pétain. For a few days Leahy was represented as sympathetic with the tendency toward collaboration, but a study of the Admiral's outspoken utterances quickly disillusioned the Nazi propaganda organs. A militant supporter of the Government's foreign policy, Leahy anticipated our entrance into the war, believed we would have to fight, and fight hard, to crush the Axis. In 1937 he had favored bringing Japan to book by clamping on a naval blockade.

—6—

Admiral Leahy was not to reach his post until January. In the meantime an event in France had focused Washington's attention on the French problem, intensifying and hastening our efforts to meet it. On October 25, Pétain met Hitler at

Montoire. The first meeting of vanquished and victor, it had been arranged by Laval, who, in his campaign of intrigue which was aimed at outwitting both the marshal and the Germans, had ambitious plans afoot. Pétain and Hitler held only a somewhat formal colloquy, the marshal being reported as stiffly ill at ease, the Chancellor torn between respect for the old soldier's age and frosty contempt for a defeatist. Such effective negotiations as went on were between Hitler and Laval. They eventuated in what Laval still speaks of as the "Montoire policy."

The negotiations were by no means satisfactory to Hitler, for, while he could act with finality, Laval had still to take into account Pétain's aloof, crotchety disposition. In general, Laval promised to try to make the French bases in the Mediterranean and West Africa available to the Nazis in exchange for a return of the French Government to Paris, the repatriation of war prisoners, and repudiation by Hitler of his supposed agreement to satisfy Italy's Mediterranean aspirations at the expense of the French Riviera and Tunisia. The fleet also was involved, Laval pledging his efforts to have it employed in convoying food ships, in "guarding" the bases, and in other activities designed to bring it into conflict with the British.

This all-out collaboration, short of open hostilities, was not, of course, effectuated. The sequel to Montoire lay in the events of December 13, when Laval was dismissed and placed under house arrest by his outraged senior.

Meanwhile, Pétain, on his return from Montoire, went to Amboise, where an emissary from Mussolini caught up with him. The Fascist spokesman warned the marshal against the "Montoire policy," enlightened him as to the full extent of Laval's purposes, and appealed to him in the name of a Latin, Mediterranean power bloc—France, Italy, and Spain—which had always had a certain attraction for the marshal. At about that moment, *Il Duce* was launching his wanton and doomed campaign against the Greeks.

The news of Montoire and gossip, diplomatic and otherwise, of increasing friction between Pétain and Laval stepped up American activity in two quarters. The island of Martinique had been a potential trouble spot since the French armistice. A sugar island, its 250,000 black population having only a thin layer of whites, Martinique was not in itself of major importance. But the harbor of Fort-de-France held the cruiser *Émile Bertin*, with a quarter of a billion dollars in gold in her hold, and the aircraft carrier *Béarn*, with six smaller war vessels which had been sent by Darlan to Martinique for refuge. The *Béarn* had been ferrying 105 American-made planes, dive bombers, pursuits, and trainers to France on June 17 in response to Reynaud's appeals. These were now parked ashore. The gold, at Bullitt's suggestion, had been on its way to New York when the blow fell. Later, it was removed to Fort-de-Saix, in the hills above the harbor.

On July 4, the British, who claimed title to the planes as part of an arrangement whereby they had assumed all unforwarded French war orders in America, levied a demand on Admiral Georges Robert, commanding at Martinique, and began to patrol the island. Inasmuch as this virtual act of blockade violated the neutrality-belt provisions adopted at Panama, the United States Government, acting for the Pan-American concert, asked the British to abandon it. After some discussion this was done, and thereafter the United States, which had re-established its consulate at Fort-de-France, maintained its own naval patrol outside the harbor.

The situation in Martinique in the fall aroused State Department concern. There were reports of infiltration by Nazi "tourists" and the arrival of German aviators from Colombia, where German interests still operated two air lines, as well as a fear that U-boats might be fueled there. A detachment of eight American naval vessels, under a heavy cruiser, maneuvered in the neighborhood of Martinique, and early in November the President sent Rear Admiral John W. Greenslade to call on Robert. Greenslade was then in Trinidad, settling on sites for the new naval and air bases. Out of their conversations grew the Greenslade-Robert memorandum, a "gentlemen's agreement," the terms of which are here first disclosed, binding the French commandant to retain the *Bertin's* gold and the aircraft in Martinique and to hold his naval vessels in Martinique waters, giving this Government ninety-six hours' notice of any intended ship movements. Under the agreement, likewise, an American naval observer was admitted to Fort-de-France by Admiral Robert; our right to naval and air patrol was acknowledged. As a separate agreement, this Government undertook to supply Martinique and Guadeloupe with food, defraying the cost from blocked French funds. The Latin Republics were, naturally, advised of these steps.

In November, several factors combined to bring the African colonies' question to the fore. In the summer, General Weygand had been sent to Algeria as Delegate General to Tunisia, Algeria, and Morocco, Darlan succeeding to the Defense Ministry. Weygand found the economy of these agricultural lands demoralized by the blockade, with civil disorder imminent. The natives were clamoring for tea and sugar; the farms, many of which had been mechanized with American machinery, required fuel for their tractors, parts for combines, etc., fertilizer, nails, wire, binder twine, bags, and lubricating oil. There were other shortages of essential products such as kerosene, coal, condensed milk for infants, and tobacco. In Vichy, where Weygand stormily was asking for assistance in obtaining these commodities, Robert Murphy, chargé d'affaires of the United States Embassy, talked with Pétain on the plight of North Africa. A native of Milwaukee, a skilled and personable diplomat, Murphy was on excellent terms with both Pétain and Weygand.

Meanwhile, in Washington, Paul Guérin, son of the president of the Morocco State Railways, was seeking permission to ship coal to his father's line. Guérin had intimate details of the economic state of the colonies. And American business interests, such as the linoleum trade, which had been dependent on Morocco for cork, were inquiring of the State Department if shipments might be resumed.

On November 15 Murphy was ordered to Algiers to make a survey and to sound Weygand on his disposition. Reaching Algiers on December 18, he found Weygand eager to enter into negotiations. On November 28, Berle and officers of the Near East Division, which handles African matters also, began a study of the economic relationships of the French African colonies involved.

Approaches were made to the British, and upon Lord Lothian's return from a visit to London in November he was persuaded of the usefulness of a U. S.-North African understanding. One obstacle among others stood in the path: negotiations had been begun by Sir Samuel Hoare, the British Ambassador at Madrid, looking to a three-way trade among Morocco, Spain, and Britain, under which tea and sugar would go to North Africa, African phosphates to Spain, and specified commodities to England. This proposal, which failed to meet the African situation, being limited to Morocco and to only a few items of trade, had supporters in the British Foreign Office.

On this side of the water Sir Arthur Salter, British shipping representative and a famous economist, protested the use of ships for this purpose, gaining support from the Maritime Commission and from Harry Hopkins, who never had approved of the French policies, Vichy or North African. Likewise, the Ministry of Economic Warfare showed reluctance to breach the blockade in the interest of American-North African trade. The President, Mr. Hull, and Mr. Berle were insistent, but the discussions, at which all these difficulties were to be ironed out, took several weeks. Finally, the Ministry of Economic Warfare sent a representative, David Eccles, to Washington to help administer the agreement, which was entered into as between Weygand and Murphy on February 28; it was confirmed by Leahy and Darlan on March 10. The story of that agreement is here sketched for the first time.

Back in France, Pétain was told that Laval had arranged with Hitler for the return of *L'Aiglon's* (the Duke of Reichstadt, Napoleon's son) body to Paris—for ulterior reasons: Pétain, on reaching Paris to receive the remains, was to be lodged at Versailles and thereafter held as the virtual prisoner of Laval and the *Herrenvolk*. This report Pétain believed, and in a stormy session of the Ministry he charged his second in command with intended betrayal, ordering his dismissal and arrest.

An American who had official business with Otto Abetz, the so-called German Ambassador to Paris, was dining with Abetz and several ranking Nazis in a Paris restaurant on the evening of December 13. News of Laval's fall reached them at dinner. Abetz, a sinuous and ingratiating intellectual who had wormed his way into Parisian cultural and social circles as an enemy agent before the war, prides himself on his worldly aplomb. The dinner talk had been sophisticated, the Nazis urbanely discussing French letters, philosophies of history, and other cultivated topics. Upon receipt of the word from Vichy their cosmopolitanism vanished. Abetz was especially moved. He flew into a rage, denouncing the French as swine and threatening to humiliate Pétain. All agreed that Hitler would, and should, march across the unoccupied zone, placing all France under the heel of the military.

It was apparent to the American that the Nazis had no advance word of Laval's disgrace. For forty-eight hours, while Abetz was in Vichy procuring Laval's release, the American momentarily expected to hear the Nazis pounding out of Paris on their way to the Pyrenees and Marseilles. Had they marched, the course of the war might then and there have changed, since the French Fleet, or a part of it, and the Mediterranean ports would have been placed at once in German hands. Whereupon the western Mediterranean would promptly have been closed to the British. The American shuddered as he waited for word of the second invasion, which did not come.

CHAPTER FIVE

"White War" in the Pacific;
Japan Joins the Axis

FIFTEEN months before Pearl Harbor Japan launched a "white war" against the English-speaking Powers and the Dutch in the Pacific. A diplomatic offensive aimed at securing all of French Indo-China as a base for the military invasion of Malaya, the East Indies, Australasia, Burma, and India on the way to a hoped-for junction with Hitler and world conquest, the "white war" rested upon a deal with the *Führer* and his tool, Laval.

In exchange for an exclusive franchise to conquer and pillage in southeastern Asia and the south Pacific, Hirohito and his samurai Government were willing to assume a full-fledged partnership in the Rome-Berlin Axis. That was the price they would pay, but they insisted on delivery of part of Indo-China before signing on the dotted line at Berlin. The Japanese were, as usual, being forehanded in dealing with Europeans. Early in September, 1940, they initiated the transaction by serving an ultimatum on the French colonial authorities at Hanoï, in Tonkin, the northernmost of the Indo-Chinese native states, a copy being handed at the same time to Laval at Vichy. A request went forward also to Berlin for its good offices with Vichy.

Here was the crux of the situation. In June, Hitler had publicly disclaimed any interest in the Asiatic and South Seas possessions of France and Holland. The Japanese wished now

ever so urgently to know if the *Reichskanzler* meant what he
said in June.

The demands levied upon the French were, in a sense, moderate. All that Japan wished—at the moment—was Tonkin,
the right to take over the air and sea bases there, garrison a
force of six thousand men, and use the railway into China
for troop transport. They were leaving Annam and Cochin-
China down the coast for later. Tonkin they could have had
without notice to Vichy or appeal to Berlin, their railway
guards already having swarmed across the province, but they
wished, even more, the formal approval of Berlin.

As Tokyo desired, the decision was made in Berlin, where
the ultimatum had been obediently referred by Laval. Hitler
gave it his endorsement. Hence, on September 19, an Imperial
Council, gathered around the timeless throne of Hirohito,
voted to join the Rome-Berlin Axis. A profound secret in
Tokyo, the American and British diplomats knew of it almost
as soon as the last councilor had voted aye, and a lady of the
British Embassy startled a Japanese Minister at dinner that
night by putting it bluntly to him:

"Why did you do it?"

Three days later the deal was confirmed when the French
authorities at Hanoï announced surrender to the ultimatum.
By that time Japanese warships lay in the harbor of Haiphong,
and Japanese war planes were dropping into the airdrome at
Hanoï. On the 27th, a politely smiling Saburo Kurusu, who
was later, as we have seen, to take part in another climactic
incident in the Pacific war, scratched his signature to a three-
power pact in the Hall of the Diplomats in Hitler's mau-
soleumlike Chancellery in Berlin, with the *Führer* and Count
Ciano watching him somewhat cynically. From some stand-
points it had been a hard bargain for the European partners.
A Japan dominating all Asia and the Pacific might not be
wholly to the liking of the Aryan master race at some remote
day of triumph. That night, Joachim von Ribbentrop, tele-

phoning his felicitations to the Japanese Foreign Minister, Yosuke Matsuoka, in Tokyo, invited him in the name of the *Führer* to visit Berlin at his earliest convenience for a talk about other aspects of the bargain.

On the day before the exercises in Berlin, President Roosevelt, closely advised about the ramifications of the new alliance, clamped down on shipments of scrap iron to any points outside the Western Hemisphere or the British Empire. Otherwise, this Government gave no public indication of concern. Mr. Hull issued a perfunctory statement, saying the pact did not "substantially alter a situation which has existed for several years." He was referring to the anti-Comintern alliance of 1936, an engagement that had gone into eclipse with the Nazi-Soviet undertaking of August, 1939. Once when asked for his view of the earlier compact's significance, Mr. Hull lapsed into the vernacular, suggesting that "if you stepped on the tail of one of them, the other two would holler." In his statement, Mr. Hull concluded that this Government had long known of the devious developments between Japan and the Axis and had been shaping its policies accordingly.

In private, the men responsible for American foreign policy had few illusions about the Far Eastern situation. The Japanese Empire was on the highroad to expansion, bound to fight any power not now involved in the European or Sino-Japanese wars should that power take a hand in either. There was, in addition, a secret protocol, which was Hitler's *quid pro quo,* committing Japan to engage the English-speaking Powers whenever the circumstances seemed ripe to the Axis. Two powers stood outside those wars, Russia and the United States, but the Soviet Union was excluded by name from the pact's provisions. Any doubts of the treaty's implications were quickly dispelled by the forthright declaration of the Tokyo *Asahi* that "a clash between Japan and America now seems inevitable" or by the Berlin Foreign Office comment: "This is an answer to the destroyer deal."

The happenings on December 7, 1941, were implicit in the Tokyo-Berlin bargain of September, 1940.

—2—

An atmosphere of crisis pervaded the White House on the morning that Matsuoka's challenge was flung to this country, though unreflected in any public utterance or other indication of anxiety. While breakfasting in his bedroom, adjoining the study, Mr. Roosevelt sent for Mr. Hull and the Under Secretary. The time had come, he thought, to re-examine the Far Eastern policy in the light of the tripartite treaty and Matsuoka's bellicose utterance. The time was awkward, with so many other things pressing in at the moment. The battle of Britain still raged, the Atlantic line's security still hung in the balance, and the President was standing a sort of psychological siege from the British, who needed so much that neither they nor we had.

Welles took a cautious line, attaching some hope to Prince Fumimaro Konoye, the Japanese Premier, a neurasthenic aristocrat, who played golf and had the manners of a Western gentleman when with Western gentlemen and a son, "Butch," at Princeton. Konoye was reported as having wept upon receipt of the word from Berlin. He had opposed the deal in the Imperial Council until the last. But Konoye's picture was being hawked in Japan, alongside those of Hitler and Mussolini, on postcards proclaiming Japan's "new day," and Konoye had been Premier when the army embarked on the "China incident." In the end Konoye always went along with the Army, but Welles and others in the State Department would find it hard, nevertheless, to abandon hope that somehow Konoye would find a way to hold the military in check.

Mr. Hull, seeming in the full morning light more than ever the gentle, white-haired sage, muttered incongruous scurrilities against Matsuoka and the other Japs. The languid Konoye did not much impress Mr. Hull, and, as for Matsuoka, the Secretary was firmly convinced that the Foreign Secretary was "as crooked as a basket of fishhooks." Mr. Hull was, however, against precipitate word or deed: he has a favorite saying to the effect that before entering a tunnel he likes to "know where I'm coming out."

The President intently reviewed the situation in the Far East, his after-breakfast cigarette in the long holder making quick, exclamatory stabs into the air. Konoye's return to the premiership in July had been the result of an army coup with overtones of attempted assassination, thirty-four soldiers having been arrested in Tokyo behind a veil of strict censorship. With him came to power the unreliable Matsuoka and an unsmiling little general, Hideki Tojo, known in the half-world of assassins, fanatics, and adventurers making up the military caste as "The Razor." Tojo, who had been head of the secret police in Manchuria, that sink of Asiatic intrigue and corruption, was Minister of War and hence the most powerful man in the Government. The coup, unseating the relatively conciliatory Prime Minister, Admiral Mitsumasa Yonai, meant the intrenching of the pro-Nazi elements. Germany's deal with Russia had eclipsed these forces, but the lightning Nazi successes in western Europe had restored them to influence. The Axis pact merely formalized a profound spiritual alignment between the aggressive Asiatics and their European counterparts.

The possibilities were forbidding. Suppose the Japanese, having sought to warn the United States away, were to strike south? They had a foothold in Indo-China; they had Hitler's blessing on their aspirations in the Dutch Indies. Heinrich Stahmer, Ribbentrop's man, who had gone to Tokyo early in September by way of Moscow, assured Konoye and Matsuoka that their rear was safeguarded, as the Soviet Union would be neutral in a Pacific war. Britain was fighting for her life on the Channel; India was divided, Australia unprepared.

Only a few battalions of bewildered French colonial troops, an odd British regiment or two in Singapore, a spineless Siam already in Japan's orbit, and some brave but outnumbered and unequipped Dutch colonials in Java stood in September, 1940, between Japan and conquest of the East. And, should the Japanese by-pass the Philippines and coolly offer the United States unimpaired commerce with Malaya and the Indies, would the American people be willing to fight for Singapore and Bandoeng? And with what, our energies being applied to holding the Atlantic line, could we fight?

Mr. Roosevelt and his conferees of that morning had no doubt of the ruthless temper of the Japanese. Their only doubt was as to when it might be brought into play. At the moment there were other counsels around the President, men in and out of the State Department and the Administration, who honestly believed the Japanese were bluffing and, if not bluffing, were too weak to put up much of a fight against the American Navy and air force. Harry Hopkins was among these activists, who, in general, urged that we polish off the Japanese first, while the British still were holding the Atlantic, so that we might be freer for any eventualities in that region. Secretary Morgenthau, a passionately loyal friend of China, also pressed for a militant line, steadily contending for economic sanctions. In the Cabinet, Harold Ickes brusquely shared Morgenthau's view. Admirals Yarnell and Leahy, among the Navy authorities, advocated joining up with the British at Singapore and taking no more nonsense from the Japanese.

Prevailingly, these men believed Japan "bogged down in China," exhausted from a long war which they regarded, somewhat wishfully, as unsuccessful. They overlooked the fact that the Japanese controlled the ports, the coastal plains, and two thirds of China's industry and, while having trouble with guerrillas, had been able to halt large-scale warfare. These advisors saw the three-power pact as a gun aimed at the United

States, but "the gun wasn't loaded." That was a favorite figure of speech with the activist groups.

Mr. Roosevelt, charged with the ultimate responsibility, in the bedroom conference elucidated a larger view—a planetary, long-range view. Our first anxiety was the Atlantic; the arch-enemy of Western, Atlantic civilization was Hitlerism. If the three-power pact were a diversion cooked up by Hitler to deflect us from our main purpose, it would not work. On the other hand, we would not yield to threats in the Pacific. Nor would we abandon either our principles or the Chinese. That, in the light of American idealism and tradition, was unthinkable. We would hold the Atlantic line. We would likewise hold the Pacific line, but, whereas the first effort would be urgent and positive, the action in the Pacific would be a delaying one.

The President's jaw snapped down on that decision. So preoccupied was he with the Far Eastern problem that, although he received visitors at his office with his accustomed cheerfulness (a factor in Mr. Roosevelt's celebrated charm is the manner in which he makes visitors seem important to themselves by paying attentive heed to what they say), he slighted consideration of the matters they laid before him. With Stimson and Knox, he also canvassed the situation and by that afternoon he had his thinking reduced to a formula, which he outlined to a somewhat surprised delegation of Congressional leaders who had come on an unrelated errand. In the President's opinion, the Far Eastern policy should be formed along these simple, basic lines:

1. We pick no quarrels with Japan.
2. We back down from no issue with her.
3. We reserve the right to use economic pressure in the hope of bringing the Japanese to reason.
4. The door, meanwhile, is to be left wide open for discussion and accommodation within the framework of our historic position in the Far East.

Mr. Roosevelt reduced this basic policy to platform rhetoric two weeks later in a Columbus Day address to the Western Hemisphere delivered from his re-election-campaign train at Dayton, Ohio. The exposition was forceful but noninflammatory, and the President chose to enlarge the policy from one applicable only to the United States to one suitable for the whole hemisphere. Avowing his desire for peace, he yet served notice that "the Americas will not be scared or threatened into the ways the dictators want us to follow," proceeding:

> No combination of dictator countries of Europe and Asia will halt us in the path we see ahead for ourselves and for democracy. No combination of dictator countries of Europe and Asia will stop the help we are giving to almost the last free people fighting to hold them at bay. Our course is clear. Our decision is made.

As for "appeasing" the "forces of evil which are bent on conquest of the world":

> We know now that if we seek to appease them by withholding aid from those who stand in their way, we only hasten the day of their attack on us. The people of the United States, the people of the Americas, reject the doctrine of appeasement. They recognize it for what it is—a major weapon of the aggressor nations.

—3—

If the President, confronted by what now stood arrantly revealed as a world-wide league of aggression, was abiding his time in the Pacific, so also were the Japanese. At that moment, the island of Hainan, off the southern coast of China, was swarming with Japanese veterans from the Chinese war; 150,-000 of them learning to fight Commando fashion in the jungles of Malaya and the Indies. On Formosa, General Masaharu Homma, who had forced European women to strip, man-

handling their men, in the blockade of the Tientsin concession, was sweating an equal number of Japanese peasants in
landing drills for the seizure of the Philippines. It was this
Fourteenth Army which captured Manila and overwhelmed
the forces on Bataan. Of all this we had little detailed information, even the efficient Chinese intelligence being able to
obtain slight data as to what went on in these islands.

If Tojo and Konoye hoped to frighten this country, their
hopes were disappointed. The tone of comment by newspapers
and public men, except for the isolationist bloc in the Senate,
was forthright. Many Americans, including Admiral Yarnell
and Walter Lippmann, thought the United States should prepare to strike now. We might be better prepared now, in
Yarnell's opinion, than six years hence; Lippmann feared
that if we sat still and did nothing "to check the conquest of
the Far East . . . we shall . . . be growing weaker." The
Government reflected its point of view by sending re-enforcements to Hawaii and the Philippines, granting a new twenty-
five-million-dollar loan to China, and warning the 16,883
Americans in the Far East to come home. Thereafter the return passage of these nationals became a first charge on ship
ping facilities in the Pacific. The public showed every sign
of approving these steps. Nor were the people diverted from
their primary concern over the Atlantic front, a contemporary
Gallup poll showing that 55.9 per cent still regarded Germany
as the "greatest threat to the United States," while only 35.4
per cent saw Japan in that light.

A pregnant result of the Axis pact was the swift solidification
of Anglo-American policy in the Far East. The hard-pressed
Churchill had yielded to blackmail in July, ordering the
Burma Road closed to munitions shipments for three months
on the pretext that Japan and China might thus be afforded
an opportunity to reconcile their differences. To this the
American Government demurred, Mr. Hull calling the action
an "unwarranted" hindrance to world trade. On October 8,

four days before Mr. Roosevelt's Dayton speech, Mr. Churchill had informed the House of Commons that the Burma
Road would be reopened on October 17, adding with regard
to the three-power pact:

> Neither of the branches of the English-speaking race is
> accustomed to react to threats of violence by submission, and
> certainly the reception of this strange, ill-balanced declaration
> in the United States has not been at all encouraging to those
> who are its authors.

A disheartening aspect of the situation was the inability of
this Government to make a sufficient answer to the appeal of
General Georges Catroux, the Governor of Indo-China, for
arms. An able and patriotic general, Catroux hoped to resist
Japanese encroachments. His sizable native army lacked
planes, artillery, and mechanized equipment. To the appeals
of Colonel Henri Jacomie, the General's emissary, we were
able to return little or nothing: only the promise of 150 planes,
World War I rifles, and other small weapons.

However, the plight of Indo-China (a fact undivulged at
the time) was the subject of consultation between the British
and Americans. The Australian Minister, Richard G. Casey,
was sounded by the State Department on shipping arms from
Australia to Indo-China, receiving the equivalent later from
this country, but the Australians felt they could not divert arms
from the defense of Britain and their own forces. If Catroux
were to make a useful stand against the Japanese, he needed
vast quantities of modern matériel. In such quantities, matériel could not be supplied by the English-speaking world,
straining every nerve, as it was, for the survival of Britain and
defense of the sea lanes.

Catroux, betrayed by Vichy and disappointed in Washington, resigned, joining the Free French in the Middle East.
The tragedy of those days lay in the contrast between the
immediate poverty in weapons and the potential capacity of

the Atlantic Powers. In Indo-China also, it was "too little and too late."

While U. S.-British policy pursued parallel lines vis-à-vis Japan after October, 1940, those lines never could be brought to meet in the realistic unity of purpose desired by the British, the Dutch, and the Australians. Mr. Roosevelt and Mr. Churchill consulted by telephone over the tripartite-pact crisis, and there were frequent parleys among the diplomats of the Pacific powers and the State Department, but the United States found itself Constitutionally unable to satisfy the wish of the others for a clear-cut definition of joint policy in the Far East. The British and the Dutch sought advance agreement on a line beyond which the Japanese could not push without danger of war—a line placed in Indo-China or, perhaps, Siam. Since the Constitution fixes the war-making power in Congress, the Administration could make no commitments entailing war.

To the British this country's Constitutional barrier to concerted diplomatic action in a crisis was an old story. The Anglo-Japanese alliance, so strengthening to Japan, came into being in 1902 partly because of the inability of the United States Government to make a reliable common front with the British in the Far East. And now in 1940 this Constitutional inhibition barred a project dear to the hearts of the British and Dutch: common use of the naval base at Singapore and concerted preparation for defense of Malaya and the Indies. Repeatedly, during the summer and fall of 1940, Lord Lothian and Minister Casey suggested joint use of Singapore's facilities; as repeatedly, Mr. Hull changed the subject.

—4—

The northern flank, engaging this Government's attention in mid-1940, sweeps across the whole of Eurasia: Trotsky's "great monolithic mass sprawled over the top of the world from the Baltic to the Bering Sea." We come to an absorbing chapter, hitherto untold, of American foreign policy in the prewar cycle: Sumner Welles' persevering courtship of the Soviet Union.

In this diplomatic passage, the principals, Welles and Constantin Oumansky, the Soviet Ambassador, were incongruously matched as to background. Welles is an old-stock Anglo-Saxon American from the "right schools" and clubs, reserved, aloof to the point of stateliness, and erroneously regarded by left-wing intellectuals in this country as a "reactionary" force in foreign policy. Oumansky was inexperienced, suspicious, and a zealot in behalf of the dictatorship of the proletariat, with manners at times verging on rudeness. They had one thing in common: the interest of his own country. Welles' wooing of the Kremlin, which, though lacking the sympathy of certain associates, who regarded it as a vain effort, had full Administration support, began at the lowest ebb in Russo-American relations since their resumption in November, 1933. On August 1, 1940, Vyacheslav M. Molotov, Commissar for Foreign Affairs, accurately described these relations before the Supreme Soviet in Moscow, saying:

> I will not dwell on our relations with the United States of America, if only for the reason that there is nothing good that can be said about them. We have learned that there are certain people in the United States who are not pleased with the successes of the Soviet foreign policy in the Baltic countries. But, we must confess, we are little concerned over this fact, inasmuch as we are coping with our tasks without the assistance of these displeased gentlemen.

At this stage it was the shallow fashion in Communist circles, here as in Moscow, to dismiss World War II as merely a struggle between rival imperialisms, Germanic and Anglo-Saxon. It thus suited Molotov, a statesman whose nose glasses, small mouth, and mild eyes give him a professorial appearance, to charge the United States with concealing "imperialist designs" in Latin America "behind a well-advertised 'concern' for the interest of the entire hemisphere." Only a week before, Mr. Welles, acting as Secretary during an absence of Mr. Hull's, had publicly condemned, perhaps with insufficient regard for the military necessity that prompted them, the "devious processes" by which the sovereignty of Estonia, Lithuania, and Latvia had been "deliberately annihilated" by Russia. In his statement, issued on July 23, Welles contrasted the forcible annexation of the Baltic republics with the cooperative principles underlying inter-American solidarity. The Foreign Affairs Commissar's accusations were regarded, therefore, as in the nature of retaliation, although the fact that they coincided with the Nazi propaganda line in the Latin Republics did not escape the notice of this Government.

Four days after his public rebuke of the Soviet Union, the Under Secretary held with Ambassador Oumansky the first of eighteen conversations that preceded the invasion of Russia on June 22, 1941, an average of two a month: a series of historic talks in which Welles, with candid patience, sought to heal the breach between Russia and the West, cautioning Oumansky against the evil consequences of the August, 1939, tie between Berlin and Moscow and offering to the Soviet envoy the friendship of this country in exchange for that link with the Nazis.

The path toward *rapprochement* was not smoothed by Oumansky, who, in the early months, reflected his Government's reserve. The Kremlin, offended by this Government's condemnation of its Baltic behavior, still resented American espousal of the Finnish cause and the "moral embargo" on aircraft shipments. In a number of incidents, the high hand adopted by the Soviet authorities had aggravated matters, a notable example being the Kremlin's refusal to allow American diplomatic authorities to visit or communicate with the captain of the *City of Flint* at Murmansk. There had been lapses of diplomatic courtesy and violations of conventions in the treatment of American nationals.

A complex of petty difficulties growing out of estrangement, the fabric of Russo-American relations was badly frayed when Welles undertook to restore it. Nor was the feeling improved by a studied derogation in certain Moscow circles of American motives in supporting the Western cause. On the Russian side, the adoption by the United States, on July 2, of export-control legislation did not help the situation. The subsequent limiting of Russian purchases of essential defense materials produced irritation, particularly since some of the withheld machine tools had been built to Soviet specifications, and the Russians doubted that we had real need of them.

Welles' patience, to the amazement of the Secretary and others, was proof against all obstacles and setbacks. Various fruitless attempts had been made to appease the Soviet Union, to wean it away from the 1939 pact of friendship and non-aggression which had freed Hitler's hands for his western campaigns.

Perhaps Welles succeeded because his objectives were not too ambitious. For one thing, this country, not being a belligerent, was not offering Russia comradeship in arms, as was Britain. The Under Secretary, moreover, was under no illusions about the coldly realistic basis of Soviet foreign policy and the proverbial Russian mistrust of other countries. Russian diplomacy, now as before 1918, is cloaked in a secrecy which may be aspired to but is seldom realized in the Western nations. Hence, there was lacking in Welles' intercourse with Oumansky the easy give and take, the informal appraisal of situations characterizing, for example, the recent conversations between British and American diplomats.

Welles' effort to come to terms with Russia grew out of his conviction that the Russo-German pact of amity was unrealistic and would not last out the war. To Mr. Welles it was a demonstrable fact that, whereas friendship between Nazi Germany and Soviet Russia was unnatural, friendship between the United States and the Soviet Union was natural. The interests of an aggressive Germany and a Russia to which peace was, at the moment, highly desirable, clashed in the Baltic, in the Balkans, and at the Dardanelles; the territorial interests of the United States and of Russia conflicted nowhere.

The Under Secretary reasoned that both these vast powers, the only great nations still uninvolved in the war, were more likely than not to be swept in before the tide of totalitarian aggression came to a halt. To Welles, in the summer of 1940, it was apparent that when that happened, the United States and the Soviet Union would be aligned on the same side. He wished now to build a bridge of good will, if possible, against the day when Germany and Russia fell out. Moreover, although Welles, unlike Cripps, Britain's sympathetic Ambassador to the Kremlin, was not drawn to Moscow on ideological grounds, he had to overcome no revulsion against the Soviet Union, believing that fundamentally Russia belonged with the Atlantic powers rather than the Nazis in the world struggle which was determining the way of life on this earth for years to come.

Already, moreover, the Soviet-Nazi friendship had given evidences of being rotten at the core. In 1940, a year before the break, while the Western World (including the Communists in America) still took the relationship at face value, Hitler was gravely disturbed by the Soviet tendency to appropriate lands of strategical value. Moscow was pressing in the Baltic; soon it would be pressing in the Balkans. Over the West also a rift appeared. The *Führer* neglected to inform Russia of his descent on the Low Countries, and the Moscow radio condemned that invasion.

In June, the Kremlin dropped publicized plans for "cultural exchanges" with Germany; work abruptly stopped on waterways linking German Poland with Russia by way of the Bug and Dnieper; German engineering and transport missions found themselves isolated; German military experts were deprived of contacts with the Red Army; instances of sabotage and border violations accumulated in the archives at Berlin and in Hitler's memory. An American correspondent, the late Ralph D. Barnes, was expelled from Germany for reporting Hitler enraged by Russia's swift appropriation of the Baltic States, especially Lithuania, and by the necessity of repatriating the long-established Baltic Germans. Barnes reported the truth.

Welles, thoroughly aware of these signs of deterioration in the Russo-German entente, promptly negotiated renewal of the U.S.-U.S.S.R. trade treaty, which was to lapse on August 6, expressing his "deep gratification" when the papers were signed. Wherever possible, Russian purchases here were approved and expedited. In August and September, one third of the export licenses granted went to charters for the Soviet Union. Tankers carried gasoline past Japan to Vladivostok; petroleum products, oil pipe, copper, wheat, and cotton flowed to that port over the grumblings of the Maritime Commission, which was not always able to find cargoes for a return voyage. In October, Russia bought 58,000 bales of cotton, talked of purchasing 500,000 bales, on Oumansky's assurances that none was going to Germany. The enlargement of Russian spindle capacity accounted, he said, for the unwonted cotton purchases. Although general exports to Russia increased during the last six months of 1940, machine tools were halted. The demands of the accelerated defense program in this country would not allow such essentials to go abroad. Yet, even here, a few exceptions were made on Oumansky's urgent representations.

—5—

Meanwhile, in the fall, the pattern of the war and of Axis relationships was rapidly changing. Hitler's failure to smash England, the complications in French policy, and Mussolini's misadventures in Greece and Albania directed Nazi activities elsewhere. The adherence of Japan to the Axis stimulated consideration of a "new order"—for Europe and the world.

Hitler infiltrated Rumania, reduced Hungary to a satellite. But before he could advance toward the Dardanelles, Suez, and the oil of Iran and Iraq, he needed new assurances from his imponderable eastern neighbor, the Russia which to Winston Churchill was "a mystery within a riddle wrapped in enigma." Accordingly, to the accompaniment of flattering articles in the press of Berlin, Rome, and Tokyo, with hints of Russia's destiny in the direction of Iran and India, Hitler invited Molotov to Berlin. Such an invitation to a Government in the Axis orbit was a command. Molotov obeyed, arousing despair in the Western capitals. As a diplomatic counteroffensive, the British had offered Stalin *de facto* recognition of the Baltic annexations, a guaranteed seat at the peace table, and a nonaggression pledge. His answer had been silence.

The Commissar for Foreign Affairs arrived in Berlin on November 12, receiving a welcome noticeable for its comparative lack of ostentation. He remained two days, seeing Hitler for a total of seven hours. Upon his departure, the Berlin press triumphantly but in vague terms proclaimed Russia's entry into the "new order," but the official communiqué merely reported an exchange of views in "an atmosphere of mutual trust that led to mutual accord." Two weeks later an official spokesman in Berlin would admit that Molotov had made no promises, but meanwhile the press in England and the United States prevailingly accepted the view that Russians had bowed to Nazi demands. Only gradually did those governments learn that Hitler, offering Russia a place in the Nazi "new order," with a partnership in his Middle Eastern enterprise and a shot at India, had been rebuffed; that Molotov had thereupon demanded, among other things, what amounted to control of the Dardanelles and a free hand in Rumania and Bulgaria.

Hitler mounted guard in Bucharest; whereupon Stalin mobilized large forces on the frontier, seizing Bessarabia and Bukovina from Rumania. Rumania and Hungary formally were inducted into the "new order" in exercises at Vienna, with Tass, the official Soviet news service, pointedly denying Nazi hints that Hungary's step had the "co-operation and full approval of the Soviet Union." In all the Balkan capitals, diplomats and journalists gossiped about obvious signs of Soviet political activity, this being most marked in Sofia and Belgrade.

On December 10, Hitler, speaking at a munitions factory outside Berlin, visualized the war as the conflict between "two worlds, two philosophies of life," one of which "must break asunder"; he boasted that with German production he could "beat any power in the world." Later that month Chinese military officers, inspecting supplies Germany was still providing for Chungking, in spite of Japan's adherence to the Axis pact, came across a significant sight in another German factory. They observed German workmen painting crossbars on a thicket of tall road signs. It seemed to the Chinese that signs showing—in Russian and German—the direction and distances between cities were being painted for every crossroads in western Russia. The Chinese, who find, strangely, that German military officers are more professionally communicative than the American or British, inquired the meaning of the signs and were frankly told that the *Führer* had ordered the *Reichswehr* made ready for an invasion of Russia.

The story, which aroused some skepticism in Army circles, was reminiscent of another example of German forethought. When the Nazis marched into Czechoslovakia they were accompanied by billposters, who soon scattered the landscape with greetings to the population, assuring them that the Nazis came not as conquerors, but as friends. In one city, the American consul, who read Polish, was astonished to see on all the billboards an appeal in Polish characters. Within an hour, other billposters had pasted the Polish matter over with sheets in the Czech tongue. The consul's report helped prepare the State Department for the impending invasion of Poland.

In December also, the Polish intelligence learned of the decision taken at Berlin, a decision in which the *Führer* overrode the judgment of General Walther von Brauchitsch, commander in chief of the *Reichswehr,* and many of Brauchitsch's Junker associates. Ever since World War I General von Brauchitsch had been firmly committed to the eastern policy of Bismarck. Wilhelm II dropped Bismarck ostensibly because of his "reinsurance policy" with St. Petersburg, which the young Kaiser had been told was a betrayal of the Triple Alliance—Germany, Austria, and Italy. That was in 1890, but Bismarckians had kept the memory of a Russian accord green, many of them attributing defeat in 1918 to the necessity of fighting a two-front war.

To Brauchitsch, Bismarck had charted the "old Prussian road," which comprised an agreement with Russia in order to gain a freer hand in the West. The geopolitics theories of Dr. Karl Haushofer, evolved in his Institute at Munich, stressed the enormous value to Germany of control of the Russian land mass. Borrowing his central concepts, even his language, from Sir Halford Mackinder, the British geographer, Haushofer, described the "world island" as the vast central mass of Eurasia and Africa, with the "heartland," immune to sea power, in Russia between the Volga and Outer Mongolia.

Haushofer, having in mind the known difficulties of conquering Russian "space," thought it preferable to gain command of the "heartland" by political and economic means. With this Brauchitsch agreed. Brauchitsch and the post-World War I generals differed, moreover, from Bismarck in that to them England was the "eternal enemy." An alliance with Russia, bringing the "heartland" into the German orbit, furnished a way to escape Anglo-American sea power, Haushofer being, in the minds of many German strategical thinkers, a providential answer to Mahan.

Brauchitsch, like Hitler, was for all-out conquest. Unlike Hitler, he was not committed, emotionally and politically, to the extermination of Communism. In approximate terms, the difference between the *Führer* and his military commanders in December, 1940, over war or peace with Russia was a collision between the "Bismarck testament" and *Mein Kampf,* with Hitler's credo victorious.

—6—

By the end of 1940 American foreign policy had hardened into a durable pattern: all aid to the democracies, a firm but unprovocative hand with Japan, helpful collaboration in the Americas, a watchful but not unkindly eye on Vichy and her colonies, and active good will toward Russia. These separate policies fitted into the whole of America's pacific mission— opposition to force, cruelty, and aggression anywhere in the world. Without essential change, they were to be administered until Pearl Harbor, with varying degrees of success and with the emphasis now here, now there, as circumstances dictated.

Two nights before the year's end, Mr. Roosevelt answered the challenge of Hitler's December 10 speech, generalizing this country's planetary policy in a fireside chat. Proclaiming the United States the "great arsenal of democracy" (in 1916 Sir Edward Grey called this country the "reserve arsenal of the Allies"), the President promised that "no bottlenecks . . . no dictator, no combination of dictators" would hamper delivery of arms to the British in their fight, "which will live forever in the story of human gallantry," but "nailed" talk about another A.E.F. as "deliberate untruth."

These points he stressed, but the President bore down heaviest on the "defeatists" and "American appeasers," who had been clamoring during December for a negotiated peace. The fact was that Mr. Roosevelt had stepped off the *Tuscaloosa* into the middle of an Axis peace offensive: propaganda, which sought at its lowest levels to saddle this Government with responsibility for prolonging the war by aiding Britain, but which seldom reached the surface of public debate. Although Hitler confined his war efforts in December, 1940, to a sustained air pounding of England and his overt diplomatic offensive to the Balkans, the month was critical in the war of nerves. Talk of peace ran through the neutral press of Europe, vague suggestions that Hitler might be willing to offer England terms before opening a new phase of the war in Europe.

The uncertainty aroused in Europe by such emanations of the Axis propaganda machine was reflected in isolationist circles in this country, engaged just then in stirring public opposition to the lend-lease proposal. Four days before the fireside chat, Senator Wheeler typically declared that the President "should insist that a just peace be worked out" and on the next day elaborated that sentiment by affirming that we did Great Britain "a great disservice in urging her to go on and fight until she is exhausted."

On the President's return to Washington, refreshed and reinvigorated, he found his advisors dismayed by the undermining effect of the war of nerves and convinced that the country was drifting into a dangerous apathy. Roosevelt's long postelection silence had, as has been noted, deflated the hopes of many Americans who saw the country's peril as urgent. Early in December the Gallup poll showed 60 per cent in favor of sending more aircraft to the British, 54 per cent for furnishing them supplies after their cash ran out. But the demonstration of Nazi failure to gain the daylight air over Britain had alleviated some fears, and the emotional intensity of the fall was abating. In the White House circle there were also apprehensions over the tardy expansion of the country's war industry. Mr. Hull, among the most disquieted of the advisors, was on the warpath when the President returned. There was talk of a national emergency week, with speeches and rallies, to awaken the public.

It happened that the President's mood matched his advisors'. At the White House the gloves were off from here on in. The future of America, of Western civilization, depended, he argued, on the people facing the facts without recourse to that wishful thinking which was the bane of democracies. First, the public must be made aware of the critical nature of their predicament, and then the conclusions from that awareness must be pushed home firmly and courageously. He determined to lay the facts before the people in unshirted fashion. Bluntly, on December 29, he began by declaring that "not since Jamestown and Plymouth Rock has our American civilization been in such danger as now." Quickly he answered the Nazi peace offensive, asserting:

> . . . the United States has no right or reason to encourage talk of peace until the day shall come when there is a clear intention on the part of the aggressor nations to abandon all thought of dominating or conquering the world.

With those Americans who were "doing exactly the kind of work the dictators want done in the United States" he was unsparing. Some of these "appeasers" went so far as to urge friendship, partnership even, with the Axis, ignoring the fate of Austria, Czechoslovakia, Poland, Norway, Belgium, the Netherlands, Denmark, and France.

> They tell you that the Axis Powers are going to win anyway; that all this bloodshed in the world could be saved; and that the United States might just as well throw its influence into the scale of a dictated peace, and get the best out of it that we can. They call it a "negotiated peace." Nonsense! Is it a negotiated peace if a gang of outlaws surrounds your community and on threat of extermination makes you pay tribute to save your own skins? Such a dictated peace would be no peace at all. It would be only another armistice, leading to the

most gigantic armament race and the most devastating trade wars in history.

. . . If Great Britain goes down, the Axis powers will control the continents of Europe, Asia, Africa, Australasia, and the high seas—and they will be in a position to bring enormous military and naval resources against this hemisphere. It is no exaggeration to say that all of us in the Americas would be living at the point of a gun—a gun loaded with explosive bullets, economic as well as military.

The fireside chat, objectifying dangers that too many Americans saw as remote and subjective, set the key for this country's efforts during 1941. A fighting speech, it was the signal for action on a wide front. Mr. Roosevelt spoke on Sunday night. The following Friday, at his press conference, he announced that Harry Hopkins was going to England as his personal observer. For one thing he wished to establish personal understanding with Mr. Churchill; he wished also to reassure the British and gain a clearer insight into the state of morale in the United Kingdom, for England had not escaped the corrupting effect of the peace *Blitz*. This the President knew. He wished to discover the extent of the softening, in what quarters the forces of appeasement had shown recovery, and how Churchill was meeting them.

Hopkins first learned of his assignment when Steve Early telephoned him where he was at work in his White House bedroom, a huge chamber with a great four-poster bed and a small desk, where Hopkins prefers to receive callers and manage the affairs entrusted to him by the President. "You're elected to go to England," said Early. Hopkins arose and ambled over to the Presidential office in the west wing.

"Did you say that, Boss?" he asked.

The President smilingly confirmed the order.

"Well, I'm going," said Hopkins. When the President looked at him quizzically, Harry amplified his announcement: "I'm going right away. I'm not going to hang around here. I know what you'll want me to do, go over to the State Department for instructions and get the views of a lot of people. I won't learn anything that way; all I need is a long talk with you." The President agreed, Hopkins called Juan Trippe, president of Pan-American Airways, found that a Clipper was leaving New York for Lisbon on the following Monday.

The President found time for a lengthy discussion over the week end, and Hopkins departed for London at 8 A.M. on Monday, January 6.

CHAPTER SIX

Warning to Moscow

MIDWAY in January, 1941, Sumner Welles warned Constantin Oumansky that Hitler had marked Russia for slaughter in the following June. A precise diplomatic technician, who weighs his words with the care of a pharmacist compounding a prescription of deadly drugs, the Under Secretary did not qualify his warning. This Government "knew" that the decision to breach the Nazi-Soviet accord had been taken in Berlin.

Oumansky neither asked for nor was supplied with corroborative detail, but, although exhibiting unconcern, he reported the conversation in full to his Government. Two months later, at a time of decision in Moscow, the Soviet Ambassador was instructed to inquire whether this Government had "confirmation" of the report from Berlin. He received categorical assurance that this Government possessed additional evidence of Hitler's intention.

The Under Secretary's purpose, fitting into the friendly matrix of the new Russian policy, was implicit: the Soviet Union was soon to feel the fury of Germany, whereupon it might look to the United States for the assistance this Government had promised to all nations resisting the Axis.

The time set by Welles for the invasion, June, should be noted, conflicting as it does with a widespread impression growing up after the event that Hitler had planned to march in May, or even April, but that his timetable had been disrupted by the uprising in Belgrade. The knowledge possessed by this Government in January was explicit on the time, virtually to the day, and the Soviet Ambassador was so advised.

Welles' warning was delivered during a military lull. Hitler, balked by his failure to break England of the fruits of conquest in the West and unhindered access to the Atlantic, had turned eastward. Now, behind a screen of hobnailed diplomacy, he was preparing to take full control of the Balkan peninsula and adjacent waters. The war on land and in the air was confined at this period to Albania, Libya, and the merciless bombardment of British cities at night, with the light retaliatory blows struck by the RAF in Germany, but the savage battle of the Atlantic waxed in intensity. So did the "white" warfare of diplomacy, in which, on all the fronts to which it was committed, this Government played a part by no means negligible in pursuit of its two major aims: defense of this hemisphere at a distance and support for the free values of the West.

Harry Hopkins, in London to bridge the personal relationship between Roosevelt and Churchill, sowed the seeds of the Atlantic Conference of the following August and consulted on means of parrying the Nazis in the Atlantic. Early in 1941, Colonel William J. Donovan, likewise a Presidential observer, ranged the Balkans and the Near East on an exploratory mission, learning from Simovich, the Serb patriot and chief of the Yugoslav air force, of the anti-Nazi coup which would not occur until March 27.

At this period the Government extended its defensive line into the North Atlantic as far as Greenland, accepting a temporary protectorate over that strategically useful island on April 9. On the day after the Nazi invasion of Denmark, Mr. Roosevelt had sent for the Danish Minister, Henrik de Kauffman, to inquire concerning Greenland's disposition. As early as May 3, 1940, the Greenland Council had asked for our protection. Meanwhile, the State Department pressed forward with its project for withholding French Africa from the Axis orbit and in the Far East presented an increasingly firm front to Japanese aggressiveness.

Welles' Russian policy bore fruit early in the new year as Russo-German ties steadily weakened. In January, Washington and Moscow signified common aims in maintenance of the Far Eastern *status quo* after the Soviet Union, extending new credits, enlarged its flow of munitions, arms, and aircraft to Chungking. A manifestation of trust occurred after the Nazis occupied Bulgaria, the Kremlin being at some pains to assure this Government of its disapproval. Russia had not been consulted, and, in light of its vital concern with Bulgarian and Balkan matters in general, this was more than a diplomatic snub.

In smaller matters also, tension was relieved. In March the full weight of the Commissariat for Foreign Affairs went into action to protect the Roman Catholic Church of St. Louis in Moscow—the "American Church"—which had been robbed five times since November, 1939, and recently desecrated. Repeated protests by the embassy had brought no relief, but now the Commissariat reported that the thieves had been brought to trial.

On the American side concessions likewise developed. Welles, as Acting Secretary, on January 21 lifted the "moral embargo" proclaimed by the President in December, 1939, during the first Russo-Finnish War. In response to Soviet representations, the Under Secretary softened references to the bombing of civilians in his accompanying statement. A Russian, Mikhail Nicholas Gorin, manager of Intourist, Inc., Soviet travel agency, at Los Angeles, was arrested when he carelessly sent secret United States Naval information, purchased from a corrupt Naval Intelligence agent, to the dry cleaners in a pocket of a coat. The Kremlin made the strongest representations for Gorin's release and deportation after his conviction as a spy, and the State Department used its good offices with the Department of Justice to effect his exchange for two Americans imprisoned under political charges in Russia.

In a relatively unimportant but striking gesture of amity, this Government assured the Russians that the Nazi propaganda machine had erred in "discovering" a rebuke to the Kremlin in Mr. Roosevelt's annual message of January 6. The President in this address again answered the Nazi peace drive by repudiating a "peace dictated by aggressors and sponsored by appeasers" and set forth his famous "four freedoms"— freedom of speech, of worship, from economic want, and from aggression. The Nazis had sought to persuade the Russians, with whom they still were on outwardly cordial terms, that Joseph Stalin had been lumped by the President with the Axis dictators. The Russians, however, understood the specified passages in the American sense.

Difficulties, of course, still arose. The lend-lease policy, as it matured, further curtailed Russia's access to essential war materials. Moscow had sixty million dollars earmarked for American purchases, much of it for goods needed by ourselves or the embattled democracies, and Oumansky pressed hard for export licenses. Over and over, Welles patiently explained that the national policy of aid to the Allies was not debatable, suggesting ever so politely that, if Russia were resisting aggression, it, too, would become the beneficiary of that policy. The discussions remained on an urbane level, although once, when the Ambassador observed that his country was "fortunately not resisting aggression," Mr. Welles, in his most congealing tones, was "interested to hear that the Soviet Union foresaw no threat to its security."

Oumansky's manner, sometimes almost hectoring, was put down to his country's pressing needs. Welles was convinced that Russia would soon be at war with the Axis. Although sound reasons existed for not granting Russia machinery which would increase her oil output or industrial production as long as Moscow insisted on trading with Berlin, Oumansky was now and then allowed a small success, and the good faith of his assurances that no American materials reached the Axis through Russia was not doubted. Indeed, a statement embodying his assurances was given the press by the State Department at his request.

Improved U.S.-U.S.S.R. relations unhappily were not reflected in the conduct of American Communists. That the Bolsheviks in this country followed the Comintern line could scarcely be doubted in the spring of 1941. When Hitler occupied Bulgaria, the Communists, up to that time involved in a coalition of convenience with Nazi propagandists and fifth columnists, picketed German consulates in New York, Boston, Philadelphia, Cleveland, Chicago, St. Louis, and West Coast cities, and William Z. Foster, the nominal leader of the party, condemned Nazi brutality. The New York *Daily Worker,* the Communist organ, continued, however, to accuse the "Anglo-American criminals" of equal guilt in waging "the most useless war in history."

The State Department, aware of the dualism in the behavior of Moscow, was able to differentiate between the Soviet Government and the Comintern's agents in this country. Before the occupation of Bulgaria the American Government had reason to believe that the Soviet Foreign Office was not too well pleased with the Comintern's activity in this country (which was, of course, in direct violation of the Roosevelt-Litvinov agreement), holding that the American Communists, as had the French, displayed too great zeal in their collaboration with the Nazis.

—2—

The movements of statesmen from country to country in the early weeks of 1941 corresponded to the acceleration of the diplomatic pace. Harry Hopkins went to London for a month's "visit" with the Prime Minister. Colonel Donovan traversed the Mediterranean basin by air. Wendell L. Willkie

likewise traveled to London as a token of political unity behind the Atlantic policy, bearing a personally written message
from the President to the Prime Minister, which ended with
this quotation from Longfellow's *Building of the Ship*:

> . . . *Thou, too, sail on, O Ship of State,*
> *Sail on, O Union, strong and great,*
> *Humanity with all its fears,*
> *With all the hopes of future years,*
> *Is hanging breathless on thy fate!*

That verse, Mr. Roosevelt wrote Mr. Churchill, "applies to
your people as it does to us."

Lord Halifax reached Chesapeake Bay late in January on
the *King George V*, and the President traveled to Annapolis
in the rain and unprecedentedly brought the new British
Ambassador ashore in the Presidential yacht *Potomac*. This
was in the *White Cliffs of Dover* stage of Anglo-American
friendship, when Britons were heroes, and before our entrance
into the war as a full ally, after which Nazi agents and their
American dupes were to produce a revulsion reflecting on our
trustworthiness as allies. Hence, the country was pleased by
Roosevelt's unconventional welcome.

Admiral Leahy got to Vichy on January 5, beginning his
vigil beside the remains of France. Presenting letters of credence—technically, the diplomat's profession of faith—to Marshal Pétain on January 8, he also brought a belated New Year's
greeting from the President, answering a delayed cable from
Pétain. The President pointedly quoted the historic slogan of
the French Republic, saying:

> My heart goes out to France in these days of her travail, and
> I pray that the French people may soon again enjoy the bless-
> ings of peace with "Liberty, Equality, and Fraternity."

For those inspiring words, Pétain already had substituted the
unexceptionable, if Fascistic, trilogy: Work, Family, State.

In January, also, Robert Murphy arrived in Washington from Algiers with the terms General Weygand stood ready to grant in exchange for a limited resumption of trade with America. And in February, Admiral Nomura, beginning his fateful mission in Washington, was met, against all protocol, at Union Station by the Nazi and Italian diplomats. His initial visit to the White House and to Mr. Hull was thereupon limited to the barest formality, his stay with the President not exceeding five minutes, although in his remarks Nomura was "happy to count you, Mr. President, as one of the oldest and closest" friends he had made during his earlier sojourns in Washington.

Hopkins landed in England on January 9. A special train ("Churchill likes to throw up special trains") met him with a guard of honor. As the Presidential envoy detrained in London, wearing a rumpled gray suit, an air of unconcern, and a disreputable felt hat that was to become famous in the United Kingdom, "All hell broke loose." London was to endure one of the heaviest night strafings of the war, and Hopkins drove to No. 10 Downing Street amidst a hail of bombs, the detonation of ack-ack guns, and the sprinkle of falling shrapnel. He didn't precisely like it.

Living in the Prime Minister's household in Downing Street, Hopkins talked daily with military men from the three services, with experts from the supply ministry, industrialists, labor leaders, journalists, and permanent functionaries of the departments, as well as with the political leaders of the Government. He found England, although victorious against the Italians in Libya and rejoiced by Greek successes, confronting a dark time. The nightly air *Blitz* smashed at the industrial cities and ports, reducing a production already far from sufficient to match that of the Continent which the Nazis were organizing. A tide of munitions and food from America was essential, "a matter of life or death" to England, as Hopkins saw it. He so informed the President in a series of three-cornered telephone talks between Mr. Roosevelt, Mr. Churchill, and himself.

The British had been caught on the horns of a dilemma, as Hopkins quickly saw. If they represented their situation to America in all its gravity, that would bolster the Lindberghs, who already were assuring the public that England was a poor bet. Emphasis on encouraging factors might be misread, producing a sense of relief that the worst was over, with a consequent relaxation of effort in this country. Hopkins, a good reporter, wished to know the real situation. He was, therefore, taken straight into the heart of the country, the British authorities showing him the best and the worst as it came. With Churchill, he traveled the country, visiting factories and camps, talking with workers, soldiers, and housewives, and becoming a familiar sight to newspaper readers as he trailed behind Churchill's square, unsmiling bulk through the English rain.

To the English people Hopkins, with his matter-of-fact expression and sartorial negligence, was a congenial figure. He had come to learn about England's staying power and the degree of appeasement sentiment in all classes. During those months, the dread possibility of an England forced or willing to withdraw from the war into the Axis orbit was a recurrent nightmare to the Administration. Hopkins, asking questions everywhere, observing, relating, and comparing, concluded that England would stick it out if given American aid. On Hopkins' reports the President was to base his confident assertions in an address of March 15, when he declared:

> The British are stronger than ever in the magnificent morale which has enabled them to endure all the dark days and the shattered nights of the past 10 months. They have the full support and help of Canada, and the other dominions of the rest of their empire, and non-British people throughout the world who still think in terms of the great freedoms. The

British people are braced for invasion whenever the attempt may come—tomorrow—next week—next month.

The British Treasury financial experts and bankers bothered Hopkins some, continually asking what terms Britain might expect in the matter of leases of munitions and repayment of loans. The former WPA Administrator and Secretary of Commerce is not pecuniarily minded. In war (or peace) a billion dollars, or pounds, to him are a mere utility, translatable in this case into terms of guns, ships, or planes with which to undo the enemy. "Why worry?" he answered these inquirers. The President would work it out some way. Hopkins puzzled the financial experts, but Churchill gave the matter no more thought than Hopkins, putting first things first, as Scripture admonishes.

Churchill is, of course, articulate, companionable, and humorous. So also is Hopkins. It was during evenings before the fire in the Prime Minister's study at No. 10 Downing Street, discussing the grave predicaments of Western civilization over the "wine of Scotland," as Churchill described it, that Hopkins resolved that Roosevelt and Churchill should meet face to face. Both men, he knew, dealt best on personal terms and not through channels. There were risks, the President and the Prime Minister being men of strong wills, self-confident and accustomed to command. Hopkins, a needler, a resourceful protagonist of an idea, determined to run that risk. One of his chief values to the President is that he clings to a course in which he believes with a persistence that few men muster in the face of Presidential indifference or opposition.

Churchill reacted favorably. That kind of high adventure, a meeting with the President, secretly contrived and executed, appealed to the Prime Minister's fondness for large gestures. Upon his return to Washington, Hopkins was to find the President agreeable, but more inclined to weigh the objections. It was a little difficult to convince Mr. Roosevelt that

Mr. Churchill actually wished to get together with him, and the President for some time doubted whether the Prime Minister could or should drop his responsibilities for that purpose.

In the last days of Hopkins' stay in London he found the sea-minded Churchill deeply troubled by the growing inability of British shipyards, subjected to bombing and over-crowded with the victims of the Nazi war at sea, to restore ships, naval and merchant, to their duties. The Prime Minister grieved at the necessity of tying up battered ships to await their turn. In the lend-lease legislation was a provision, urgently sought by the British, for repairing ships in American yards—a measure which severely strained this country's neutral status under international law.

In the last few days before he took off for America Hopkins learned that two big vessels had been badly punished, with no way available for their restoration. "Get them going, start them off," he told Churchill. "The bill will be passed, and the President will take care of them by the time they arrive."

The return of Hopkins, with his circumstantial accounts of England's behavior under fire and of the character, determination, and color of Churchill and other influential figures in English life, clarified Roosevelt's understanding of the transatlantic phase of the common task. Hopkins' first mission to England had been a success; his second would be even more useful.

—3—

Meanwhile the "great debate" over lend-lease raged through the United States, in Congress, but also, as the President was to observe, "in every newspaper, on every wave length—over every cracker barrel in the land." Congressional committees endlessly took testimony. For the isolationists, making a last stand on Bill 1776, as lend-lease was reminiscently numbered, Charles A. Lindbergh was the star witness. In flat contradiction of Hull, Knox, and General Marshall, the flier denied that America was in danger of invasion, declared that the loss of the British Navy would not seriously affect this country, and refused to acknowledge a preference as to which side should win the war.

A passionate, searching debate, thoroughly ventilating the issues, the lend-lease controversy reached an end in Congress on March 11 when both Houses passed the conference measure. A half-hour later the President signed the bill and five minutes thereafter approved a list of items for immediate shipment to Britain.

A defense measure, House Bill No. 1776 placed this country in a tacit, nonshooting alliance with Great Britain and all other nations which, by their belligerency, were helping to keep war away from our shores—a fact well understood by the Axis.

The President called it the "aid-to-democracies bill," pledging a "total effort" to build a "vital bridge across the oceans—the bridge of ships which carry the arms and food for those who are fighting the good fight." To Churchill it was a "new Magna Charta," and the London *Economist* read in it a "declaration of interdependence." Subsequently, Churchill was to rank passage of this bill with three other great climaxes of the war: the fall of France, victory in the battle of Britain, and the Nazi attack on Russia.

With the bill's adoption, Dr. Gallup reported the President's popularity had advanced from 55 per cent on Election Day, the preceding November, to 72 per cent. The Senate had passed the bill by 60 to 31, the House by 260 to 165, overwhelmingly confirming the Administration's policy. "This decision," said the President, addressing the White House Correspondents' dinner in Washington on March 15, "is the end of any attempts at appeasement in our land; the end of urging us to get along with the dictators; the end of compromise with tyranny and the forces of oppression." So it seemed, and was, this country's frontiers being now in the English Channel and the Sea of Japan, the people, expressing their will through Congress, having put them there.

The adoption of lend-lease abated one of Churchill's gravest worries. But another, almost equally corrosive, remained. It was one thing for the United States to become the "arsenal of democracy," fabricating the arms of war; it was another to get the finished product across the Atlantic. On February 9, during the heat of the lend-lease debate and while Hopkins was still, as the Prime Minister described it, his "frequent companion," Churchill addressed the American people by air, over the heads of his own public, in a moving assertion of Britain's will and capacity to resist. This speech, its Churchillian rhetoric marching like the Guards on parade, ended:

> Put your confidence in us. Give us your faith and your blessing, and, under Providence, all will be well. We shall not fail or falter; we shall not weaken or tire. Neither the sudden shock of battle, nor the long drawn trials of vigilance and exertion will wear us down. Give us the tools, and we will finish the job.

Taken as an assurance that Britain was not asking another American Expeditionary Force, the speech had enjoyed Hopkins' approval. A great deal of consideration was given by Churchill and Hopkins to methods of checkmating the Nazis in the battle of the Atlantic, though Churchill ignored the problem in his speech. Emphasis on it would have complicated further the lend-lease debate. But once Congress and the President finally had acted, the demand for safeguarding the Atlantic shipping lanes again burst into prominence in the press and in the councils of those Americans alive to national imperatives.

A phenomenon often remarked during the defense period was the carrying over into the thinking of Americans concerning World War II the mental images of World War I. Whenever war was mentioned, people thought of expeditionary forces, of trench combat in Flanders, of lending dollars to the Allies—until Roosevelt outmoded that concept. Now, when they considered the job of helping get the goods to England, they fell back on the technique of the convoy, which was an American contribution to the earlier war. The President had found an alternative, however, for that slow, plodding escort of merchant flotillas in the swift, ranging protection of the patrol.

That answer to the cry for convoys would come at the end of April. Throughout April, the President, with the March toll of Allied shipping losses—437,730 tons—fresh in mind, advanced steadily along this line. On April 9, he announced the transfer of ten Coast Guard cutters, ships resembling destroyers, to the British for their convoy service. On that day also, it will be recalled, he accepted the protectorate over Greenland. The next day he asked Congress for legislation enabling him to requisition and pay for sixty-four foreign merchant vessels immobilized in United States ports, this figure not including the two German and twenty-eight Italian merchantmen subject to lawful seizure as things stood. On April 11, after characterizing the Axis drive into Yugoslavia as "wanton," he acted to enlarge the flow of supplies to the Middle East by withdrawing the southern end of the Red Sea from the list of combat zones. This authorized American merchantmen to carry supplies to Egypt via the Suez Canal.

At a press conference in the last week of April, Mr. Roosevelt disclosed that to American naval craft had been assigned the task of patrolling the sea routes to Europe up to a point he did not specify, but which was tacitly understood to be in the zone of Iceland. British forces had occupied Iceland, without impairing that ancient democracy's sovereignty, in May, 1940. On this patrol duty, United States men-of-war and aircraft were to police the Great Circle route from American waters eastward, on the watch for Nazi raiders, surface or undersea. If such were found, patrol craft were to wireless clear warnings to all ships in the vicinity and stand by to hold the raiders under observation. Should an armed British vessel pick up the warning and detect the enemy, that was, technically, no business of the United States patrol forces.

The practice of patrolling to safeguard American rights on the high seas was not new. Under the Declaration of Panama, a neutrality strip roughly three hundred miles offshore had been designated. That strip the Navy had patrolled on behalf of all the Americas since the beginning of the war. In the North Atlantic the range of the patrols had gradually been extended. To make the wider patrol effective, units of the main fleet in the Pacific had to be detached.

—4—

In February the United States undertook new activities and responsibilities in widely separated quarters of the French overseas empire, one under Vichy, the other flying the Free French cross of Lorraine. On February 5, Karl de G. Mac-Villy, a Tennessean, a former journalist, and a veteran Foreign Service officer, arrived in Noumea, the capital of New Caledonia, and soon thereafter opened an American consulate. A large island rich in nickel, New Caledonia lies to the east of the middle of Australia on the Clipper route to that continent. Strategically important to the defense of Australia and New Zealand, New Caledonia is the jewel of French Oceania. South of New Caledonia lie the New Hebrides, administered as a condominium by France and Britain, and far to the east are the Society Islands, of which the capital is Tahiti. These constitute Free French territory, governed in the name of the committee in London by a remarkable Frenchman, Admiral Georges Thierry d'Argenlieu, who in peacetime is Father Louis de la Trinité, a Carmelite monk and Catholic intellectual, a contributor to the *Revue des études carmélitiques,* and a lecturer at the Catholic University in Paris.

The decision to dispatch a consul to New Caledonia had been expedited on the motion of Ernest Gruening, Governor of Alaska. As a guest on the first Pan-American Airways flight to New Zealand, Dr. Gruening visited Noumea, observed its importance to Pacific defense, and on his return took up with Adolf Berle our lack of official representation. Soon thereafter Consul MacVitty was on a Clipper bound for Noumea, with instructions to co-operate with the authorities in "effective control." Under that eclectic policy, which has been applied throughout the French imperial holdings by the State Department, MacVitty has remained in official contact with D'Argenlieu and his Free French administrators. Word that the United States dealt in French Oceania with Governor d'Argenlieu, instead of Vice-Admiral Jean Decoux, Vichy Governor of Indo-China and nominal proconsul of the Pacific islands, did not reach the public until a year later. In March, 1942, D'Argenlieu made public the terms of his recognition by Washington.

The criteria employed by the State Department since Sedan in all matters relating to France, metropolitan and colonial, have been pragmatic. What would work best for the United States, the Western cause, and the French people? The situation, with the democratic world everywhere on the defensive, was fluid and varied. A uniformly doctrinaire position based on aversion to the Fascistic complexion of Vichy and sympathy for Free French aspirations might have produced a more heroic but a less useful policy.

In February, Robert Murphy returned to North Africa with the American terms for agreement with Weygand, terms which also bore the imprint of His Majesty's Government. The articles as negotiated by Mr. Murphy and General Weygand on February 28 were simple:

No war materials were to go to North Africa. Nothing could

be re-exported under any form or by any subterfuge. No excessive stocks could be accumulated, all imports from America being for current consumption. A special account was to be set up by the United States Treasury in the Franco-American Banking Corporation of New York, through which blocked francs held in the French Government account could be "unfrozen" to meet any adverse money balance running against North Africa. In case the balance ran against the United States account, dollar exchange could not be used to meet it. That was to prevent dollars from falling into Nazi hands. Furthermore, all cargoes were to proceed on French vessels tied up in American ports. This avoided burdening British, Allied, American, or neutral tonnage. Moreover, after each voyage the ships had to return to this country.

These routine stipulations were safeguarded by a provision for policing the agreement. Control officers, attached to American consulates, were to have easy access to harbor installations, railway and truck stations, warehouses, and oil-storage plants. In practice, twelve control officers were sent into North Africa, supplementing the consular staffs maintained at Casablanca, Algiers, Tunis, and Oran.

These observers enabled the United States to watch North Africa "like a thousand hawks" (Mr. Hull's phrase). The control officers, young men with military or naval training, had been chosen specially for aptitude in weighing the meaning of developments in ports and airdromes. Such scrutiny was open and legitimate, for, implicit in the contract (which could be terminated at any time), there was Weygand's assurance that the Nazis and Italians would be held strictly to the letter of the armistice terms governing the status of the colonies. To this promise the Delegate General cleaved in all details and through several crises. Until Weygand's removal as viceroy upon Nazi insistence in November, 1941, he held the victors at bay throughout North Africa.

The thin-lipped, irascible, immensely dignified little French general, moving briskly about his capital, Algiers, made no secret of the fidelity with which he was executing the political provisos of his compact with Murphy. On his part, Murphy, still counselor of the Vichy Embassy on special detail, was, in effect, accredited to the Delegate General; during his absences, Felix Cole, the Consul General, acted likewise. Partly because of Murphy's excellent personal relations with Weygand, partly because of Weygand's real antipathy to the Axis, and partly because of the colonies' vital need for food, fuel, and farm equipment, the agreement worked to the benefit of the Atlantic powers. An ·added safety factor was the distribution of petroleum products through American oil firms, long established in North Africa, which saw that gasoline and Diesel oil got only to legitimate customers and in legitimate amounts.

Repeatedly, Weygand clashed with the armistice commissions; unbendingly he opposed measures, Nazi-inspired and transmitted through Vichy, calculated to relax the guard he had set over the three colonies. Thrice he stood between Vichy and surrender to the Nazis.

So it happened that the French African ports were held out of Nazi use for many months. "If the *boche* wants North Africa, let him come and take it," Weygand repeatedly told the collaborationists of Vichy and Paris. To his American friends, Weygand would say:

> If you people were to come in strength, with sufficient air force, mechanized divisions and reserve, we would not resist, but join you. Not the British, but the Americans. We would join in holding these colonies away from the *boche*.

But America was not at war.

At any time after June, 1940, Hitler could have marched down through the unoccupied zone and across Spain, besieging Gibraltar and crossing the Mediterranean to French North Africa, with a moderate-sized army. Or he could have taken the shorter route from Italy to Tunis. Yet to have done so would have exposed a long flank to the British and thrown part of the French-Fleet into the hands of the Allies, and we have seen that after December, 1940, Hitler was determined to remove the Soviet threat to his rear. A bloodless surrender at Vichy and Algiers was quite another thing. This strategical difficulty faced by the Nazis in southwestern Europe throws light on the steady diplomatic pressure exerted in Vichy and Algiers.

And at what cost was North Africa isolated? Three tankers of oil products and six cargoes of other merchandise passed from this country to North Africa until Weygand's removal brought a suspension of the North African agreement by the State Department.

Meanwhile, at Vichy, Admiral Leahy had the discouraging task of maintaining the Western World's contacts with unoccupied, hungry, distracted, and victimized France. The little French watering place, first exploited by the Romans and now the seat of palace politics and the shabby intrigue of defeat, was to be a virtual prison for the Ambassador. For two reasons he scarcely dared leave Vichy. The success of his mission depended upon unbroken, firm, and personal contact with the aged marshal. Secondly, when he traveled elsewhere, the spontaneous demonstrations of French affection opened the population to retaliations and gave rise to the danger of incidents.

Leahy's life, after taking over his post in January, became circumscribed within the bounds of the doctor's residence overlooking the Allier, which served to house the Embassy, his home in the Gould villa, five blocks distant, and Pétain's suite in the Hôtel du Parc. The Ambassador walked the block and a half from the Embassy to call on Pétain in the modest apartment serving the Chief of State as dwelling and office. As Pétain spoke no English and Leahy had no French, the American customarily took along the First Secretary of the Embassy, H. Freeman Matthews, as interpreter.

The personal relations between the marshal and the admiral, stiff at first, gradually relaxed into an affability sometimes difficult to translate. Pétain, still erect, his well-cut features still remarkably firm, his eye haughtily direct despite his eighty-five years, received Leahy in his drawing room, incongruously furnished with the elegant satin-and-crystal finery of a French de luxe hotel. Occasionally, he indulged in a mannered, General Staff jest. An epicure, the marshal generally limited his wit to comments on food and drink, sometimes straying into more carnal bypaths.

A plain man to whom food was, by and large, a utility, Leahy had no wit with which to match Pétain's Gallicisms. But out of the somewhat Gothic official meetings between the skeptical French medievalist and the forthright American salt there grew an arresting association. The admiral's candor, at times outspoken to the point of embarrassment, had been counted upon by Mr. Roosevelt to establish a bond. It did. In the steamy half-light of conspiracy at Vichy, Leahy's bluff honesty shone like a good deed in a naughty world.

Pétain grew to rely on Leahy's word, to dread his blunt reminders of France's obligations to this Government, and, above all, to trust his reports and his judgment on affairs in France and abroad. In the nature of things, the American Ambassador was one of the best-informed men in the unoccupied zone. He had a specially selected staff, there were hundreds of Americans and friends of America all about, highly placed and acute to trends, and there were the American correspondents, objective as usual. If Pétain's immediate circle sought to insulate him from certain facts and situations, there was Leahy, always ready with a straight answer.

Steadily, the Ambassador hammered home the sincerity of this country's support of the British and the democratic cause, its desire to see France restored as a bulwark of the West, and the inexorable meaning of its slowly gathering industrial and military might. Darlan might minimize America's strength and cast doubt on her will, as he did, but Pétain was inclined to believe Leahy. In the protracted, anxious, painful tug of war between Washington and Berlin over Vichy, Leahy had to contend with devious forces and, overshadowing the improvised capital, the weight of the Nazi *Wehrmacht*—only two hundred miles away.

Early in 1941, reflecting Leahy's status, the purchased press and radio of Paris began to agitate for a breach in Vichy-Washington relations or, at the least, for the removal of Pétain to Paris, away from the Ambassador's influence. From time to time, the Marcel Déats, the Jacques Doriots, and the Jean Luchaires of Paris journalism called Leahy, in varied terms, the "most powerful individual" in the unoccupied zone, the "real ruler" of that remnant of France. In April, 1942, Luchaire would assert that Leahy had "ruled France through intermediaries for eighteen months." Leahy was the "arch-*saboteur*" of collaboration; he was accused of bribing Vichy not only with United States funds but with the French assets "frozen" in America.

Simultaneously, and from motives totally different and thoroughly decent, American liberals, committed to the Atlantic cause, were also agitating for a rupture with Vichy and the recall of Leahy. Particularly did they oppose sending food to France.

—5—

The food sent by America to France was, by any humanitarian standard, little enough, but it had political effects far out of proportion to its bulk: a few thousand tons of concentrated milk and vitamins carried over in the spring of 1941 on the "milk ships" *Cold Harbor* and *Exmouth* and scrupulously distributed to infants and schoolchildren by the American Red Cross. And later, to relieve Vichy's dependence on 800,000 tons of wheat being dangled by the Nazis in Paris as the price of concessions, two shiploads of flour (13,500 tons in all), with eight hundred additional tons of milk and 30,000 layettes, were sent over.

Small as were the milk shipments quantitatively, they supplied a supplementary ration to 90 per cent of the two and a half million children in the unoccupied zone. That ration is now unavailable. They brought a tide of gratitude so heartfelt as to be genuinely embarrassing to Americans in France, especially to the Red Cross staff and Commissioner Richard F. Allen.

The arrival of the *Exmouth* at Marseilles took the Ambassador and Mrs. Leahy to that port early in April. They went, with misgivings, at the insistent invitation of the French committee assisting the Red Cross. The Admiral had been correctly advised by his own doubts: the journey turned into a series of demonstrations that sapped the Leahys emotionally, alarmed the French authorities, and momentarily threatened physical harm to the throng French themselves.

Demonstrations occurred all along the road to Marseilles. The news of their progress preceded the Leahys by telephone, and, in each village, crowds, waving flags, saluting the Ambassador, and cheering America, slowed the car. This triumphal procession exhausted the Leahys. Once they reached the Grand Hotel in Marseilles, word spread, and thousands of *marseillais* soon appeared in the Canebière, shouting for the Ambassador to appear *"au balcon."* After consulting the local authorities, the Leahys made a brief appearance. The admiral found the authorities badly worried. Only a few months earlier, on October 9, the sixth anniversary of the assassination of King Alexander and Foreign Minister Barthou, the people had poured into the streets, piling flowers high around the memorial and fighting the gendarmes in a surge of resentment only too patently aimed at the Nazi conquerors.

With difficulty the police cleared the Canebière. They had locked up all the known Gaulists and other sympathizers with England and the Third Republic, they threw a cordon around the neighborhood, and yet the people came, saluting the admiral, cheering America, and singing *Tipperary* in recollection of Franco-Anglo-American solidarity in 1917 and 1918. Leahy promptly asked that there be no opportunity for a demonstration on the next day, when he was formally to receive the *Exmouth* at the pier. Thus, police lines kept away all but the five thousand invited guests.

The demonstrated popularity of Leahy * and the American flag nettled the Nazis. As one result of the Ambassador's experience, Admiral Darlan struck out mention that the flour was a gift of the American Red Cross from news of its arrival, overruling the Vichy Foreign Office, which had initialed a routine Red Cross release. Inasmuch as the Red Cross avoids political coloration or dispute, Darlan's suppression of credit was not carried to Pétain. But the bakers of France rectified Darlan's intentional oversight. The flour, being baked, was handed out gratis to all persons having bread cards on three successive Sundays, beginning the last Sunday in May. The flour had reached the bakers in sacks bearing large red crosses and the lettered name: AMERICAN RED CROSS. In an overwhelming majority of bakers' show windows, these empty flour sacks were conspicuously draped during the distribution. Thereafter the source of the bread was no secret.

At about this time a story, which may or may not be apocryphal, began to be told of a curious ritual to be observed in working-class bistros. In each public house hung a large lithograph of Pétain. Recently the proprietors had been all but compelled to purchase and hang a comparable picture of Admiral Darlan's beside the marshal's. Here and there, it was said, drinkers, lifting their glasses to the marshal's likeness, toasted not Pétain but *putain*, a word meaning prostitute. Pointedly turning away from Darlan's picture, they then drank to "the other admiral," meaning Leahy.

* The demonstrations at Nice, whence the Leahys had gone after receiving the *Exmouth* men, were even more wildly enthusiastic than those at Marseilles.

The flour ships, as has been said, reached Marseilles on May 14. By that time Darlan was deep in the spring collaboration of 1941, a *rapprochement* growing out of his visit to Berchtesgaden on May 11, which profoundly disturbed Washington-Vichy relations, produced Vichy resistance to the Free French and British in Syria, and led, among other threatening matters of that tense season, to the President's declaration of unlimited emergency on May 27 and another widening of the Atlantic patrol. This second attempt by Hitler to bring unoccupied France firmly into the "new order" transcended in intensity the effort lodged through Laval at Montoire. It ended the honeymoon phase of Leahy's mission, testing his mettle until, with the doughty support of the President, Secretary Hull, and General Weygand, he restored Franco-American relations to a workable basis.

In withholding credit for feeding Frenchmen from America, Darlan was merely executing orders. He had been told, moreover, that there should be no more free bread from the United States. In the third week of May, the Vice-Premier sent for Commissioner Allen to announce a change in policy. Hereafter, the United States Government must allow the Vichy Government to purchase wheat in this country, using its "frozen" francs. Vichy wished the Red Cross to attend to its distribution, but the French people must know their own Government was feeding them. In that case, Allen replied, the Red Cross would have to withdraw.

Before departing, Allen called to pay his respects to the marshal. The flour ships still were being held in Marseilles, although a condition of the transaction had been their immediate return to a United States port. When Pétain made the usual polite inquiry as to whether anything was lacking to the departing visitor's well-being, Allen spoke of the detained ships. The marshal manifested angry surprise. "The ships shall be released according to agreement," he declared. Within forty-eight hours the vessels had sailing papers.

—6—

The implications of Hitler's grabbing of Hungary and Rumania—that is, that he was bent on a Balkan detour—had focused Washington's attention on that front. The President thought it advisable to have a broad survey of the situation in Albania, where the Greek army held the initiative against Mussolini's halfhearted invading forces, as well as in the rest of the peninsula, which was under the iron fist of Nazi diplomacy. For the task Secretary Knox nominated his old friend, Colonel Donovan, who may be presumed to have seen more of the world's wars since 1918 than any other American.

A former Assistant Attorney General and a onetime Republican candidate for Governor of New York, Donovan, because his hobby is the study of war, was especially equipped for wartime observation. Apart from that qualification, he had recommended himself to the President by the accuracy of his judgment of Britain's prospects in the late summer of 1940, at a time when professional military observers were still pretty much dazzled by the Nazi campaign in the West.

Donovan flew first to London, via Lisbon, for talks with Prime Minister Churchill and friends in the British military establishments. January 6 found him in Cairo. From Egypt he went to Greece, visiting the front. Two weeks later he was in Sofia, where he saw King Boris, Premier Philoff, and Ivan Popoff, the Foreign Minister. Donovan's visit to Bulgaria coincided with reports, emanating from Ankara, of renewed negotiations for a Bulgar-Turko-Greek entente, a lower Balkan front, which, however, did not materialize.

The Gestapo already had Bulgaria in its grasp, although the Government mustered sufficient courage to suppress a Nazi-inspired press campaign against the United States and Britain during Donovan's stay in Sofia. Already contemptuous of the Bulgarian Government, the Nazi secret police boldly ransacked the Presidential emissary's rooms in the Grand Hotel on the day of his arrival, and when he reached the station to take a train for Belgrade on the 22nd, his passport was missing. Complaints to the Bulgarian authorities were, of course, futile. The Orient Express was held up for twenty minutes while Donovan vainly searched for the passport, and he was obliged to leave for Yugoslavia without it.

A citizen of Sofia turned in the passport, wrapped in an old newspaper, at the city's lost-and-found bureau on February 15. The Nazi propaganda agencies, which seemed inordinately irked by Donovan's presence in the Balkans, jeered, on the air and in press releases, at the American as a fumbling diplomat, so careless as to lose his passport. Without, of course, admitting the stealing of the passport or the rifling of Donovan's luggage, the Nazi radio outlets throughout the Balkans—as well as Nazi propaganda directed at the United States—claimed darkly to have found documents in his possession implicating him in a scheme to forge an anti-Axis front in that region and plunge the Balkans into war. It suited certain American isolationists to accept the Nazi imputation without checking. Had they checked, they would have learned that Donovan purposely carried no papers, made no notes, and delayed writing a report until he was back in Cairo on the road to London and home.

The fact that wherever he went, Donovan threw his counsel and his impressive influence as the President's personal representative against the Axis was, of course, no secret. Scrupulously he made no commitments, beyond the general promise of this Government to assist all nations resisting Nazi encroachments or aggressions. But the Nazis, cognizant of the enormous prestige of the United States in the hard-pressed Balkans, were well advised in seeing a threat in Donovan's circuit of those capitals. Although Donovan's role was primarily an observer's, the people in the Balkans construed his pres-

ence as an earnest of Mr. Roosevelt's concern for their plight
and took heart from it.

The influence of America reached its apogee in Yugoslavia,
to get ahead of the sequence of the Donovan story for a moment. On March 27, the day of the Simovich coup, the leading
newspaper of Belgrade, *Politika,* spread three photographs
across the top of its first page. The young King, Peter II,
looked from the center, on one hand General Dusan Simovich, the new Premier, and on the other President Roosevelt.
Arthur Bliss Lane, the American Minister, as will be recalled,
was a symbol of hope to Belgrade during the great patriotic
demonstrations that accompanied the overthrow of the Regency, two days after its pact with Hitler.

Those manifestations of friendship for this country are well
known. Not so well known are the circumstances of Colonel
Donovan's visit to Belgrade, beginning on January 23. After
the uprising, the Nazi propagandists, echoed as usual in certain isolationist circles in this country, charged Donovan
with a share in the responsibility. They alleged, further, that
he had helped induce the coup by misleading the Serb patriots
as to the support they might expect from the United States.
Later the Nazi line was to change, and by April, 1942, Hitler
would be charging that the coup was "instigated jointly by
England and Moscow."

The facts regarding Donovan, as might be supposed, are
otherwise. There was no occasion for Donovan to offer help
to the Serbs who brought about the revolt. They had direct
information concerning the American attitude from the able
and passionately devoted Yugoslav minister in Washington,
Constantin Fotitch, who had discussed the matter with Mr.
Roosevelt on several occasions. The President and Sumner
Welles had assured Fotitch that this country's pledge of help
under the pending lend-lease legislation would be honored,
but Mr. Roosevelt had declined to assure Yugoslavia publicly
to that effect. Private assurances were forwarded to that

Government, but Minister Fotitch, an acute observer of the American scene since 1935, had few delusions about the volume of assistance or the speed with which it might be forthcoming.

Fotitch was agitating resistance from Washington. From the short-wave station WRUL also, exhortations were going forward to the Yugoslavs to rise against the Regency. These activities, while helpful, were incidental: revolt was in the Serbian heart.

In Belgrade, Donovan called on Prince Paul, the Regent; on Premier Dragisha Cvetkovich, Foreign Minister Alexander Cincar-Markovitch, and the Croat leader, Vladimir Matchek. They seemed vaguely sympathetic to the democratic cause but fearful of the Axis. In response to their questions, Donovan asserted that the American Government and people expected Britain and her allies to win the war in the end, no matter how present prospects appeared, and that this Government intended throwing its industrial power more and more into the balance.

With General Simovich, Donovan entered a more bracing climate. Simovich, a veteran of Serbia's fight for freedom during World War I, had been banished to an obscure post by the Regency because of his anti-German sentiments, being recalled only through the insistence of the officers of his air corps. Able, fiery, devoted to Serbia's independence and the memory of the Axis-martyred King Alexander, Simovich voiced the distrust of much of the army for Cvetkovich and his War Minister, General Neditch. Should the appeasement-minded Regency yield to Hitler, said Simovich (and he suspected that it would), the air force and sympathetic officers in other branches would rise, depose Prince Paul, and seat the young King on the throne. The plans were already worked out in great detail.

This sensational information Donovan laid before General Sir Archibald Wavell in Cairo, reporting it thereafter in London and Washington. Whatever influence, if any, it had on the British decision to help form a Balkan front in Greece is probably known only to the responsible British authorities— Wavell, Sir John Dill, Eden, and Churchill. In Washington the report helped this country shape its policies in advance of the actual insurrection. Unhappily, the Nazi descent on Yugoslavia gained its objectives so swiftly that American supplies, had they existed in abundance, could not have been made available to the Serbs.

The point of the Donovan story, borne out by collateral evidence in Washington, is that the Serbs needed no outside pressure to rise and exert themselves against German aggression. Until the last moment, the leaders of the coup neglected to establish contact with the British, doing so then only as the result of Fotitch's insistence. Only one staff talk was held with the British, and that after the invasion. Certain that the Serbs must and would fight, with or without aid, Fotitch, a roly-poly intellectual, an amateur of the piano, and a gourmet, was indefatigable in soliciting the moral and material help of the English-speaking Powers, hoping for much and expecting little unless resistance was prolonged.

The Nazis seemingly were not aware of the Donovan-Simovich conversations until after the colonel had left Belgrade for Istanbul and Ankara. Donovan then became conscious of redoubled Gestapo surveillance and obstruction. At the last minute, for example, the Vichy French authorities forbade his crossing Syria by plane, declaring his visa invalid, and he was obliged to go to Cairo by a much less advantageous route. Back in Egypt, Donovan visited the Libyan front. He then flew to London, crossing to Dublin, at the request of British and American authorities, in a vain attempt to persuade Eamon de Valera to grant air and naval bases to Britain, before returning to Washington with a comprehensive report on affairs in the eastern Mediterranean.

CHAPTER SEVEN

The Hull-Nomura Conversations—
War in Russia

MR. HULL's conversations with Admiral Nomura, a long-range exercise in diplomatic futility if measured by abstract standards, began on the Japanese Ambassador's motion in mid-March, 1941, and lasted almost unbrokenly until December 7. In spite of them, war did come. Whether the talks deferred war for nine months, or whether the time merely was utilized by Tokyo in massing military power for conquest of the Pacific area, cannot be known with certainty until such day as the Japanese archives are opened, and the diaries, letters, and memoirs of the Nipponese war lords see the light. On the American side the perspective is unclouded. This Government hoped, against its better judgment, for a comprehensive settlement of Far Eastern problems and, failing that, nursed a more limited and pragmatic hope that hostilities might be staved off for as long as the Japanese were willing to talk.

At Nomura's request, the conversations proceeded privately and, so closely was the secret guarded in the vast rumor chamber of Washington, their existence became known only when Winston Churchill divulged it upon his return to London from the Atlantic Conference. Until Pearl Harbor this Government was not at liberty to disclose their substance without the consent of Japan, and the conversations were, as is notorious, unfinished business when the Japanese bombers arrived over Oahu. This happens to be the first authoritative disclosure of the course of the conversations, and even this report must be *ex parte* and incomplete, including only Mr. Hull's part and, because of limitations of time and space, not even that in full.

When the statesmen first met, the Far Eastern crisis, chronic since the summer of 1940, was simmering again, after having come to a boil in February. Contemporaneously with Nomura's chilling reception in Washington, the Japanese had disposed five men-of-war in the Gulf of Siam, concentrating a battle fleet in Haiphong harbor as well. This naval display sent a tremor from Singapore through the Antipodes to Washington and London. In Malaya, the High Commissioner hurried bomber re-enforcements to the north, also mining Singapore waters. In the Indies, the Dutch called merchantmen into neutral ports, canceling all sailings, while the Australian and New Zealand war cabinets regarded the Japanese movements with the "utmost gravity." In Washington, the State Department again warned all women, children, and "nonessential" men in Japan, China, and Malaya to take the first ship home, and the President pointedly assured a press conference that war, if it came in the Pacific, would not diminish aid to Britain and her allies.

The motives behind the Japanese demonstration were not at the moment clear. Had they intended coercing Siam into yielding air bases not too readily forthcoming? Or was it a trial of the nerves of the Pacific powers? Whatever the motives, the war scare, if scare it was, failed to frighten the West. And when a Tokyo "spokesman," taking cognizance of the foreign reaction, branded reports of Japan's aggressive intentions as merely "sensational," Sumner Welles astringently retorted that this Government was "far more interested in the deeds of other nations" than in the patter of their "spokesmen."

Although the conclusion is not unimpeachable, it may be plausibly inferred that Nomura's desire for parleys with Hull arose in part out of the stiffness with which the Pacific powers confronted the February naval demonstrations. The basic motivation for the Hull-Nomura conversations lay, of course, far deeper in the past than February. U.S.-Japanese relations had been almost continuously critical since Stimson vainly moved heaven and earth in 1931 toward a concert of the West against Japanese appropriation of Manchuria, the first symptomatic outburst of the ugly new imperialism carried forward by Germany and Italy in Europe and Africa and resulting finally in World War II.

Roosevelt and Hull faithfully pursued the Stimson policy of nonrecognition of the Manchurian conquest and, although Hull tempered the high-spirited tenor of Stimson's diplomatic notes, this Government maintained, in the ten years between 1931 and 1941, steadfast opposition to Nippon's mad ambitions—ambitions pursued with increasing boldness and cynicism. In April, 1934, Japan asserted what was tantamount to the overlordship of China. In the following December, Tokyo served notice of a desire to terminate the Washington Naval Treaty with its subsequent modifications, thus returning the sea powers to competitive conditions. The notice, a clear sign of warlike intent, threw the United States and Great Britain into closer collaboration in terms of sea power. Two years later Japan signalized her break with the English-speaking Powers and her true affinity with the European neobarbarians by signing the anti-Comintern pact with Berlin. In July, 1937, the blooded and irresponsible Japanese Army began its conquest of China, an event which at once evoked from Secretary Hull the strongest condemnation and an offer of his good offices.

At no moment in the dreary ten-year period of lust and loot in the Far East did this Government condone a single offensive act by Japan. The face of the United States steadily was averted from the vicious militarism of Tokyo and in 1937, after the "China Affair," this Government renewed positive efforts to check Japan's course. Protest followed protest as the lives, rights, and property of Americans, as well as of Chinese and Europeans, were put to the hazard of Japanese arrogance.

The weapon of economic sanctions was early examined, being considered at the Brussels Conference in 1937. This meeting of signatories of the Nine-Power Treaty of 1922, shunned by Japan but attended by the Soviet Union, which had not been present at Washington, vetoed sanctions largely because of the Constitutional and traditional inability of the United States Government to undertake the obligations of collective action. Anthony Eden, voicing a realistic view on behalf of Great Britain, was unwilling to undertake economic warfare unless the United States and other nations agreed to support such steps with military commitments. Britain and the Netherlands stipulated a collective guarantee of their Far Eastern possessions against Japanese armed force as a condition of economic penalties. The Soviet Union took a similar line.

This Government, inhibited against pledges of future warlike action, was forced to drop its campaign for sanctions at Brussels. Nevertheless, in June, 1938, it proceeded on its own, initiating in the "moral embargo" on shipment of airplanes and parts to Japan a consistent, steadily maintained, and constantly tightened course of economic warfare that reached its grand climax in the "freezing" order and total embargo of July 25, 1941. In that summer of 1938, American bankers and exporters felt the discouraging influence of the State Department in the matter of credits to Japan. Gradually, the "moral embargo" was widened to take in raw materials useful in the manufacture of aircraft, such as aluminum and molybdenum, and plans and plants for the manufacture of high-test aviation gasoline. In July, 1939, came notice of denunciation of the 1911 Treaty of Commerce and Navigation. The treaty had a six-months' clause, bringing it to an end in January, 1940. Then in July, 1940, acting under the National Defense Materials Act of July 2, Mr. Roosevelt began applying embargoes on war goods, starting with scrap iron, through control of export licenses.

The underlying rule governing Washington's economic warfare on Tokyo called for impeding Japan's brutal schedule as seriously as possible without giving outright cause for fresh aggressions or provoking military retaliation against the United States. Upon that formula, the diplomatic and economic measures undertaken by this Government against Japan after June, 1938, were maintained with complete realism.

By January, 1941, when the Konoye government overcame objections by Admiral Nomura to accepting the Washington mission, the economic warfare was telling on Japan. Nomura came on an errand of appeasement. Carefully chosen because of his friendly association with highly placed Americans, including the President, Nomura, known as an old-fashioned Japanese liberal, was charged with obtaining relaxation of this Government's punitive measures. For the accomplishment of that end he was, however, insufficiently supplied with diplomatic valuables. He brought, as we shall see, nothing valid with which to trade.

The immature, self-deluded quality of the Japanese military mind was thoroughly manifested in this *démarche*. In the Japan of the Kwantung army's ascendancy, since 1931, it is the Army which determines national policy, the Foreign Office being merely assigned the task of phrasing intercourse with other nations in European language. The Foreign Office, handed impossible jobs, contents itself with clothing communications in idioms and clichés calculated to beguile the Occident. This accounts for the high-flown tone given to the most sordid, transparent, and self-serving statements of Japanese intention.

The Nomura mission foundered on a fundamental misconception, a misreading of American policy that could only have been nourished in a stubbornly encased mentality. Japan,

arriving late at the idea of the state, came abreast of the West
in technology with breath-taking strides. It lagged, however,
in applying political and social lessons. Thus, although Japan
embraced mass production, its economic structure continued
to approximate eighteenth-century mercantilism. And, while
it adopted a constitution and granted manhood suffrage, Japan
integrated its state around an exaggerated, Oriental concept
of the divine right of the dynasty—a type of integration outmoded in the West.

Moreover, Japan embarked upon an imperialism that was
losing favor in the West, a reactionary and backward impulse
to subdue other peoples and annex and rule their lands by
naked force. That form of territorial imperialism, obtaining
its widest national sanction in Japan after 1931, had fallen
under the ban of the West increasingly since the turn of the
century and emphatically after World War I. This new distaste was exemplified, to cite familiar instances, by this Government's decision to fulfill its pledges by withdrawing from
the Philippines and by Britain's cession of autonomy to Ireland, the legalization of the British Commonwealth, and the
relaxation of rule from Westminster in India, Egypt, and
elsewhere in the Empire.

The Japanese, like the Germans, failed to comprehend our
new concept of international association. Hitler made the
same mistake about Britain. Hence, his attempts to forge an
alliance with London, based on mutual recognition of hege-
monies, his on the Continent, Britain's world-wide, failed in
the middle thirties. Japan fell into similar error with this
country. Out of an obvious belief that the United States, too,
wished special and improper privileges in the Far East, Japan
was to offer this country a partnership in plunder, a joint
Japanese and American overlordship in the Pacific area (ex-
cepting China, which was to be reserved for Japan alone),
against the interest of all other powers and the native peoples
themselves.

There was no bait there for Washington. The United States had advanced far beyond such primitive ideas of world organization and association. Throughout the Hull-Nomura conversations, the United States considered the rights and interests of all governments and peoples involved: the Chinese, the Russians, the Siamese, the Burmese, the British, the Dutch, and the Malayans. The gap between Japanese and American aspirations for the Pacific area was, quite naturally, unbridgeable.

—2—

The Secretary and the Ambassador met, as has been said, some sixty times. Two thirds of the conversations took place at night in Mr. Hull's apartment, until the spring at the Carlton Hotel and thereafter, after his removal, at the Wardman Park. Meeting in the Secretary's library, the conferees sat in the hospitable presence of intimate photographs. Testifying to Hull's steadfastness in the faith, on the wall was a bronze plaque reading: "The Woodrow Wilson Award—to Cordell Hull, Unremitting in His Labor to Remove the Economic Barriers to Peace."

The mechanics of the historic talks were simple. Nomura, tall for a Japanese, genial, and with his one good eye beaming friendliness, usually arrived on time. At the earlier conferences Nomura was accompanied by Colonel Iwukuro, of the Japanese Army, and Mr. Wikawu, an officer of the Co-operative Bank of Japan.* At Mr. Hull's side was Joseph W. Ballantine, Assistant Chief of the Far Eastern Division of the State Department, born in India of American parents, who had served this country as a diplomat in Japan for twenty years.

Inasmuch as the Ambassador preferred to use English, there was little call for Ballantine's linguistic skill. His principal chore was translating Nomura's English, delivered with Jap-

* Iwukuro and Wikawu returned to Japan in July, 1941.

anese syntax and inflections, into American English. Occasionally, the Ambassador would repeat in Japanese some statement made to him by the Secretary and ask Mr. Ballantine whether he had understood Mr. Hull correctly. Usually Nomura showed a clear grasp of the Secretary's utterances. The night sessions tired Mr. Hull (one lasted more than four hours) and, added to his daily stint at the State Department, wore down his strength.

Because the great decision of war or peace rested with Tokyo and not with the conferees, the conversations remained unrewarding and inconclusive. Nomura was in steady touch with his Government. The lengthy formulas submitted from time to time and the instructions to Nomura were, as usual with the Japanese, minutely specific. On the infrequent occasions when he was late, Nomura excused himself on the ground that the decoding of a message had taken longer than he expected.

A great chasm—the width of two worlds—fundamentally separated the statesmen, however congenial the secret sessions might be. Mr. Hull's world was that of the orderly nineteenth century, when imperial ambitions could be satisfied without provoking war between the continents, or even the great powers themselves, and the powers professed regard for the law of nations. A liberal century, its spirit was humane, its keynote progress. Nomura's world stretched back to the Emperor Jimmu, traversing centuries of samurai militarism, unmodified by Christian idealism and scarcely touched by democratic individualism. When the American spoke of international relations, he was mentally referring to the Good Neighbor policy; at home, Nomura's superiors had in mind the Tanaka Memorial, a blueprint for world conquest by force which had been disowned by Japanese statesmen, but which their deeds confirmed, from the "Mukden incident" to Pearl Harbor and thereafter.

Nomura belonged, it was true, to what the Secretary called

the "peace crowd over there," but a peace crowd with only a lingering influence. The Admiral, widely traveled in the West, an admirer of the English-speaking Powers, professed a genuine desire for peace. Like many older naval officers, he saw Japan's future as a great foreign-trading power: as the banker, ocean carrier, and fabricator for the Far East—a destiny corresponding to that of Britain in the nineteenth century. He thought Japan should exercise a moderate political and commercial sway over China and the rest of the Asiatic mainland. Japanese of this school never had been reconciled to the "China incident," believing that the ill will stored up against Japan by such army excesses as the "rape of Nanking" far overcame any superficial advantages of conquest. Nomura feelingly deplored the prospect of war with the United States. Unlike the Army ruffians in command at Tokyo, Nomura neither overrated German might nor underrated the warlike capacities, resources, and will of the English-speaking nations. Foreseeing Germany's inevitable defeat in this war, he feared that Japan, if plunged into hostilities, faced ruin also, a calamity requiring decades of good faith and hard work to overcome.

Of Mr. Hull the Ambassador asked patience. His Government, he thought, would settle the "China incident," withdrawing its forces, sooner or later, but not under pressure from the West. It was the Secretary's shrewd judgment that Tokyo could not withdraw from China because, apart from the "face" involved, a couple of hundred thousand civilian "carpetbaggers" had followed the troops into occupied China, appropriating large industries and small shops alike, taking over civil administration, driving taxicabs, peddling opium, establishing houses of prostitution—an evil, venal swarm. Having despoiled the Chinese of their property, homes, and businesses, these "carpetbaggers" (a term of more than ordinary opprobrium to the Tennessee-bred Mr. Hull) needed the Army to protect their lives and ill-got gains.

Until the end the conversations were to remain "explora-

tory," never reaching the dignity of negotiations. In part this
was due to the fact that Nomura actually had nothing to offer
in the way of concessions. Declining to recede in the matter
of China, he also was unable to discuss Japan's withdrawal
from the tripartite pact with any point or meaning. He "talked
around it," but it was plain to Mr. Hull that Tokyo regarded
the Axis relationship as the cornerstone of its foreign policy.

To understand the role played by each conferee, it should
be recalled that it was Nomura who had initiated the conversations. Japan was the suitor. This Government sought
nothing of Japan and at no time levied demands or volunteered formulas. The American position was that if Japan
lived up to its treaty responsibilities, the law of nations, and
ordinary international decency no parleys were required.
Nevertheless, the President and Secretary of State were willing
to discuss any issues raised by the Japanese at any time.

As for the Japanese, the war party obviously hoped to get
this country to sanction its aggressive program, isolating America from China and, by extension, the British. It is now plain
that Nomura's mission called for a sort of "legalization" of
Japan's Chinese conquest. Had the United States agreed to
Japan's overlordship in China, no matter how tenuously, and
endorsed Nippon's claim to a peaceful primacy in southeastern
Asia, Tokyo would have gained a much-sought-after cloak of
legality. In this connection, Japanese experts at the State Department refer to the characteristic Japanese passion for justification. For example, a Japanese judge will commonly go to
almost any length to obtain a confession before sentencing
a prisoner, no matter how patent his guilt, wishing the culprit
to condemn himself and thus relieve the court of responsibility.
During the Hull-Nomura conversations, Tokyo wished this
country to share the guilt for her aggressions. The Japanese
also, it goes without saying, hoped to obviate armed conflict
with the United States in the Far East, for then, with Britain

engaged elsewhere, the further conquests in mind would be easy.

On May 12, two months after the conversations opened, they reached their first climax. The Easter pact with Stalin had safeguarded Japan's northern flank. On the 12th, in the most ambitious and exhaustive statement of the Nipponese position during the entire discussions, Nomura offered this country an "*entente cordiale*," a mutual recognition of U.S.-Japanese supremacy in the Pacific area. In a long preamble, the Japanese announced the hope that, by a joint effort, the nations might establish a just peace in the Pacific and by the rapid consummation of an *entente cordiale* arrest if not dispel the gathering clouds of world war. The document breathed a note of urgency: for such a decisive act, protracted negotiations seem ill-suited and weakening. It was, therefore, suggested that the two Governments agree at once on principles and adequate instrumentalities . . . binding both Governments in honor and in act, leaving secondary questions to a more leisurely conference.

A fair-seeming proposal, the memorandum assayed down to the same old story, the underwriting by the United States of Japanese ascendancy over China. Stripped of high-sounding verbiage, the passages dealing with a China settlement called for special Japanese rights in the mainland republic excluding other nations—in short, a commercial hegemony similar to that already established in Manchuria. This, of course, violated the American principle of equal opportunity, as the idea that China should remain in economic subjection to Tokyo was equally unacceptable. Politically, the Japanese proposed to keep a stranglehold on China by the device of a common front against Communism, which would authorize the maintenance of Japanese armies of unspecified size in that country for an indefinite period.

In exchange for this proposed betrayal of China—never for a moment considered by our Government—the Japanese, as usual, offered no compensation. The *entente cordiale* envisaged no *quid pro quo*. Tokyo remained adamant against any relaxation of her Axis ties. The May 12 memorandum set forth only what had been discussed previously—that is, Japan reserved the right to interpret her responsibilities under the tripartite pact as she deemed fit without reference to the opinion of Berlin or Rome. That this vague and meaningless undertaking could not be accepted by the United States aroused surprise, real or feigned, in Japanese embassy circles.

Toward the end of May, the State Department prepared and submitted to Nomura a "rewrite" of the May 12 memorandum, phrasing it in conformity with American policy as expressed in Mr. Hull's Four Points. The Four Points called for (1) maintenance of the *status quo* in the Pacific area except by consent of the peoples involved, (2) full respect for the sovereignty of all nations (including China) great or small, (3) noninterference in the domestic affairs of other nations, and (4) equality of commercial and cultural opportunity everywhere in the Far East. Constituting a sort of Good Neighbor policy for the Pacific area, the American position in 1941 rested on the substantial basis of a policy that had been continuous since John Hay phrased the Open Door principle. Thus, Mr. Hull was quoting the soundest American doctrine.

To a nation embarked upon a dynamic, expansionist movement by arms, the Four Points were, of course, uniformly repugnant. So, while the conversations remained on a correct and urbane level, Mr. Hull felt from time to time that the Ambassador was "looking over my shoulder to see what there was to back up my words."

Until June 21, the Secretary and the Ambassador met frequently and by no means unpleasantly (Nomura's chief recreation was motoring, and he reported to Mr. Hull with enthusiasm on each new journey into the country around Washington), getting nowhere, but helping, perhaps, to fend off the evil day. For a couple of weeks in June, the Secretary received Nomura while ill in bed with a stubborn summer cold. Several times, the Secretary tested statements of "the old codger" Nomura for veracity, gratifiedly finding no discrepancies. The Ambassador had asked for the meetings, and there was, thought Mr. Hull, always the off chance that the Japanese militarists—"those damned swaybacks"—might come to their senses.

Mr. Hull's ordeal during the trying, prewar months of 1941 —months during which the State Department, was, as he phrases it, being "rawhided" steadily by those who wished an aggressive line with Tokyo—was unique in the records of American statesmanship. Although he considered the chances of preserving peace not better than one in fifty, the Secretary resisted impulses toward cynical impatience, believing that lone chance worth striving for and certain that, in any event, the time he might thus be purchasing was well worth the effort.

—3—

Meanwhile, other conversations affecting U.S.-Japanese relations were going forward in Berlin and Moscow. On the night of September 27, 1940, it will be recalled, Ribbentrop telephoned Matsuoka the *Führer's* invitation to visit Berlin. At that high point of Nazi prestige such an invitation was little short of a command. In March, Matsuoka, whose mission it had been to take Japan out of the League of Nations and into alliance with the European despots, went to Berlin and Rome by way of Moscow, his visit coinciding with Axis defeats in Albania and in the Mediterranean. A convivial, with the impudence of a small boy or a clown, Matsuoka engaged in rough-and-tumble debate with Hitler, who employs tantrums as an expedient of statecraft. He also accepted the gift of a motorboat from *Il Duce* and wrote a complimentary poem to the girls of Italy.

Hitler presumably called upon his ally to execute the secret protocol binding Japan to attack America and England at a time suiting Axis convenience. When Matsuoka insisted that he had not been empowered to make such a fateful decision, Hitler reputedly resorted to violent behavior. The American Government, hearing of a clash in the Chancellery, doubted that Hitler really wished Japan to go on the warpath—for reasons that shall soon be examined. It was thought that Hitler might have been testing Japanese sincerity. The appeal he made three months later to Tokyo to open up a Pacific front was not disingenuous, and Japan's failure to move in the summer of 1941 for a time produced a rift in Axis harmony. In April Hitler was not ready. Nor was Japan. Training had not been concluded on Formosa and Hainan.

On Matsuoka's journey into Europe he merely passed through Moscow by train. On his return he tarried. He arrived on April 7. Eighteen days before in Washington, the Soviet Government had asked for "confirmation" of Hitler's intention to attack Russia that summer. At the same time, the American Government advised the Soviet Union that Matsuoka's chief errand in Europe was the negotiation of a nonaggression treaty with Russia, freeing its rear for a war on the English-speaking Powers. It was this Government's opinion, volunteered to the Kremlin, that Russia would be better served if it kept Tokyo on the anxious seat instead of entering into a hard-and-fast agreement. This counsel the Kremlin was to reject.

One obstacle to amity between Russia and Japan was the historic rivalry for the hegemony of eastern Asia which had produced the Russo-Japanese War of 1904. This continuing collision of interest along a common frontier had twice within three years produced hostilities: at Changkufeng, Siberia, in 1938, and in the Nomonhan area of Mongolia in 1939. Another barrier was Russia's friendship for Chungking. Matsuoka pressed his project on arrival at Moscow, but met with evasion. The atmosphere of Moscow was rather flagrantly anti-Axis.

Radio Moscow read Greek war communiqués ahead of the German, and a commentator put high Britain's chances in the war.

In the huge, pink-walled Kremlin, conferences went on fruitlessly from Thursday to Saturday. Matsuoka was to depart for home on the evening of Easter Sunday. When he took leave of Stalin Saturday afternoon, the Japanese was certain there would be no treaty. He accordingly gave that night over to conviviality. Next morning his sleep was disturbed by a call from the Kremlin. At 2:30 P.M. a convention had been signed, and at five o'clock Radio Moscow carried its terms—a five-year agreement not to wage war on the other party. Supplementary terms seemed to favor Japan. Russia recognized the puppet state known as Manchukuo and abandoned long-standing claims to the Japanese half of Sakhalin Island and to border pockets in Manchuria. In exchange, Japan recognized Soviet influence in Outer Mongolia. The "China incident" was not mentioned in the public announcement, but Russia would continue to supply Chungking. From the face of the terms, an uninformed observer would be forced to conclude that Moscow, not Tokyo, had been the suitor.

If the overnight reversal by the Kremlin was strange, what shall be said of Stalin's effusive farewell to Matsuoka? The Foreign Minister's train was to leave the Siberian Station at 6:09 P.M. Unprecedentedly, Stalin turned up, striding down the platform in high spirits and shaking hands heartily with Matsuoka, his staff, and the Axis diplomats, who had turned out in the interests of solidarity. The procedure left Matsuoka puzzled all the way across Russia and Siberia. He was still a little perplexed when he reached Manchuria, informing the press that he hadn't expected to return with a Russian treaty. "It was," he said, "negotiated in ten minutes." There had been, the voluble Foreign Minister confided, considerable talk by Stalin to the effect that, after all, they were Russians and Japs, Asiatics together. Unless the Thursday-to-Sunday indifference was merely mystifying mumbo-jumbo, something must have happened to make a neutrality compact with Japan suddenly of the utmost desirability to the Kremlin. A search for the answer will repay future archivists.

The news of the Easter treaty startled the Western World, although Mr. Hull professed to see little in it. Its significance, he felt, could be "overestimated"; it was merely "descriptive of a situation which has in effect existed between the two countries for some time past." The only doubt had been as to whether they would put it in writing. This Government's policies remained "unchanged," though the agreement did, however, represent a blow to American diplomacy. It was so interpreted by many observers, who, seeing that the treaty freed Japan for adventures in southeastern Asia, yet overlooked the realities which may have driven Russia to it— namely, the threat from Berlin.

The Soviet Union was far from helpful in clarifying the situation, *Pravda,* for example, unctuously parading the pact as a triumph of the "Soviet policy of peace." That official Soviet journal even had the effrontery to denounce as "fabrications" dispatches in the English-speaking press calling attention to the "deterioration of relations between the Soviet Union and Germany. . . ." With an illumination perhaps unconscious, *Pravda,* however, did cede credit to *The New York Times* for observing that ". . . Russia is following its own policy," adding as its own commentary this substantial truth:

> It is time to understand that the Soviet Union is conducting its own free and independent policy, entirely free from foreign influence. This policy is determined by the interests of the Soviet State and the interests of peace.

At the same time the controlled Tokyo press was hailing the pact as a "new sword" in Japan's hands against the Western powers.

About few international undertakings has there been so

much obfuscation. The English-speaking press, unaware that Hitler's timetable called for a march on Russia within two months, continued to regard Stalin's act as one of unmitigated treachery toward the West.

In Berlin, the press hailed the Moscow understanding as a consummation of Axis desires. Official Nazi opinion coincided with the prevailing view in the West that Hitler had decreed the accord, forcing his satellite, Stalin, to sign on the dotted line. That interpretation conflicted with the strong presumption of Washington that Hitler had not been consulted and that, far from being pleasing, the news from Moscow infuriated him. This Government's advices indicated that the *Führer,* moreover, had not pressed the pact on Stalin and Matsuoka, as he was to claim on June 22, in his statement justifying the invasion of Russia. It was believed that Hitler had been of two minds during Matsuoka's visit. Japan was an asset to hand: should he use her, either against the English-speaking Powers or Russia, or should he withhold Japan from a course of conquest which might prove embarrassing to him were he to gain undisputed sway in Europe. At the moment, moreover, Hitler was meditating the most ambitious of his peace offensives against the West, hoping to ease his position there before launching into Russia.

Nazi diplomacy in the spring of 1941 would have taxed the ingenuity of Richelieu. Hitler's erroneous intelligence advices convinced him that he could reduce the Russians before fall. In that case, having set up a puppet state, would he not need an uncommitted Russia as a means of exerting leverage on Japan? There seems little doubt that he urgently reminded Matsuoka of Japan's obligation to strike at America and Britain. Such an attack might contribute to the diplomatic enterprise just then taking form in the devious mentality of Berchtesgaden.

The convolutions of Nazi diplomatic strategy in the spring of 1941 led into labyrinthine paths, yet this Government, in the light of its knowledge of Hitler's central objective of the summer, had an insight into the maneuvers of Berlin necessarily denied to the public. Washington, having cautioned the Kremlin against a tie-up with Tokyo, was naturally displeased with the pact. In fact, the Moscow treaty temporarily withered the tender shoots of U.S.-Soviet *rapprochement*. Oumansky gathered almost at once that his appeals to a "most favored nation" status, guaranteed in the U.S.-Soviet commercial treaty, weighed as nothing against the supervening "aid-to-democracies" policy as enacted by Congress. Export licenses for the Soviet Union simply were not to be had. Although Washington understood the urgency of Russia's danger on her western borders, it could not overlook the fact that Moscow was now bound by treaties of friendship with both ends of the Axis.

A few weeks before June 22, the Soviet Ambassador grumblingly informed a State Department officer whom he met socially that he thought of going away for the summer. "I might as well go home," he added. "I can do nothing in Washington."

−4−

A clear understanding of the Nazi-Vichy collaborationist coup of May, 1941, is impossible without reference to Hitler's peace gamble in the West. Additionally, all Nazi moves of the period must be read in relationship to the impending war on Russia.

On May 10, Rudolf Hess dropped out of the Scottish skies, bearing peace overtures to a group of Britons he had been led to believe would co-operate with his mission. England was to have "generous terms," retaining command of the fleet and British Empire at the price of ending hostilities, replacing the Churchill Ministry with a collaborationist Government, and recognizing Nazi hegemony on the Continent. The general nature of the Hess errand, so closely guarded in May, 1941, has been no secret since Mr. Churchill lifted the curtain in his speech of January 27, 1942, wherein he added the comment that "the only importance attaching to the opinions of Hess is the fact that he was fresh from the atmosphere of Hitler's table."

Simultaneously the "war of nerves" broke in full force on England and America. In broadcasts slanted for England, the Nazi propagandists disparaged American aid, stressed the undoubted pacifism of the American public, and quoted isolationist leaders in this country (to whom the wish was father to the thought) on the absence of a unified national will. At that moment, the military picture was black for England. Her forces had retired from Greece, been whipped out of Crete; her North African army had been forced back into Egypt, and the war on the seas was going badly. There can be no doubt that constant hammering on America's equivocal spirit and the laggard state of her munitions effort disquieted England.

The emphasis in the war on America's nerves turned on England's shaky military position. Ceaselessly, this country was told that Britain was through. "Why prolong the war?" ran the refrain. "Why not assist the British to make peace while they still have their fleet and Empire intact?" Word of the supposed availability to England of such a "generous" peace somehow reached men in public life, evoking from Senator Tom Connally (D., Tex.) a celebrated *gaffe*. Connally, an Administration leader, a supporter of the country's foreign policy but notoriously indiscreet, observed in an interview: "As far as we're concerned, if England keeps her independence and her Navy, that is all that she can ask. It is their war, after all." Subsequently, when questioned concerning the background out of which his utterance came, Connally denied having information that England had the choice of keeping her "independence and her Navy." Connally added that he had only been "playing a hunch," but such talk was current in Congress and elsewhere, and the enemies of this Government's foreign policy, unreconciled after their defeat on lend-lease, made the most of it.

In Pittsburgh, for instance, Senator Wheeler, posed for an America First mass meeting this question: "If the British Isles and the British Navy are our first line of defense, wouldn't it be sensible to bring about a peace that would save the British Isles and the remainder of the British Fleet?" Philip La Follette, former Governor of Wisconsin, assured an America First rally in Baltimore that the war was lost to the "disintegrating British Empire," and in Philadelphia, Lindbergh, before a similar gathering, voiced identical sentiments, adding a call for new national leadership. As the President's third term was only four months old, the aviator's demand was promptly construed as a veiled hint of insurrection, an imputation which he rather ambiguously denied.

The Hitler drive on Vichy proceeded from the same motives as his attempt to estrange and divide the Anglo-American coalition: the protection of his rear in the west against his forthcoming campaign in the east. Beyond that general objective, it served also to damage this Government's efforts to hold on to its diplomatic front in Vichy France. That phase was not lost on Senator Wheeler, who saw in the "closer collaboration between France and Germany" added evidence of the "futility of our getting into this war."

Darlan made his eager pilgrimage to Berchtesgaden on May 11. Exactly a week before, Ambassador Leahy, concerned over the trend at Vichy, had obtained from Pétain a renewal of his pledge that he would not exceed the armistice terms in Germany's favor. The marshal's pledge was soon, however, to be impaired in respect of Syria, and, but for Leahy's heroic representations and Weygand's firmness, it might have gone altogether out the window.

At Berchtesgaden, Hitler, cordially receiving the collaborating admiral, declared the time had come for France and Germany to draw more closely together. In token of his good will the *Führer* offered, in exchange for certain concessions, the repatriation of 100,000 French war prisoners, officers and noncoms who also had served in World War I. In deference to French military pride, Hitler offered Darlan the right to organize a skeleton air force; in deference to prostrate French finances, he agreed to review the arrangement whereby Vichy paid $8,000,000 a day for the upkeep of the army of occupation. In practice, Hitler did send home the veteran prisoners, a few French army planes were reconditioned and placed in service, but the sum exacted for the army in France remained unchanged. For his part, Hitler demanded access to military supplies in the colonies, assistance to Nazi arms in Syria, the right to use French possessions as Nazi bases, and employment of the fleet by the French for convoying food ships and other patrol duties. The last condition was, of course, designed to bring the French Fleet into conflict with the British. The Nazi demands, it will be seen, corresponded closely to, exceeding somewhat, those accepted by Laval at Montoire. Should the Vichy Government refuse these reasonable terms, Hitler could not, he warned Darlan, answer for the consequences.

On May 13, the day of Darlan's return to Vichy, Leahy again saw the marshal. This time the atmosphere had changed. Pétain was vaguer, although he insisted that Darlan had not agreed to "military collaboration." The next day, Pétain presided over a full cabinet in the Pavilion Sévigné, out of which came reports of the most conflicting nature. A communiqué merely announced unanimity, saying obscurely that the "effect of these negotiations will be felt soon." On the 15th, Pétain explained. Darlan and Hitler had arranged a "closer collaboration" in economic matters and "this new interview permits us to light up the road into the future." Pétain's rosy optimism was to be short-lived.

That day Washington pondered news of collaboration in

matters other than economic. The day before, thirty German warplanes reached Iraq, where Premier Rashid Ali was resisting a British penetration, and at least fourteen had landed en route in Syria at airdromes under Vichy control. Hitherto unpublished, the details of those landings have some interest. Three Messerschmitt 110's refueled at the great airport of Rayak, halfway between Beirut and Damascus in southern Syria. At Damascus, four Condor troop carriers and four Heinkel 115's, bombers, were serviced by French and German ground men, and at Aleppo three Junkers paused before flying into Iraq. The planes, believed to have come from the Italian island of Rhodes, bore Iraqi insignia and the Iraqi colors of green, a shade which approximated the French blue. As soon as the British in Palestine had received word of the landings, the RAF bombed the airports at Damascus, Palmyra, and Rayak without, however, destroying any of the Iraq-bound aircraft.

That was by no means the whole story of collaboration in Syria. General Henri Dentz, the Commissioner-General, a flabby but ambitious officer, acting under the instructions of Nazis on the ground, already had sent two trainloads of arms and motor fuel to Iraq on the 12th. Two more were to follow on May 25 and 27. The trains, rising out of Syria, had to enter Turkey, where they joined the tracks of the Istanbul-Bagdad railway, which crosses a corner of Syria on its way to Mosul and Bagdad. To the Turks, presumably on guard against violations of their neutrality, Dentz vowed that the matériel was bound for French border garrisons in Syria.

Syria was, of course, a mandated territory, France only the trustee appointed by the League of Nations. To American protests based on that ground, Dentz mendaciously replied that the German planes had been "forced down." In Vichy, Pétain, when cornered by Leahy, stonily insisted that the shipment of war munitions fell within the armistice conditions, a contention unacceptable to the Ambassador and his Government. On the point of Vichy's present intentions regarding the African possessions and the fleet, Leahy was met with evasions.

The news from Vichy and Syria produced the most acute reaction in this country, raising again, as it did, the specter of Dakar. Since Sedan no aspect of American defense had more troubled the dreams of official Washington than the status of that African peanut port. Should Hitler be handed the North African ports as bases, that meant Casablanca; Casablanca meant Dakar. It was only a step from the mainland to Madeira and the Cape Verdes; another fairly long leap to the Azores. As the President had pointed out, the Azores lay nearer to our shores than Hawaii.

With Hitler poised at Dakar and in possession of the Atlantic islands, Brazil, friendly though it might be, and the rest of South America below the bulge, would have to give thought to the possibility of "getting along" with the Nazis. To South American statesmen, conscious of their dependence on Anglo-American sea power in resisting the Axis, the significance of Dakar was even more immediately apparent than in Washington. The Brazilians, to mention only one Latin American Government and people, had taken a grave risk, gratifying to us, in throwing in their lot with the United States before the outcome of the war had been clearly indicated. We did not wish to let them down. Throughout the southern continent there existed small doubt that the United States proposed to defend the continent all the way to the Horn; the only doubt concerned our military capacity. Over and over candid friends from below the Isthmus reminded Washington that they had no desire to become "another Poland." Such psychological factors accentuated American anxiety regarding Dakar and the Atlantic islands.

—5—

This Government lost no time in combating Vichy's collaborative intentions. On the 15th, Mr. Roosevelt employed his skill at public persuasion, replying to Pétain with an appeal to the French people, which was broadcast to France by short wave, to stand by the American tie and their tradition. Reminding the French that their Government had promised not to exceed the armistice terms, the President sharply advised Vichy that such a commitment and its fulfillment were minimum conditions for a "France which demanded respect for its integrity." Ending on a note of rather surprised inquiry, the President allowed himself to question that Vichy would actually "lend itself to a plan of voluntary alliance," delivering up to the enemy France and the colonial empire, "including French African colonies and their Atlantic coasts, with the menace which that involves to the peace and safety of the Western Hemisphere."

A bold and telling counterstroke in the political warfare over France, the President's statement invoked an immediate and, as it turned out, maladroit fire from Vichy, Paris, and Berlin. A Vichy communiqué sought to blame the fall of France on her "desertion" by the United States Government. The Coast Guard had been given custody of thirteen French vessels in American ports, including the giant liner, pride of the French merchant marine, the *Normandie,* and in the American press demands increasingly found voice that the United States seize the French possessions on this side of the Atlantic. On all these counts, the inspired French-language press in Paris charged Roosevelt with "blackmailing Pétain" to keep him out of the "new order." Nazi short-wave beams poured out propaganda warning America to stay out of Europe, cautioning the American people that their President's "interference" with Hitler's projects would "unite all Europe"

—three hundred million Europeans, against "one hundred and thirty million Americans in the United States and forty million Englishmen in a ruined and defeated England."

But the Nazi propaganda output was soon brought into closer accord with the peace offensive. Almost before the sound of "blackmail" had faded from the air waves, the Paris radio was importuning the President to throw his influence behind peace. That sort of intervention in Europe would, it seemed, better suit Hitler's purpose. That type of intervention likewise suited certain isolationists in this country, Senator Wheeler, for example, urging the President to call a peace conference. In this cause Pierre Laval enlisted. The Quisling from Auvergne sent for an American United Press correspondent and read him an avuncular lecture for transmittal home, its general burden being that Americans had failed to realize that

> . . . this isn't a war like other wars; it's a revolution. . . . In the rebuilding of Europe, you Americans can play a magnificent role. But you can do it only in peace. . . . Reflect well before you throw yourselves blindly into a great adventure.

Mr. Roosevelt naturally ignored the mediation proposals. Whereupon the Nazi propaganda machine reversed itself. Unless the President acted soon, he was warned, all France would be mobilized behind the Axis. In Berlin, Grand Admiral Erich Raeder chimed in circuitously, warning the United States by way of the Japanese news agency Domei that Germany could only view the Atlantic patrols as "aggressive." Raeder suggested that their extension would bring an unspecified but ominous reaction. Mr. Hull dismissed Raeder's observations as "a well-known German practice" intended to frighten the United States out of the plain path of its Atlantic policy.

The transatlantic "white" war was growing in intensity

day by day. Meanwhile, the battle of the Atlantic came closer
home when the Nazi battleship *Bismarck* burst out into the
the Atlantic on a raiding career, sinking the battle cruiser
Hood and itself falling victim to air and surface blows from
the British Fleet. On May 21, Henry S. Waterman, the American consul at Bordeaux, reported the landing of 140 American
survivors of the Egyptian merchantman *Zamzam*, which had
been boarded and sunk by a German raider in the South
Atlantic.

The President answered, on May 27, in a fireside chat,
Hitler's peace offensive and the hemispheric threat implied
in Nazi-Vichy collaboration. This speech, a searching analysis
of the world situation and a grim recapitulation of America's
determination to sail the seas on her own terms, concerned
the safety of Americans, North, South, and Central. A seafaring man, glorying in his country's historic role on the sea,
Mr. Roosevelt was on familiar and inspiriting ground. His
audience outside the White House was estimated at 85 million
listeners.

"The war," he stated bluntly, "is approaching the brink of
the Western Hemisphere itself. It is coming very close to
home." Thus far Hitler's "plan of world domination" had
been thwarted by the "epic resistance" of the British Empire
and the "magnificent defense of China." Unless the Axis
gained control of the seas, its defeat was certain; and to do
that they must first "capture" Britain. "The battle of the
Atlantic," he found, "now extends from the icy waters of the
North Pole to the frozen continent of the Antarctic." He
pointed to the increasing sinkings of merchant vessels by Axis
raiders and submarines, "great numbers" of them "actually
within the waters of the Western Hemisphere."

Turning to measures of protection, the President read to
his listeners a lesson in strategy. In this war, one step led to
another. Czechoslovakia had been conquered from Austria,
Norway from Denmark, Greece from Albania and Bulgaria.

"The attack on the United States can begin with the domination of any base which menaces our security—north or south." The intentions of the aggressors could not be accurately foretold, but, in view of the "sudden striking force of modern war," it "would be suicide to wait until they are in our front yard." Therefore:

> Old-fashioned common sense calls for the use of a strategy which will prevent such an enemy from gaining a foothold in the first place. We have, accordingly, extended our patrol in North and South Atlantic waters. We are steadily adding more and more ships and planes to that patrol. It is well known that the strength of the Atlantic Fleet has been greatly increased during the past year, and is constantly being built up. . . . We are thus being forewarned; and we shall be on our guard against efforts to establish Nazi bases closer to our hemisphere.

The "national policy" now called for getting all aid to the British, by safeguarding the sea lanes wherever necessary; it called also for setting a watch on the bases that Hitler's machinations might deliver to him—on Casablanca, on Dakar, on the Azores and the Cape Verdes. Henceforward, American cruisers, taking the whole Atlantic for their task, would be patrolling the neighborhood of those threatened harbors and islands, guarding against surprise occupations by the Nazis and their allies. To enforce this Atlantic policy more adequately, the President declared at the conclusion of his address a state of unlimited national emergency.

The implications of the widened Atlantic patrol in the Roosevelt policy of defense at a distance were not fully comprehended at the time. That the United States was now guarding cis-Atlantic bases was minimized in the public understanding by the declaration of national emergency. There had been considerable agitation for the seizure of Dakar and the Atlantic islands, and a rumor gained wide credence that an expedition aimed at Dakar actually had been sent from Norfolk. Actually, we were only to watch the crucial spots, but, as the President pledged in a fighting finish:

> We in the Americas will decide for ourselves whether and when and where our American interests are attacked or our security threatened. We are placing our armed forces in strategic military position. We will not hesitate to use our armed forces to repel attack.

—6—

Since Mahan and for a half century, the keystone of American naval strategy had been an undivided battle fleet: a concentration of striking power in whichever ocean seemed at any given time to hold the greater menace. The Panama Canal had seemed a naval necessity in part because it enabled the united fleet to shift rapidly from ocean to ocean. With the widened Atlantic patrol, the one-ocean policy had to go.

A justification was, of course, found. Air power provided it. The strategists agreeing with the new policy (many admirals went along only reluctantly, some not at all) estimated that the southwestern Pacific might be held largely with air power. Its geography seemed to lend itself to air tactics; its many islands useful as steppingstones, the South China Sea itself barely more than six hundred miles from Manila to Hong Kong. So it happened that in the spring of 1941, the emphasis was placed on re-enforcing the Philippines and Hawaii with aircraft.

In advancing to new ground on May 27, Mr. Roosevelt, as usual, was abreast, not ahead of, the popular trend. American blood was up in May, 1941. Upon Donovan's return from his tour of the Mediterranean fronts and capitals, he flatly declared that if it were "to our advantage to declare war, we should declare war." Talk of methods "short of war" was beginning to draw belittling barbs in the interventionist press.

The public will, as reflected by the Gallup barometer, likewise showed a hardening in that direction. Whereas in April, 87 per cent of the pollees voted against the abstraction, war, by May only 81 per cent did so. In May, 68 per cent were willing to accept participation in the war if necessary for Allied victory; 71 per cent favored convoys (patrol) to Britain, if the Government deemed them necessary; 71 per cent opposed peace negotiations at that time; 82 per cent believed we would be at war before ever a peace conference met.

As a reflex of the Vichy-Nazi crisis, the Senate, by 59 to 20, authorized the Government to seize 102 ships in American ports belonging to nations occupied by Hitler. In Congress and throughout the country, as nearly as might be determined by the available measuring rods, the national policy had overwhelming support. Four former Presidential candidates—Willkie, Alfred E. Smith, John W. Davis, and James M. Cox —endorsed the Atlantic-patrol speech. From nation-wide groups of citizens came expressions of vigorous backing, and two leading isolationist newspapers, the St. Louis *Post Dispatch* and the Detroit *Free Press*, announced a change of heart. "The die is cast," said the *Free Press*, "we are in the war." Although technically premature by six months, the sentiment was widely held.

The usual minority report—reverberations of the Nazi peace offensive—was brought in, *The Chicago Tribune* finding "the suggestion that the United States is about to be attacked . . . in some other continent and the defense must start there dangerous as it is absurd"; Lindbergh accusing Mr. Roosevelt of desiring "world domination," and Wheeler being convinced that the President had "surrendered to the warmakers." Whistling in the dark, the America First Committee, an antiwar group chiefly engaged in opposing support of Britain, announced that "our fight is almost won," and forty Congressmen renewed their campaign to "keep our country out of 'shooting war.' "

In Europe, the President's answer to Nazi encroachment

generally was interpreted as a step toward war. Thousands of Britons remained up until 5:15 A.M. to hear the address, and the newspapers cut deep into paper stocks to publish the text in full. The London *News Chronicle* predicted that "guns . . . will speak next," the *Star* thought Mr. Roosevelt had signed Hitler's and Mussolini's "death warrants," but Mr. Churchill merely observed that the "tremendous decision" brought him "indescribable relief." To DNB, the Nazi news agency, Mr. Roosevelt was "cramming war down the throats of the American people," and the verbarian Virginio Gayda described the speech as "plethoric, subtle, alarmist, aggressive, and yet extremely equivocal and confused." Two days late, the Soviet Union's censors allowed three paragraphs to be published; Vichy scissored all references to France, Dakar, or the Atlantic bases generally.

The Central American Presidents united in adhering to the declaration, while Manuel Avila Camacho of Mexico saw all American nations acting as a "democratic unit." Below the Isthmus there was wide press approval. Roberto M. Ortiz, the incapacitated President of Argentina, believed the address "merits frank adherence," but his substitute, Ramón S. Castillo, reaffirmed Argentina's neutrality.

—7—

In Vichy, Admiral Leahy was encountering heavy weather. Pétain, when he could be seen, spoke with reserve; Darlan blustered, in a moment of exasperation, publicly attacking the United States for "meddling," an accusation to which Leahy retorted with emphasis. The French press in Paris continually pricked at the American Ambassador for "interfering" with the "will of France" to co-operate in the "new European order."

American pressure against collaboration was exerted in Washington as well as Vichy. On June 5, Mr. Hull addressed the French people. Reviewing at a press conference the numerous benefits this Government had extended to France in defeat, the Secretary expressed "frank concern," reported that Leahy was still in the dark about Vichy's true intentions, and called reports of Nazi-Vichy collaboration "scarcely believable . . . despite indications appearing in our preliminary reports."

The contest with Hitler over the will of Vichy went forward in Washington on still another salient. Mr. Hull, in repeated interviews with Gaston Henry-Haye, called the French Government sternly to account for its dalliance with Berchtesgaden, demanding fulfillment of Pétain's pledges. A new note entered the parleys when, after the middle of May, this Government began to press Pétain through Leahy and Henry-Haye for a written memorandum of his pledges.

Mr. Hull pulled no punches with the Vichy Ambassador. When, on May 25, Henry-Haye called to protest Coast Guard surveillance of French merchant vessels in United States ports, the Secretary grasped the opportunity for another blunt homily. One trouble with Vichy was its instability, he observed. Its official press shilly-shallied, one day denouncing the United States for "interference," the next day meekly proposing to hand over its African colonies to this Government for safekeeping. The Nazi element, it seemed to Hull, had got the upper hand. If that were true, Vichy France could look for no further friendship from the "peaceful, liberty-loving nations."

"Co-operation with Hitler," the Secretary told the little Frenchman, "is an act of brigandage. If you continue you will become a nation of brigands." As Leahy was doing in Vichy itself, the Secretary spoke of the risks France ran, not only in the matter of ships, but in the matter of food for the children of metropolitan France and supplies for the French possessions. A knuckling under to Hitler now might mean the stripping of all French possessions from the homeland through the fortunes of war. Much might be spared France if Pétain would renew his pledges—in writing.

The supplying of French arms to the Iraqis, at the behest of Hitler, stirred Hull to new wrath. Pointedly he asked Henry-Haye what effect he supposed such behavior would have on the "gentlemen's agreement" between Admiral Robert in Martinique and this Government. When, on June 8, General Dentz signified his intention of fighting the incursion of the Free French, under General Catroux, supported by the British, into Syria, Mr. Hull demanded of the French Ambassador:

"Why didn't you fight the Japanese in Indo-China?"

The battle for Syria between two parties of Frenchmen, the Vichy contingent being also engaged, with the backing of the Germans, against the recent ally England, shocked and angered this Government and large sections of the American population. Vichy France reached a low in American esteem, from which it was not to recover. At this time also news of the sinking of the American merchantman *Robin Moor* in the South Atlantic, her passengers and crew having been set adrift inhumanely in small boats hundreds of miles from shore under an equatorial sun, fanned the flames against Germany and quickened American preoccupations over Dakar and the islands of the South Atlantic. In France, Laval and Darlan, fearful that collaboration again was slipping through their fingers, went to the public for support against the steady pressures being applied by the United States. Laval baldly used his familiar argument of expediency, while Darlan "urged the French people to conquer their illusions and consent to sacrifices," warning them of the prospect of utter destruction at the hands of a chagrined *Führer* should they resist.

From Mr. Hull these exhortations brought a fresh blast on June 13. The attitude of the Vichy Government was "a matter of the deepest disappointment and sorrow" to him. It was clear that Germany had prevailed upon Vichy to do "Germany's fighting in the Syrian area of the general German ad-

vance." Moreover, Laval and Darlan were asking the French
people to curry favor with Hitler by repudiating their history
—"all the French traditions, institutions, liberties, interests,
culture, and the entire way of life which made France
great. . . ." To the Secretary, parenthetically, "The general
adoption of Hitlerism would set the world back five to ten
centuries." He spoke directly to the people of France in conclusion, saying:

> It remains to be seen whether the French people accept
> this preposterous status and thus pave the way for them to
> find themselves assisting Hitler as his cobelligerents in his
> desperate effort to conquer Great Britain and secure control
> of the high seas. In the prevention of such a possibility, both
> the French people and the people of the United States have a
> common interest of tremendous importance to the future.

At Vichy the diplomatic struggle was going against the
United States and the Atlantic cause. Not so at Algiers. In that
capital of North Africa, the fiercely proud Weygand, pledged
equally with Pétain and Darlan against extralegal concessions
to Berlin, declined to compromise his honor. Weygand's commitment rested on the reciprocal terms of the North African
agreement. As so often before, and after, the viceroy did not
see eye to eye with Vichy. In the first week of June, Pétain was
persuaded to send for him.

Austere, jealous of his prerogatives, Weygand was on terms
of punctilio with Pétain, his military senior and Chief of the
State. Darlan roiled him. The demands levied by Darlan on
Weygand at Algiers and Vichy called for the gradual infiltration of the North African port cities, including Casablanca,
by Nazi "experts," a sharing of the defense of his viceroyalty
with the Nazis, and a campaign to be initiated in North Africa
against the Free French in Equatorial Africa. Weygand categorically rejected all demands. In a series of stormy sessions
with Darlan, the general refused to exceed the armistice terms,

refused to launch an expedition against other Frenchmen, and made no secret of his disapproval of Dentz's action in Syria.

On the rock of Weygand's resistance collaboration broke in June, 1941. Gradually, Pétain resumed easier intercourse with Leahy, the fever subsided in Darlan, and Hitler, approaching the zero hour for the march into Russia, allowed the issue to cool.

At that moment, the peace offensive, still actively maintained, took first importance in the Chancellor's western plans. Certain voices in high Nazi circles assured Hitler that the attack on Communist Russia would rehabilitate him with large groups in England and America, softening the will to resist in those countries. Thus, when Ambassador Winant returned to Washington, on his own motion, for a personal report on the state of affairs in England, including the still delicate matter of Rudolf Hess, the Nazi propaganda stream played disquieting rumors over that event. Winant, said the Nazi broadcasts, had brought back an ultimatum from a beaten England: "Either you come in, or we get out of the war." The Nazis sought to create the impression that England was ready for peace, the decision resting with America; and certain American newspapers accepted this construction. An interview by John Cudahy, former Ambassador to Belgium, with Hitler appeared in *Life,* containing a toplofty assurance from the *Führer* that he had no aggressive designs across the Atlantic.

Mr. Roosevelt at a press conference countered these Nazi sallies in the war of nerves. Referring to gossip concerning the purpose of Winant's return and Cudahy's report on Hitler's intentions, he branded both as products of the Nazi propaganda factory. On his desk, he said, lay confidential intelligence reports establishing that Dr. Joseph Goebbels' line for the friends of the Nazi cause in this country was (1) Hitler has no designs on America, and (2) Winant has brought back peace terms England must accept unless the United States is willing to go to war. In answer, the President observed that

Winant hadn't brought back "even the tenth cousin of a peace offer." Winant himself, in a confidential talk with a group of Senators, reported that Britain was far from despair, its production increasing satisfactorily, and, while the blows at Crete and in the Libyan desert had been staggering, Churchill remained confident that he could hold Suez and the oil fields of Asia Minor.

The war of nerves, nevertheless, had harried Britain more than could be revealed at the time and than can be, in certain respects, even now. Abandonment of the ferocious air assaults on London synchronized with Hess' arrival, the last all-out night attack on the metropolis also occurring on May 10. The enforced secrecy over Hess' motives, his message, and the circumstances under which the fanatical No. 3 Nazi had reached British soil told obliquely on British morale after the first thrill of exultation had passed.

The military war was, however, approaching one of its great climaxes. Sir Stafford Cripps flew home from Moscow in the first week of June, and on the 12th Churchill made a crushing answer to the peace offensive. Speaking in St. James' Palace, surrounded by six members of his Cabinet, the High Commissioners of Canada, Australia, New Zealand, and South Africa, and the Prime Ministers or their representatives of North Ireland, Belgium, Czechoslovakia, Norway, Yugoslavia, Luxembourg, Greece, Holland, Poland, and Free France, Churchill promised on behalf of all to "fight on till life is gone, or victory won," pledging that as for Hitler

. . . with his tattered lackey Mussolini at his tail and Admiral Darlan frisking by his side, he will find no peace, no rest, no halting place, no parley.

Unlike 1940, the summer of 1941 would see no lull either in the war of guns or words.

—8—

The news that Hitler had invaded Russia, thus opening a two-thousand-mile front across Europe and producing a realignment of forces, reached Washington simultaneously with a premature heat wave on the Sunday morning of June 22. It found Mr. Roosevelt nursing a slight throat infection at the White House and Mr. Hull preparing to rise from his sickbed to depart two days later for the cool repose of White Sulphur Springs, in West Virginia. Mr. Welles, comfortably encased in imperturbability against the heat, motored in from his estate, Oxon Manor, in Maryland. None of the three was surprised by the dispatches. Mr. Hull had telephoned Mr. Welles at home, advising an early declaration of support for the Soviet Union after speaking with the President by phone. That day Mr. Roosevelt saw Mr. Welles and Lord Halifax, talking also with Harry Hopkins and telephoning Prime Minister Churchill, but no major decisions were made either in Washington or London. None was needed, for the event, which struck the public with tremendous impact, had been long anticipated by the Governments of the English-speaking Powers.

The news came as an immense relief to Mr. Churchill, not only because it had been hopefully awaited, but also because it released the speech he had been rehearsing for two months. During that period the Prime Minister's friends had been required to give attentive ear to his rolling phrases and to varied epithetical allusions to Hitler. When Churchill went on the air at three o'clock that afternoon he was pronounced by them as letter perfect. Affirming that he had been for twenty-five years a "consistent opponent of Communism," recalling that he had given Stalin "clear and precise warnings" of what was in store, the Prime Minister concluded that "any man or state who fights against Nazism will have our aid." He had earlier confided the same assurance to Ivan M. Maisky, the Soviet Ambassador in London.

In Washington, no public speech was delivered, no statement made until the next day, but, like Churchill, the President and Welles already had given thought to the phraseology in which their reaction should be clothed. Upon returning to Oxon Manor on Sunday, Mr. Welles drafted a statement of this Government's policy, which early on Monday morning he took to the White House for a breakfast conference with the President. Only the President and the Acting Secretary participated in the important task of formulating this country's policy toward defense of the Soviet Union and what was to be a united Anglo-American-Russian front against Nazism. The statement was made public at noon of Monday the 23rd by Mr. Welles at a press conference. A great deal of Welles' moral indignation, a quality unsuspected by those who observe only the rather formally professional Wellesian exterior, shone through the statement, as when, at the outset, he observed:

> If any further proof could conceivably be required of the real purposes and projects of the present leaders of Germany for world domination, it is now furnished by Hitler's treacherous attack upon Soviet Russia. We see once more, beyond peradventure of doubt, with what intent the present Government of Germany negotiates "nonaggression pacts."

The "word 'honor,' " Mr. Welles went on, "is unknown" to the present German Government, whose "sworn engagements to refrain from hostile acts against other countries . . . are but symbols of deceit . . . and dire warnings . . . of hostile and murderous intent."

There was an "immediate issue." Should the "plan for universal conquest, for the cruel and brutal enslavement of all peoples, and for the ultimate destruction of the remaining free democracies . . . be successfully halted and defeated?" To this Government the answer was clear: " . . . any defense against Hitlerism, any rallying of the forces opposing Hitlerism, from whatever source these forces may spring, will hasten the eventual downfall of the present German leaders, and will therefore redound to the benefit of our own defense and security."

Welles crowned the argument with a sentence concisely expressing the American policy: "Hitler's armies are today the chief dangers of the Americas."

The satisfaction felt on June 22, 1941, by Roosevelt and Welles in Washington and Churchill and Eden in London over the opening of a new front against the evil force of Nazism was mixed with apprehension lest a quick victory be won by Hitler—a triumph which would magnify and concentrate his powers for new onslaughts against the West. Until the *Reichswehr* actually moved across the border zones at dawn of that day, the American and British leaders could not be wholly certain that something might not happen to alter German plans—a last-minute reconsideration by the *Führer*, a decision to exact a price which Stalin (whose dread of a war with the Third Reich was an open secret) would pay for peace, or even an army revolt, repudiating the campaign in the East.

The opposition of the commander in chief, Colonel General von Brauchitsch to the Russian campaign was well known in the English-speaking countries. Russia had been surprised, a circumstance not wholly clarified yet in Washington and London, in view of the expectation with which those capitals awaited the action. Stalin had, it seems apparent, been taken in by the Nazis until the last moment. One factor may have been his belief that the army under von Brauchitsch would not actually march.

Known also to Washington was the fact that Nazi party strategists steadily had assured Hitler that the Russian venture would be merely a brief detour. In a matter of weeks, they told him, he could return to the main task, the reduction of England. Not until December 19, when Hitler described

Russia in a speech as Germany's "most dangerous enemy of all times," would England be relegated to second place. That would be after the break with and humiliation of Von Brauchitsch. On the day after the invasion the German Foreign Office left no doubt about the order in which the enemies then appeared when a spokesman called the invasion of Russia only "a phase in our general struggle against England." And a few weeks later, Dr. Goebbels was to explain the Russian campaign in the Munich *Neueste Nachrichten* as "a preliminary condition for the decisive battle against England." The Chancellor and his circle evidently had not the slightest doubt of a prompt liquidation of the Eastern front.

England moved to the side of Russia at once, ahead of the United States, which was, of course, still a nonbelligerent. London's need and opportunity were more immediate. Not for six weeks would the American Government's resolve to take full advantage of the new front be formulated, yet only four days after the invasion this Government offered technical assistance, broadly implying also that the Soviet Union's difficulties with export licenses for machine tools and war equipment were at an end.

Ambassador Oumansky called at the State Department on the 26th, where Acting Secretary Welles recalled his warnings of January and March and assured his somewhat chastened visitor that previous differences were "past history." Oumansky, regretting the vigor with which he had formerly pressed his demands, observed that he had thought well enough of the warning in January to report on it "in full," a fact which Welles dryly assured him he had known.

The June 26 conversation was the first in a series leading up to an exchange of notes on August 2 between Welles and Oumansky, the former pledging on behalf of this Government "all economic assistance practicable for the purpose of strengthening the Soviet Union in its struggle against armed aggression." Soon thereafter this Government would be show-

ing its good faith by a strong, if fruitless, effort to pry little
Finland, so recently the object of American admiration, out
of the war and its place in the Axis orbit.

—9—

The Government, braced for the invasion, proceeded along
a foreordained path. Not so with two groups in America which
had for several months been vying, if on different levels, in
their efforts to dissuade this country against further participation in the war. These disparate groups, the American Communists and the isolationists outside the Comintern ranks,
reacted divergently. To the vocal isolationists, in Congress
and out, Hitler's war on Russia seemed as gratuitously helpful
as an answer to prayer. If the Administration was pleased by
the fortuitous addition of a large and perhaps powerful enemy
to the ranks of those fighting Hitler, the isolationists were no
less gratified at the disparagement which they believed association with "Joe" Stalin would bring to the anti-Axis cause.
The Communists, caught flat-footed in their puerile and high-
pitched campaign against the American foreign policy, had
to revise their strategy between editions, so to speak, lumber-
ing awkwardly and with poor grace into support of this Government insofar as it would support Russia.

The America First isolationists, typified by their acting
chairman, General Robert E. Wood, of Chicago, construed
the event as giving the *coup de grâce* to their opponents, the
interventionists. Wood described the invasion as "the entry of
Communist Russia into the war," prophesying that it would
"settle once and for all the intervention issue. . . ."

The invasion moved Senator Robert A. Taft (R., Ohio),
the leading candidate among those defeated for the Republican Presidential nomination by Wendell L. Willkie in 1940,
to an unaccustomed hilarity, the Ohioan proposing "Packages
for Petrograd," an obvious take-off on Bundles for Britain, a

voluntary and large-scale enterprise which had clothed many thousands of bombed-out Britons. Taft added, in a more characteristic vein, that "a victory for Communism would be far more dangerous to the United States than a victory for Fascism." A gleeful note ran through isolationist comment. Senator Wheeler, believing that the addition of Russia to the anti-Axis bloc irretrievably ruined the prestige of that bloc in this country, proposed that the United States could now "just let Joe Stalin and the other dictators fight it out."

Herbert Hoover, exhibiting his persistent distaste for the Administration's brand of international association, put the case on a rather more elevated footing, although he, too, could not resist a gibe. Said Hoover:

> We now find ourselves promising aid to Stalin and his militant Communist conspiracy against the democratic ideals of the world. Collaboration between Britain and Russia . . . makes the whole argument of joining the war to bring the Four Freedoms a gargantuan jest.

The first public reaction to the news of June 22 tended to bear out isolationist hopes. There was something infinitely consoling to the plain American, exasperated on the home front by the impudence of the Nazi Bundists and the shrill nonsense of the Communists, in the thought of these two alien and (to them, at the time) equally offensive regimes battering each other to death on the plains of Poland, the steppes of White Russia, and in the Crimea. Wheeler's lighthearted dismissal of the conflict evoked a sympathetic response in the first days of invasion from many who mistrusted his motives and disliked his views.

But before long the public attitude veered away from the isolationists. However heartening it might be to witness the head-on collision of Hitler and Stalin, that was not, as Welles had pointed out, the "immediate issue." The call was for a discriminating, not a blanket, judgment; not for "a plague o' both your houses," but for an appraisal of American interest in the light of the new circumstances. Soon the majority of Americans were showing a deeper insight into the problem through a democratic flexibility of opinion, which was remarkably displayed over the whole prewar period.

The isolationists, guilty of a summary judgment, had again misread the public mood. What they had overlooked was that, ingrained as had become American aversion to the type of despotism practiced in Moscow, we had no fear of Russia. The Nazi regime was an immediate threat, not only to our way of life and our political system, but to our independence as well. Furthermore, should the Nazis achieve a swift victory over Russia it was apparent that their threat to our security would be enlarged. There were other factors in the orientation of public approval toward the aid-to-Russia policy. Apart from the Nazi regime itself, Germany was not too popular in American thinking—in part a hold-over of the rancorous estimates of German character formed in World War I.

Apart from its absolutist regime, the American people liked Russia, much as they like China and the Chinese. The Iowa farmer or Detroit motor worker might regard his preinvasion Russian counterpart as impractical and perhaps a bit dumb, but he had a certain fondness for him; and, as for Russia itself, his feeling was one of curiosity and sympathy for another huge continental country, rich and fruitful, and having many of the climatic and physical characteristics of his own. Moreover, when Americans stood off and looked impartially at the two systems locked in a death struggle, they found certain points in favor of the Russian. Both harbored grave evils from our point of view, but, while the Nazis sneeringly vituperated democracy, the Soviet Union paid it the tribute of calling themselves democratic and of adopting, although not practicing, a democratic constitution. The Russians had also repudiated that bane of the Nazi system (the czarist, as well): racial prejudice and persecution. Finally, Americans had no national heritage of animosity toward Russia, for our vital interests had never conflicted.

Twice this Government had intervened on Russia's behalf and in its own interest. Theodore Roosevelt, having backed the Japanese in their war with Russia, reversed himself toward the end to preserve the balance of power in eastern Asia. He supported the Russians at the Portsmouth Peace Conference, incurring universal disfavor in Japan. In thousands of Japanese homes "Teddy's" photograph was turned to the wall, and anti-American riots in the cities cost many lives and much property damage. Woodrow Wilson, fearful that Japan might gobble up the Russian maritime provinces, thus unsettling the Asiatic balance after World War I, sent American forces into Siberia charged with blocking Japanese aggression. They succeeded, adding another tally to Japan's long count against America.

In the summer of 1941 America and Russia were, as Walter Lippmann noted, again "separated by an ideological gulf and joined by the bridge of national interest." The United States needed Russia, and Russia needed the United States. Self-interest and not sentiment dominated the relationships between Washington and Moscow. It was the isolationists, although the thought would no doubt surprise them, who took the soft and unrealistic attitude.

By whatever intellectual and emotional processes the American people arrived at their conclusions, there was no doubt, as July and August disclosed a stubborn resistance on the part of the Soviet armies and people, that public opinion approved of aid to Russia. The magazine *Newsweek,* surveying the volume and character of mail received by Congressmen and Senators on war issues, found in July that epistolary opposition to such aid was "insignificant." Somewhat later, when the isolationist minority in both Houses sought to exclude Russia from the benefits of lend-lease, it polled few votes.

The lot of the American Communists was even less happy

than that of their fellow isolationists of the *bourgeoisie*. Already they had incurred the displeasure of the Soviet Foreign Office by a somewhat too enthusiastic collaboration with the Bundists. On June 22, their patent allegiance to a foreign power required an about-face startling in its abruptness. The case of *The Sunday Worker,* New York, was revelatory. In its issue of that day, the *Worker* denounced reports of a rupture in relations between Germany and Russia as "lying" emanations of the capitalistic imagination, affirming that "the American people want none of this war."

In its Monday issue, the *Worker* published a manifesto by William Z. Foster, the Communist party's national chairman, and Robert Minor, acting national secretary, denouncing the invasion of Russia as an "attack upon the peoples of the United States and the entire world." Foster at once called a national convention of the party to reverse the party line. The convention resolved to support the United States Government in its "crusade" against the "hateful, barbaric, imperialistic dictatorship of Hitler" on certain conditions. Among them was one that the American *bourgeoisie* must cease its "persistent slanders and attacks against the Soviet Union." In exchange, no doubt, although it was not so stated, the American Communists were to cease their abuse of the American system.

—10—

The consequences of the great climax of June 22 spread—as was the case with the fall of France and Britain's successful resistance—in ever-widening circles. First they ruffled the Sea of Japan, setting forces in motion that led directly to the war in the Pacific. The sequence of events, actions and reactions of Tokyo on the one hand and Washington and London on the other, sheds an immediate and searching light on the path by which war came to America.

The word, unexpected in Tokyo, of the invasion of Russia

found Foreign Minister Matsuoka entertaining Wang Ching-wei, chief of Japan's puppet Chinese State, at a theater party. Excusing himself, Matsuoka saw Konoye, and together they repaired to the Imperial Palace to explain the vast new convulsion to Hirohito. Matsuoka's number definitely was up. The loquacious, overbearing, and irresponsible Foreign Minister, by leading Japan into both the Axis pact and the Easter neutrality treaty with Stalin, had seated the perplexed Government of Nippon firmly on the horns of a dilemma, and the Tokyo regime had sustained another disillusionment concerning the fidelity of the German ally. Matsuoka caught the blame on all counts, and before the week was out the powerful organ of mass opinion in Tokyo, *Nichi Nichi*, was openly demanding his official head.

Ten days after Hitler marched, or on July 2, the ninth Imperial Council since the Meiji Restoration of 1868, meeting at the Palace, turned the event to Japanese account. A new bargain with the Axis was struck. General Ott, the German Ambassador, had asked for a repudiation of the treaty with Moscow. To this the Tokyo Government saw no insuperable objection—for a price: undisguised occupation of all Indo-China with Vichy's sanction, the legalizing of a conquest which could easily have been made by *force majeure*. Upon Ott's agreeing, the trade was consummated—lacking only Vichy's assent—by the Imperial Council, which, at its close, issued only the brief announcement that Japan's "fundamental policy" had been determined. Again, the extremity of Europe had been Japan's opportunity.

Twenty-four hours later, on July 3, Sumner Welles informed Ambassador Oumansky that the Japanese Imperial Council had solemnly agreed to breach the pact of April with Stalin and to attack Siberia at a time as yet unspecified. Mindful of the January warning, Oumansky received the word with evidences of dismay. "This," he said, "is very serious." For reasons which will be examined hereafter Japan elected first, of course, to move south.

A few days later the Under Secretary further advised the Soviet Ambassador that acute pressure was being put upon Tokyo for an early stroke at Vladivostok. By that time the Kremlin had itself observed signs of deterioration in its relations with Tokyo. One example had to do with transit visas. After prolonged negotiations the Soviet Union recently had won the privilege of such visas for nationals who wished only to pass through Japan. Three days after the Imperial Council, the Japanese consul general at New York refused to grant further transit visas, citing a new ruling on the point. Only a straw, its direction was not lost on Moscow.

The Konoye Ministry wasted little time in reorienting itself. Two weeks after the Imperial Council, on the evening of July 16, Prince Konoye motored out to Hayama, where the Emperor maintained one of his country residences, to announce that the Cabinet had resigned. Hirohito returned to Tokyo the next day and, after a series of confabulations, charged Konoye with creating a new Ministry—sans Matsuoka. The Army had disposed of Mr. Facing-Both-Ways. Konoye's new cabinet numbered fourteen, half of whom came from the Army or Navy. Vice-Admiral Teijiro Toyoda, a former naval attaché in London, and a brother-in-law of a director in the house of Sumitomo, one of the "big five" of Japanese industry and commerce, replaced Matsuoka. Since the great commercial interests of Japan preferred peace, dreading a war that would destroy trade with the other Pacific powers, Toyoda's appointment evoked some hopes in Washington and London of a turn toward the West. It was, however, noted that the anti-Western General Tojo, "the Razor," remained as War Minister.

The Imperial Council firmly had fixed Japan's steps on a *Drang nach Suden,* for, although the Japanese had been required to satisfy Berlin of their treacherous intentions toward the Soviet Union, the pledge to void still another treaty was at the moment merely a bargaining point: the bargain itself being the means of smoothing the drive toward the rich south.

Mr. Hull, as we have seen, went to White Sulphur Springs two days after the Nazi attack on Russia. The vain and protracted effort to bring Nomura to agreement on principle had disappointed him, wearing down his strength. On June 21, Secretary Hull sent the Japanese Ambassador a second "rewrite" in response to the memorandum of May 12, and on June 22, the Secretary, receiving Nomura in his bedroom, suggested that the Japanese position required further clarification. As usual, he left the door open for renewed discussion. In view of "the importance of the understanding" the Japanese had proposed in the *entente cordiale* memorandum of May 12, he asked Nomura to keep in touch during his absence with Maxwell Hamilton, Chief of the Division of Far Eastern Affairs, and Mr. Ballantine. The Secretary was kept informed of their conversations by telephone.

During Mr. Hull's stay at the West Virginia resort, the Ambassador sought, however, to reopen the personal conversations with the Secretary. On July 4, Mr. Hull declined to receive the Ambassador (who had arrived unannounced), pleading the state of his health. He thought nothing could be gained by another talk at that point. Nomura had submitted nothing new to Hamilton and Ballantine. Not for more than a month did the Secretary again receive the Ambassador.

CHAPTER EIGHT

Atlantic Charter

HARRY HOPKINS' second visit to London, in July, 1941, was not prompted solely by the Russo-German war, although that development, with its bearing on Britain's desire to share its lend-lease aid with Moscow, motivated the journey in part. Ostensibly, he was being sent solely on British lend-lease·matters, the job of allocating and expediting supplies to the democracies having been placed on his shoulders by the President. Also high on Hopkins' agenda was the face-to-face meeting that he never had allowed the President and the Prime Minister to forget. The war in Russia, with its ominous repercussions in Tokyo, seemed in July to make such a conference between the two leaders even more advisable, if not, indeed, essential. Hopkins carried, therefore, the President's full consent to arrange for the subsequent meeting at sea.

Since the invasion, assistance to Russia had been much talked about in White House councils. Gradually a policy of all aid was formulated amid a multiplicity of opinions that raged most around the question of Russia's capacity to resist. There was no agreement here. The General Staff, professionally impressed by the quality of Brauchitsch's army, prognosticated pessimistically. Scarcely any of the generals thought the Red Army would be able to make a stand short of the Urals. At the State Department there was somewhat more hopefulness. Oumansky's categorical optimism had some effect, as did the nature of the requests he was pressing—machine tools, oil-drilling equipment, and other goods which would be useful only in case of a long war. At the other pole from the General Staff stood Joseph E. Davies, the indefatigable and persuasive former Ambassador to Russia, who was cheerfully predicting at the White House and in the public press that Russia's resistance would "amaze the world." He was everywhere in those days urging that this country improve the opportunity offered by Russia's willingness to destroy Nazis.

Mr. Davies' confidence in Russia's staying power carried undoubted weight in forming this Government's opinion. Twice he stated the case to Sumner Welles, acting as Secretary of State, in the early days of July. In his important book, *Mission to Moscow*, published late in 1941, Davies, in a diary notation after one of these conferences, accurately said of Welles: ". . . a mind like a Swiss watch . . . a thoroughgoing individualist, a democrat . . . heart and head in this fight to save this country from the menace of Nazi victory." Seeing the President, Davies besought him to send personal assurances of help to Stalin.

On July 8, Davies attended the swearing in of Senator James F. Byrnes as an Associate Justice of the Supreme Court at the White House, later going to Harry Hopkins' room for a talk about Russia. On the wall was a military map of Europe. Davies indicated the spots in the Urals where Russia had developed war industries which presumably lay out of Nazi reach unless the Soviet Union should fall apart or surrender. Davies emphatically assured Hopkins that neither of these eventualities would happen. He referred his host to his reports, while Ambassador, on the Soviet Union's industrial and military strength—memoranda since published in the above-mentioned book.

While in Russia, Davies had the advantage, apart from his own enormous and objective curiosity, of the insight into Russian military affairs possessed by his military attaché, Colonel Philip Faymonville, one of the few foreigners who had gained the confidence of the Red Army leaders. Faymonville, now assigned to routine army duty in this country, had a high regard for the Red Army's training, spirit, and equipment. Before Hopkins' departure, Davies sent him a brief of his reports and views, along with Faymonville's findings, on the military prospects for Russia.

Hopkins flew to Britain on a bomber, on July 17 reaching London, where the press made much of his arrival and quoted his trenchantly expressed confidence that Anglo-American industrial power would "whip this fellow Hitler." At No. 10 Downing Street, he plunged into consultations with the Prime Minister on broad phases of the transatlantic supply problem, on detailed arrangements for the forthcoming Roosevelt-Churchill meeting at sea, and on the new elements introduced into the situation of the Western powers by the war in Russia.

On two aspects of the Russian problem the Prime Minister and his American guest were in agreement. Both discounted the gloom of the military men, as dense in London as in Washington; both doubted that the democracies were taking as full advantage of the Russian "godsend" as they should. Hopkins had been fortified by Davies' reports and enthusiasm, which also impressed the Prime Minister. Churchill had respect for Davies' judgment in Russian matters. Twice, in 1937 and 1939, when the Ambassador was in London, Churchill, then a fractious Member of Commons, had questioned him about conditions in Russia.

"The Red Army is going to be a tougher nut to crack than our people, and yours, believe," Churchill said to Hopkins. And indeed, the two men in London who believed most in Soviet endurance were Churchill and Hopkins. This was, of course, in the second half of July, when the Nazis still were carving huge bites out of the Ukraine and White Russia. Thus, the hopefuls had little, however, in the way of current evidence on which to base their optimism. The reports of the military attachés shed no real light, the Kremlin maintaining its cloistered reticence despite Anglo-Russian alliance and

American assurances of aid. Ambassadors Maisky and Ouman-sky could contribute little in a factual way. At this point Churchill suggested: "Harry, why don't you go and have a look for all of us?"

Hopkins, having cabled the President and having received his prompt approval, reached Moscow on the evening of July 30. Met at the airport by Ambassador Laurence A. Steinhardt, Hopkins went at once to see Joseph Stalin at the Kremlin, passing the early evening with the Soviet statesman and re-turning on the next day for another three-hour conversation.

In Moscow, Hopkins had another baptism of bombfire, watching from the roof of the American Embassy, in Mokho-vaya Street, a block from the Kremlin, while, for the seventh time, the Nazis attempted to shower explosive and incendiary bombs on the city. A tour of Moscow by motor the next morning astonished the visitor, the damage being demon-strably "insignificant." Candid with the press within the lim-its imposed by the secret nature of his errand, Hopkins told interviewers that he had offered Stalin assistance on the Presi-dent's authority. Stalin, vowing unbreakable resistance to Nazi aggression, had given him a note for the President.

What Hopkins could not disclose was that, in his two ses-sions at the Kremlin, Stalin had unlocked the inner chamber of Soviet defense secrets, parading before his visitor a wealth of evidence attesting Russia's armed and industrial might. Here were the figures, heretofore hidden from all foreigners and all but a minute number of Russians themselves, on (for example) tanks: types, quantities, production capacity both as to present flow and prospective volume. Stalin revealed the position of his reserves—information battalions of SS men would gladly have died for—both men and machines. He spread before Hopkins tabulations on manpower, broken down according to branch of service, together with statistics on the ratio of fully trained soldiers to those in training. All aspects of transport—rail, truck, and shipping—were taken into account. The reports on the war industries fascinated Hopkins, bearing out impressions he had received from Davies' reports.

"All of that is for you to see, if you wish," Stalin said. "You may go anywhere, to any front, to any factory, and find out if what I have shown you is true." Hopkins, satisfied of the essential veracity of the volunteered information, replied that he hadn't the time to make a personal survey and that, in any case, he believed one unnecessary in view of the abundance of the corroborative detail.

At the end Stalin indulged in prophecy, saying: "The Germans will never get to Moscow this year."

Upon handing Hopkins the note for the President, Stalin asked him not to disclose the secret information to anyone except Mr. Roosevelt. The President could then do as he liked with it, Stalin relying upon him to use it most effectively. Hopkins had made "some heavy commitments across the table," as his part of the bargain. He also proposed that representatives of the three Powers meet in Moscow on Russian supply problems, a proposal that gained Stalin's ready consent. It seemed to Hopkins that such a conference was almost a necessity if the English-speaking Powers were to gain exact insight into Russian needs.

Hopkins brought out of Moscow a rigorous but favorable impression of Stalin as a tough-minded, single-purposed man, granitelike in demeanor but straightforward. Hopkins also is straightforward, approaching people with an uncomplicated Midwestern openness. Unawed by the Soviet leader, Hopkins met him on friendly terms and had no trouble establishing an easy working relationship. There were no social trimmings to his calls at the Kremlin, the hours of conference being packed with exhaustive consideration of vital matters.

Hopkins also carried away a half-forbidding, half-respectful view of the wall of secrecy behind which the Kremlin is immured, a wall higher and less penetrable than the brick surrounding that ancient enclosure. "The Russians know how to keep a secret," he was to observe to Churchill.

In Moscow, Hopkins had heard from the Red Army men of their confidence in Faymonville, and upon his return to Washington Hopkins busied himself in digging the colonel out of his Army assignment and getting him started back to Russia. The President approved of this step, and when a certain resistance presented itself at the War Department, Hopkins cut it short by saying: "You might as well get his passport ready, because he's going over." It was apparent to him that no other American military man would have half the chance of sitting on the inside at Moscow.

Back in England, Hopkins was obliged to disappoint Sir Stafford Cripps, who asked what he had discovered. Mr. Churchill, informed of Stalin's injunction to hold it all for the President's ear, was content to wait. Two days after Hopkins' return, he sailed on the ill-fated *Prince of Wales* as the Prime Minister's guest, with Churchill and his Foreign Office, Army, Air, and Navy staffs, for the rendezvous with the President.

— 2 —

The bargain by which Japan cleared its path to the south provoked prompt retaliation from Washington. Vichy yielded on July 21, turning over, as Welles was to put it, "an important part of the French Empire" to Japan. On the 29th Darlan and the Japanese Ambassador at Vichy, Sotomatsu Kato, signed a treaty pledging the "two Governments to co-operate in military matters for the defense of French Indo-China." The terms of the common defense were covered in secret protocols. In announcing the treaty, the Japanese observed with blatant disingenuousness that they had acted to forestall "Anglo-Saxon aggression." This Government was not to receive until August 2 a text of the Tokyo-Vichy agreement, showing the complete and willing capitulation of the French Government.

On July 25, the United States "froze" Japanese funds, amounting to 131 million dollars, in this country. At the same time, and at the request of Chiang Kai-shek, Chinese assets totaling 262 million dollars were likewise tied up to prevent resources under control of the Japanese invaders being used against the democratic front. With the Japanese securities and commodity markets plummeting to their lowest depths since the "Mukden incident of 1931," Tokyo followed suit, locking up 217 millions of American assets in Japan. Great Britain, Australia, New Zealand, Canada, and the Netherlands East Indies—these furnishing, with the United States, virtually all of Japan's effective foreign market—promptly took action similar to that of Washington.

This move, described by *Nichi Nichi* as "one step from armed warfare," and certainly a milestone in the descent into war in the Far East, was put into effect with a casualness noteworthy in view of its import. The brief, matter-of-fact "freezing" order had been long prepared. It lay, awaiting only the signatures and seal, in Under Secretary Welles' safe. For months, the activist faction in the Administration had been urging such an order, similar to that already applied to the European members of the Axis, as a prelude to a complete embargo on trade with Japan. They had sought to bring pressure on Secretary Hull through the President, saying, in Mr. Hull's own paraphrase of their exhortations: "Why don't you stand up to the Japanese, show some courage, and get in there?" But Mr. Hull, with the support of the President, had resisted that definitive and drastic act.

Mr. Hull was, as he said, "down in the Virginia mountains," when word of Vichy's surrender reached Washington. Much improved in health, he was still following the day-to-day developments in foreign policy by telephone with Sumner Welles. When this happened, the Secretary felt that the time had come to act, to put an end to the sterile conversational attempt to appease the war party in Tokyo. There seemed no other road open. He advised Welles to consult the President about "freezing" Japanese assets. The President likewise could see no other way by which we could call the Japanese to account. All the other economic weapons in our arsenal had been expended without result. By the new incursion southward, the Japanese had given irrefutable evidence that they proposed to push on beyond China into an area vital to us. In the face of that open signal, further commercial relations with Japan plainly amounted to arming an enemy. The "freezing" order was, therefore, signed, sealed, and proclaimed.

Only the day before, the President, informally addressing members of a voluntary committee of civilian-defense leaders, explained in homely, idiomatic detail what he had been trying to get at with Japan. Because the White House still considers those impromptu remarks the clearest expression of the Government's policy vis-à-vis Japan, they are here fully republished. At the moment Harold L. Ickes, as Oil Administrator, was asking consumers on the East Coast to curtail their use of gasoline because of transportation shortages. Referring to that situation, the President said:

All right. Now I am—I might be called—an American citizen, living in Hyde Park, New York. And I say,"That's a funny thing. Why am I asked to curtail my consumption of gasoline when I read in the papers that thousands of tons of gasoline are going out from Los Angeles, on the West Coast, to Japan; and we are helping Japan in what looks like an act of aggression?"

All right. Now the answer is a very simple one. There is a world war going on, and has been for some time—nearly two years. One of our efforts, from the very beginning, was to prevent the spread of that world war in certain areas where it hadn't started. One of those areas is a place called the Pacific Ocean. . . . There happened to be a place in the South Pa-

cific where we had to get a lot of things—rubber, tin, and so
forth and so on—down in the Dutch Indies, the Straits Settlements, and Indo-China. And we had to help get the Australian
surplus of meat and wheat and corn for England.

It was very essential, from our own selfish point of view of
defense, to prevent a war from starting in the South Pacific.
So our foreign policy was—trying to stop a war from breaking
out down there. At the same time . . . we wanted to keep
that line of supplies from Australia and New Zealand going
to the Near East. . . . So it was essential for Great Britain
that we try to keep the peace down there in the South Pacific.

All right. And now here is a nation called Japan. Whether
they had at that time aggressive purposes to enlarge their empire southward, they didn't have any oil of their own up in
the north. Now, if we cut the oil off, they probably would
have gone down to the Dutch East Indies a year ago, and we
would have had war.

Therefore, there was, you might call it, a method in letting
this oil go to Japan, with the hope—and it has worked for two
years—of keeping war out of the South Pacific for our own
good, for the good of the defense of Great Britain, and the
freedom of the seas.

A method of purchasing time for the democracies, the Far
Eastern policy had been under fire for several years. Direct
fire from the friends of heroic China in this country, their
names being legion; lateral fire from those who, seeing the
national interest clearly, if impatiently, believed we should
take a more aggressive line regarding the approaching conflict in the Pacific. These critics, whose ardent counsel suited
Mr. Roosevelt's own temperament better than a negative,
patient, waiting game, had the inestimable advantage of being
without responsibility. To the President and Mr. Hull the
problem still was one of proportion, of keeping first things
first. The danger in the Atlantic was the more immediately
menacing. The Pacific could wait. Accepting the verbal be-
laborings of the group that wished to "crack down" on Nippon

at whatever cost, the President and his Secretary of State played out the string, secure in the knowledge that appeasement was more than a term of well-bred invective. It was also a strategical weapon, useful, perhaps even essential, in approaching a two-ocean war with a country exposed and psychologically unprepared.

The Government knew that the Japanese had held in reserve, throughout the China war, large stocks of war supplies, especially metals and oil: a quantity sufficient for a major campaign elsewhere. This was the Japanese insurance fund against embargoes. The reserve, of course, was not large enough to enable them to ignore economic penalties of that sort: it was intended, on the contrary, to assure them the military power to resist the enforcement of embargoes or any other serious interference with their plans. A primary aim of American policy was therefore to avoid provoking the Japanese to the use of armed force, while gradually applying economic pressure. Each action taken was delicately calculated to weaken Japan's capacity for aggression, without shutting the door to a peaceful settlement in the Pacific. Mr. Hull is convinced that but for this careful handling the Japanese would have attacked in the fall of 1940, in which case they would have met no resistance worthy of the name short of Australia or India (and perhaps not even there); or in the spring of 1941, in which case Hitler might have found it unnecessary to invade Russia. It must be remembered that, from January, 1941, on, the State Department had information as to Hitler's intention to turn eastward. Until the assault on Russia actually was launched, the possibility was always in the mind of our Government that hostilities in the Far East might change Hitler's plans, encouraging him instead to throw his full force against the sea powers of the West.

The crucial question posed by the "freezing" order is why, in the light of the President's explanation, it was clamped on at all. The order was construed by the Japanese as provocative.

Moreover, it was perhaps unnecessary. Trade with Japan, the further supply of oil and other commodities useful to their war effort, might have been halted by export restrictions and pre-emptive buying, based on the valid plea that our rapidly expanding war production required all the critical raw materials we had and that could be supplied from the South Pacific. Indeed, the export of critical materials already had shrunk to a small stream. The order did supply the Japanese war party with an additional argument for domestic use in their attempt to persuade the people that Japan was being "encircled." But, as has been noted, the freezing order seemed to be the only effective weapon left in our economic arsenal. And the way was always left open for its relaxation in return for a change in Japanese policies.

Indo-China was an imperial prize. A group of native States gathered into an administrative entity by France, it is larger in area than metropolitan France. Its population of twenty-three millions is approximately that of Spain. Rich, fertile, strategically useful to a power wishing to command the ocean route from Europe to China, Japan, and Siberia, it possessed, moreover, an excellent naval station in Cam Ranh Bay, its anchorage covering the space of 15,000 acres and steeply surrounded by mountains. The French had begun to develop Cam Ranh Bay into a modern naval base in 1936, stopping work in June, 1940, but a fair foundation remained upon which the Japanese might build.

The Japanese began to move into the colony in force before the ink had dried on the treaty. Soon there were 48,000 troops in the southern states, 12,000 in Saigon, the "Paris of the Far East," alone. A considerable advantage of having Indo-China was that Japan could now proceed to develop advance bases for troops, repairs, and supply hundreds of miles nearer its southern objectives than the Japanese archipelago itself.

As a countermove, the President expedited the re-enforcement of the Philippines and Hawaii. Major General Douglas

MacArthur, a Field Marshal and commander in chief of the Philippine Army, was restored to active duty in the United States Army, with the rank of Lieutenant General, and placed in command of all armed forces in the islands, the Philippine Army being mustered into United States service. Meanwhile, the decks were cleared for action in China, the Marines in Shanghai and Peiping and the half-dozen gunboats of the Yangtze River patrol being ordered withdrawn to Manila. Mr. Roosevelt was also throwing in this country's lot more decisively with Chungking. He had sent Lauchlin Currie, one of his administrative assistants, to Chiang Kai-shek for a survey of China's needs. Currie's visit was followed by the appointment of a military mission under Brigadier General John A. Magruder and by the Chinese generalissimo's retention of Owen Lattimore, an American recommended by the President, as his political advisor. Tokyo interpreted the Magruder mission as evidence of a Sino-American military alliance. At the same time, volunteer pilots from the American Army and Navy were arriving in China in growing numbers, and the Burma Road was being improved, American engineers reorganizing its thoroughly inefficient traffic system.

The Government's moves in the Pacific, as always, escaped the barbed denunciations applied by the isolationist party to similar advances in the Atlantic. Yet the public, on the showing of the Gallup polls, remained indifferent to the isolationist distinction between the oceans, supporting the Government in the Pacific in about the same ratio as in the Atlantic. A test of sentiment in July had disclosed 62 per cent of the testees voting to check Japan, even at the cost of war. That was roughly the proportion steadily expressing itself in favor of aiding Britain to defeat the Nazis at the risk of war.

Although Vichy France escaped retaliatory action by this Government, Washington leveled at it the strongest disapproval, a disapproval heightened by the certainty that Vichy had made an abject, sordid, and unnecessary surrender of

French interest in Tokyo *cum* Berlin. It was one thing to yield honorably to superior force in Indo-China, another to enter into a pseudo partnership with the Japanese aggressor against the Western powers.

Actually, Vichy's only hope for the retention of Indo-China lay in Western success, yet the men of Vichy readily betrayed French interests for considerations which can scarcely be imagined.

On August 2, with the text of the common-defense treaty before him, Welles issued a statement, declining to accept the impudent Tokyo-Vichy French explanation of its act as a move to forestall Anglo-Saxon occupation and serving notice that France's relationship to its overseas possessions must hereafter be the subject of pragmatic study based on each case as it arose. Welles thereby laid down the policy of "manifest effectiveness," saying that this Government would be influenced by the care in each instance exercised by Vichy France in endeavoring to "protect these territories from domination and control by those powers which are seeking to extend their rule by force and conquest, or by the threat thereof."

At the moment, peril was intruding itself from quarters other than southeastern Asia. Welles himself, at a press conference late in July, disclosed apprehensions concerning Axis pressure on some of the remaining independent countries in Europe. He meant Spain and Portugal, and successful Nazi manipulation of those countries meant the Azores, Canaries, and Cape Verdes. Meanwhile, Berlin and Paris were pressing Vichy and Weygand for a treaty of "common defense" analogous to the shameful transaction over Indo-China. The attempt to wrest the African colonies out of Weygand's firm grasp would reach a head in August, producing a new crisis for Vichy. It was in July, 1941, that the President told Congress:

"I do believe—I know—the danger of today is infinitely greater."

He knew, a fact withheld from the public in the Western nations, that the Nazi timetable called for launching a drive on Gibraltar, the western Mediterranean, and the Atlantic islands on October 15. Believing that Brauchitsch could break Russian resistance by September, the *Führer* proposed to move south in the fall, expecting to have all Europe in his physical possession by Christmas. To that end, the diplomatic offensive against the French and the countries of the Iberian peninsula went forward remorselessly in midsummer.

The Governments of Portugal and Spain, at the time Welles spoke, were undergoing an unbelievable pressure of promises, bribes, and threats, but mostly threats. Both countries were to resist, Portugal because the scholarly, modest dictator, Dr. Manoel Salazar, declined to repudiate the two-hundred-year-old alliance between Britain and Portugal; Spain because—a fact not generally known in the West—the Army command and a fair portion of the hierarchy never had been incorporated into the Nazi orbit. Serrano Suñer, the Foreign Minister and chief of the Falange, might wish to deliver Spain to the Axis, but the Army kept a wary eye on him. The generals had observed what had happened to their opposite numbers in Italy, the bishops did not relish having Spain a province of Nazidom, and the British, because they represented a counterbalance to the Axis, had surprising sources of strength in Spain Furthermore, the British were remedying the worst of Spain's undernourishment with grain from Argentina, thereby gaining mass sympathy.

In July also General Marshall, testifying before the Senate Military Affairs Committee, declared that the United States had been in imminent peril for two months and that, should he tell all he knew, it "might result in something like the sinking of the *Maine* or the Zimmermann note."

The Chief of Staff would not particularize, but it was assumed in educated quarters that he referred to a Nazi *Putsch* aimed at Bolivia, just then in process of being nipped by a

strong Bolivian Government. Early in June, the British censorship had uncovered a correspondence between Major Elias
Belmonte, Bolivian military attaché at Berlin and a political
adventurer, and Ernst Wendler, a Nazi consul in Bolivia, incriminating Wendler, a German named Schroth, head of the
Lloyd Aereo Boliviano (a line until recently under German
control), a former Finance Minister named Victor Paz Estens-
soro, and others. Belmonte had been the strong-arm mercenary
of Germán Busch, the first and last dictator on the totalitarian
order in South America. Busch, who had seized power in July,
1937, by a coup, had killed himself on August 23, 1939, ending
his regime. The constitutional Government following Busch,
fearing Belmonte's propensity for violent intrigue, sent him
to Berlin.

This was no paper conspiracy. A total of five thousand
Germans, Bolivians of German descent, and non-German Bolivians had been organized by cells into a disciplined band.
They had a flourishing press, operating openly, three clandes-
tine radio stations, and a foothold in the Army. The letters of
Belmonte, who was acting under instructions of the appropriate Nazi agency, flowed on, incriminating more and more
ringleaders. In one of the concluding letters, before President
Enrique Penaranda del Castillo proclaimed a state of siege
and quashed the conspirators, Belmonte wrote Consul Wendler: "The situation is ripe for revolt. . . . I think, however,
July is the most favorable for action."

Exposure of the planned coup struck the Foreign Office
spokesman in Berlin as "nonsense." President Roosevelt had
turned all the South American states into his "stooges," the
spokesman added, with, no doubt, a touch of rue. A strategical
reason for Germany's recurrent interest in Bolivia as a spear-
head of Nazi military infiltration into South America is that
the country lies inland from the sea and hence might be supposed to be immune from the outreaches of American sea
power. High in the Andes, Bolivia is also difficult of access by

land. It could be made into a mountain stronghold, and in Berlin there had been and would again be talk of establishing an impregnable Nazified state on the roof of South America.

—3—

On August 3, Mr. Roosevelt sailed out of the harbor of New London, Connecticut, on the yacht, *Potomac,* bound, so far as official Washington (except for a handful of men) and the public knew, on a typical Roosevelt holiday cruise in New England waters. So closely was the secret held that even Mrs. Roosevelt did not know the historic nature of the cruise. Mr. Hull, who had returned from White Sulphur, issuing a statement in which he blasted the Axis for employing practices in governing subject peoples "rooted in savagery and barbarism," was aware of the encounter that lay ahead. In order to preserve secrecy, the Army and Navy people assigned to the conference were stealing off, almost incognito, to fly or to sail on the *Augusta* and the cruiser *Tuscaloosa* for Newfoundland.

Sumner Welles, who headed the President's political staff, as General Marshall and Admiral Stark directed the military, flew from Boston to the place of meeting, there boarding the *Tuscaloosa.* The President and Welles had been preparing for the meeting for eight days before Mr. Roosevelt departed, discussing principles which, it was hoped, might grow out of the conference as a declaration of war, or peace, aims. Those subjects lay near Roosevelt's heart. The case for the democracies, he felt, should be put, simply and emphatically, before the war grew much older and before the United States became a belligerent. It should, moreover, be a joint declaration.

As early as January, 1941, the President had offered in his Four Freedoms a basis for the kind of world worth striving for after the war. But that was too generalized, having the disadvantage, in addition, of being unilateral, like Wilson's Fourteen Points. Both the Fourteen Points and the Four Freedoms had been launched in messages to Congress. They bound no-body but their authors. Morcover, when President Wilson undertook to negotiate with Prince Max of Baden for a truce on the basis of his points, they still, strictly speaking, bound no one else, the President not having thought it necessary to gain the sanction of Lloyd George and Clemenceau, an over-sight that by no means eased his tasks at the Paris Conference. Mr. Roosevelt wished to avoid that obvious pitfall. He en-visaged an agreement with the British on broad political and economic principles while we were still at peace and before the emotional intensities of the belligerent state blurred our clear vision of the desirable. Mostly, he wished to commit the British, grimly fighting for survival, to a postwar program. Welles carried along working drafts for a declaration, the product of several conversations in the oval room.

The American flotilla gathered in the "Newfoundland bight," as Churchill was to put it, on the morning of August 10. In the late afternoon the *Prince of Wales* dropped anchor near the *Augusta*, and the semaphores conveyed an invitation to Mr. Churchill and five of his ranking companions and Hopkins for dinner in the President's cabin on the *Augusta*. Churchill, in his plain, brass-buttoned reefer, the uniform of an Elder Brother of Trinity House, brought with him Hop-kins, Sir Alexander Cadogan, Permanent Under Secretary for Foreign Affairs and Mr. Welles' opposite number, as well as the chiefs of the Army, Navy, and Air Force.

At the dinner for fourteen, a comradely occasion informed by Mr. Roosevelt's raillery and Mr. Churchill's soberer wit, the oppressive weight of Japan's relentless drive southward, concern over Russia's capacity to retreat and endure, and the whole budget of global worries were dismissed for the moment as the Britons and Americans devoted themselves to getting acquainted in preparation for the work ahead.

That work began the next morning as the assorted naval craft lay at anchorage, with the sound of protective aircraft seldom out of hearing. On the way across, Churchill had dictated his own draft of war aims. An after-breakfast conference in the President's cabin on the *Augusta* was given over to a reading of the American and British drafts and some desultory talk of principles, limitations, and form. The work of drafting a united statement was then assigned to Welles and Cadogan, who retired to Welles' quarters on the *Tuscaloosa* for the first of a half-dozen sessions. The military authorities similarly paired off, either on American or British ships, the Army men with the Army, Air Force with Air Force, Navy with Navy. In these "pockets," as Welles termed them, the fruitful technical work of the conference at sea went forward.

The crisis in the Far East claimed first attention, resulting, as we have seen, in Churchill's agreement to the President's policy of delaying hostilities without invoking a "deadline." That agreement represented a unifying of English-speaking policy in the Pacific. In the discussions about a deadline, it was generally held that the geographical limit should be set in the south at Cam Ranh Bay and that the Japanese should be warned not to develop or further fortify that base under penalty of war. But it was Hopkins' report, made first to the President alone and by him communicated next to Churchill and his own people and, finally, to all hands, which most stirred the pulses of the Atlantic Conference. The President, optimistic by nature, received the detailed, circumstantial news of the magnitude of Russia's forces and her effort, with something like elation. Churchill, too, was rejoiced, the report bearing out the surmises of himself and Hopkins in London and offering the most substantial military hope of the war for Britain.

At first, when Hopkins, at the President's suggestion, summarized the Kremlin's case for the generals and admirals, he met with skepticism. After all, Hopkins was not a military man, and the generals, still dazzled by Brauchitsch, found it hard to accept Stalin's flat pronouncement that the Nazis could not take Moscow in 1941. As Hopkins related what he had heard and seen in ever more convincing detail, even the hardest-bitten of the military chiefs began to concede that a new face was being put on the Soviet Union's capacity to hold the Nazi avalanche. By the third day, a spirit of buoyancy over the outlook in Russia compensated in some degree for the gloom over the Pacific.

The Atlantic Charter reached final form on the third day. Lord Beaverbrook had arrived meantime and had joined the little group in the President's cabin as they listened to a reading of the draft prepared by Welles and Cadogan. Also present was Hopkins. The President and Prime Minister read the articles aloud, Mr. Roosevelt reading the preamble, which described the document as a "joint declaration of the President of the United States of America and the Prime Minister, Mr. Churchill, representing his Majesty's Government in the United Kingdom, who deem it right . . ." Here, the Prime Minister interrupted:

"Shouldn't we say 'being met together deem it right'?" he asked. "Being met together" it was, and so appears in the official text—a stout Anglo-Saxon phrase, reminiscent of Milton or the Book of Common Prayer.

All went well until the fourth article. The first—". . . their countries seek no aggrandizement, territorial or otherwise"— passed without comment. The second embodied Churchill's phraseology: ". . . they desire to see no territorial changes that do not accord with the freely expressed wishes of the peoples concerned." That was a heavy gun put at the disposal of political warfare in Germany. It plainly constituted a pledge against dismembering the Reich, a pledge subsequently strengthened and applied as to Germany by Mr. Churchill in a speech that had Mr. Roosevelt's full sanction. The third round was Roosevelt's: ". . . they respect the right of all peoples to choose the form of government under which they will live; and they wish to see sovereign rights and self-government restored to those who have been forcibly deprived of them." That, of course, offered assurances to the subjugated peoples of Europe.

As drawn by the President, the fourth article, dealing with equal economic opportunity and access to raw materials, had been controversial from the start, arousing a lively debate on the first day. Churchill lacked the President's freedom in the premises. His Government was committed to Empire preference under the Ottawa conventions, he had no authority to undo that commitment, and, furthermore, he represented only the Government of the United Kingdom and not that of the Dominions, which were equal partners in the Ottawa agreements.

A bit unwillingly, the President was obliged to take a compromise there, the article reading in final form:

> Fourth, they will endeavor, with due respect for their existing obligations, to further the enjoyment by all states, great or small, victor or vanquished, of access, on equal terms, to the trade and to the raw materials of the world, which are needed for their economic prosperity.

The compromise, as is apparent, lay in the "existing obligations" clause.

That hurdle passed, the going was smoother. Number five represented a blending of American and British phraseology. It pledged the signatories to "bring about the fullest collaboration between all nations in the economic field, with the object of securing for all, improved labor standards, economic advancement and social security."

The sixth article followed Roosevelt's language: ". . . after the final destruction of the Nazi tyranny, they hope to see established a peace which will afford to all nations the means of dwelling in safety within their own boundaries, and which will assure that all the men in all the lands may live out their lives in freedom from fear and want." The phrase "all the men in all the lands" came, however, from Churchill, who begged leave to amplify the President's prose at that point, the added phrase being sonorously Churchillian. The sixth article comprehended, without enumerating, the Four Freedoms.*

Numbers seven and eight closely followed the United States draft. They read:

Seventh, such a peace should enable all men to traverse the high seas and oceans without hindrance;

Eighth, they believe that all of the nations of the world, for realistic as well as spiritual reasons, must come to the abandonment of the use of force. Since no future peace can be maintained if land, sea or air armaments continue to be employed by nations which threaten, or may threaten, aggression outside of their frontiers, they believe, pending the establishment of a wider and permanent system of general security, that the disarmament of such nations is essential. They will likewise aid and encourage all other practicable measures which will lighten for peace-loving peoples the crushing burden of armaments.

A reassuring harmony of purpose as well as mutual trust were exhibited during this conference on the final draft. Apart from the compromise on the fourth article, the views of Roosevelt and Churchill were fully represented.

—4—

For the first time in their century and a half of separate existence the United States and Great Britain had been joined in a written alliance. Its end was the destruction of Nazidom and the construction of a peaceable, free, and kindlier post-

---

* Upon this failure to specify a pledge of religious freedom the isolationists were to pounce, supposing that the President had omitted it "out of consideration for the new ally, Joe Stalin." In submitting the charter to Congress, the President disposed of that quibble.

war world based on a concert of the Atlantic Powers. The Atlantic Charter fittingly recalled in its name this country's long-standing Atlantic policy and, with the inter-American compacts of solidarity from Montevideo to Havana, constituted formalization of that "Atlantic System" Henry Adams had observed in 1906.

Much of the generalized character, as well as the initiative, for the Atlantic Charter came from Roosevelt. Churchill agreed unreservedly to its definitions, but his principal aim at the moment (as pointed out at that time by one of the authors of this book in his syndicated newspaper column) was the "destruction of the Nazis and the perpetuation of the British Empire. What else happens is secondary to him, and would be to any responsible man in his position."

Back in 1930, before the "Mukden incident" and before Hitler's rise, Churchill, writing for *Scribner's,* imagined the result of a victory for Lee at Gettysburg.* He saw, first, the division of this country into two republics and, secondly, its reunion in 1905 through the efforts of Theodore Roosevelt and Prime Minister Herbert H. Asquith.

Thereafter, the "Re-United States" and the British Empire were, in Mr. Churchill's fantasy, linked in a "Covenant of the English-speaking Association," which, by its conjoined weight, averted the First World War after the assassination at Serajevo. Under the Association's charter, common citizenship was granted throughout the English-speaking world, the peoples deeming "themselves to be members of one body and inheritors of one estate." In Churchill's description:

> The flexibility of the plan which invaded no national privacy, which left all particularisms unchallenged, which altered no institutions and required no elaborate machinery, was its salvation. Without prejudice to their existing loyalties and sentiments, they gave birth in themselves to a new

---

* The article was based upon a recent tour of Civil War battlefields, the Prime Minister being among the British students of that War.

higher loyalty and a wider sentiment . . . they were associated by indissoluble ties for the maintenance of peace between themselves, for the prevention of war among outside Powers and for the economic development of their measureless resources and possessions.

Churchill, a sturdy nationalist in 1930, as in 1941, envisioned then a sort of closed, Anglo-Saxon corporation. With the Atlantic Charter, and its subsequent enlargement by President Roosevelt in his address of February 23, 1942, to include the "whole world," Churchill became committed to a far wider association. As of August, 1941, Roosevelt was in a position to take a broader view, being still nonbelligerent and removed by distance and British resistance from the Nazi peril. By temperament and intellectual habit also, the President has been more inclined than the Prime Minister to make the world his province, to consider global problems in broad, sweeping strokes. Both men think in strategical terms; both, weaned on Mahan, understand the importance of the seas as highroads of commerce and conquest. Neither Roosevelt nor Churchill fears the implications of responsibility in terms of power.

A European scholar now in this country, who has been studying the Munich Institute of Geopolitics for its influence on Nazi policies, recently remarked that Roosevelt alone, among Western leaders, was a match for the strategical thinking that has been going on in Germany between wars. Understanding the interrelationships of climate, geography, economics, soil, politics, and cultural tradition almost by instinct, the President, said this authority, is himself a "one-man Institute of Geopolitics."

Because of these Roosevelt and Churchill aptitudes, the Atlantic Charter avoided more Wilsonian blunders than merely the First World War President's insistence upon making his Fourteen Points a unilateral statement, lofty in tone and withheld from the consideration of his European part-

ners. Two things Mr. Wilson did not understand—power politics and economics. The conferees off Newfoundland did not
shrink from taking military and naval power into their hands.
Where Wilson left the disposition of armies and navies to an
unformulated society of nations, which turned out in practice
to be a postwar league of victors burdened with contradictory
ideals, Roosevelt and Churchill realistically assumed the burden of disarming the aggressors after this war and of themselves policing the peace until such time as a genuine association of self-governing nations might be established.

The perfectionists of 1917 made a great point of an abstract
freedom of the seas. By this they meant unhindered use of the
seas for commerce by belligerents and neutrals alike in time of
war. They failed, however, to apply the same standards to
land warfare. Under their definition of the rules of war,
navies would be permitted only to engage navies or, presumably, take part in military operations against enemy bases. The
reverse of the shield went unnoticed, nothing being said
against the land blockade or against the destruction or appropriation of goods moving in commerce on the land or, indeed,
against land war on civilians and their property. The Wilsonian principle of freedom of the seas, which swiftly vanished
from consideration at Paris, penalized the sea powers at the
expense of the land powers, such as Germany. Mr. Wilson, of
course, could have had no such motivation, although he must
have been aware of German interest in and advocacy of such
a provision. He may have forgotten that the United States was
no longer a weak, seafaring country, as in 1812, seeking vainly
to affirm its rights to trade with both great belligerents in
Europe, England and Napoleon's France, without molestation
by either. That plank in the Fourteen Points was dated by a
full century.

Roosevelt and Churchill, sea-power men, brought the freedom of the seas up to date, merely expressing their confidence
that the kind of co-operative peace they had in mind—the Pax

Anglo-Americana of the Atlantic Charter—would enable all nations to use the seas in the pursuit of their legitimate errands in time of peace.

Although commentators everywhere, in Europe as in America, sought at once to draw parallels between the Fourteen Points and the Atlantic Charter, the similarities were more fancied than real. Both, it is true, arose out of American concern for an orderly, pacific world, both looked forward to some type of world association, and both renounced territorial aspirations or other forms of national aggrandizement.

But there were profound differences. Wilson's bias was almost wholly political. Only one of his points—that pledging equality of trade conditions—took economic factors into account. Three of the Charter's articles included economic bases for an enlightened and prosperous world. The social bases likewise were stressed by Roosevelt and Churchill, as in the pledge of the "fullest collaboration . . . with the object of securing, for all, improved labor standards, economic advancement, and social security."

Profiting by Wilson's experience, Roosevelt and Churchill steered clear of specific commitments in the territorial reorganization of Europe after this war. Eight of the Fourteen Points dealt with boundary and related matters, and by and large those were pits unwittingly dug by Wilson himself for his own entrapment and the embarrassment of the peace settlements.

The Germans, by angry repetition and with the assistance of such Britons, Frenchmen, and Americans as had managed to work up a sense of guilt as well as disillusionment between wars, had fairly well discredited the Fourteen Points. That assault on the Wilsonian charter, in fact, played a part in the rise of the Nazis, Hitler gaining the acquiescence of numerous Germans by endless iteration of the lie that Germany, unbeaten militarily, had been defrauded by Wilson at Paris. That lie was palatable to the Germans. Not so the truth, which was that, beaten in the field and facing mutiny and civilian revolt, the German leaders used Wilson's declaration as a device with which to escape the consequences of defeat. Because of the wholesale slanders of the earlier document, the Atlantic Charter's edge as a propaganda instrument was blunted upon its announcement, comparisons between the two documents serving in the minds of many to tar the Charter with the stick of the Fourteen Points.

But that was an early reaction. At first, the genuinely liberal and democratic character of the pledges was interpreted cynically in certain quarters. This country was in the midst of a convulsive debate on the precise limits of our participation in the war, and the passions and rancors of that debate colored the thinking of some. As time passed, however, and the articles were studied with greater composure, it was seen that these were honest pledges, entirely in harmony with the developing enlightenment of British and American policy—pledges that could be honestly kept.

The reception of the Charter in England also, as in America, was conditioned by other matters. The English, hoping that Churchill would have been able to get the United States into the war during the conference at sea, felt let down by the long-range nature of the declaration. Fighting for their lives, the British were thinking in military, not political, terms.

It is no secret that Churchill's standing with his people has varied somewhat according to the relative success of his American policy. The fact that the Prime Minister had an American mother, knew America well if unflatteringly, and got on so congenially with Roosevelt and his subordinates helped his popularity at home, especially during the year in which Britain fought alone and desperately desired America's help. Widely popular in this country as a symbol of what the British call pluck and of what we are likely to call guts, Churchill has been a continuing asset to Britain. His broadcasted speeches had an audience second only to Mr. Roosevelt's. But, it seems under practical analysis, that his people expected too much of the Prime Minister if they thought he could cajole, wheedle, or stampede this country into belligerency. Mr. Churchill caused Americans to think better of Britain, but not of war. If and when this country went to war, it would be for vital American reasons.

Britons, like Americans, are not too familiar with the political and strategical motives that stir the other country to action. Nor is the inevitable collaboration of the Atlantic Powers in defense of their common ocean any better understood in England than here. It was not fair then to blame Mr. Churchill because he had been unable to persuade Mr. Roosevelt to declare war while off Newfoundland. In the cool light of national interest, the British went to war against the Nazis not because they were Nazis but because they had the strength, the malevolence, and the will to threaten the political independence and well-being of England and the British Empire. Similarly, the United States supported Britain with constantly increasing fullness not because it liked England (which, however, it prevailingly does) or because it detested the Nazis (which it likewise does), but because our national and hemispheric security was involved, and we were willing to go to pretty far lengths to sustain the civilization of which we were a part.

Churchill's chief value to the British cause in America was a certain tough-minded understanding shared with Roosevelt in matters of strategy and world politics generally. Both are nationalists. Neither allows sentimental regard for the other country to interfere with the interests of his own. Neither has pulled his punches with the other. Hence, it was easier for Roosevelt to do business with Churchill than with a different type of Prime Minister.

—5—

An outgrowth of the Atlantic Conference second in importance only to the linking of the English-speaking powers was, however, the confirmation, unifying, and strengthening of Anglo-American policies toward the Soviet Union. A joint Roosevelt-Churchill message, drafted at sea and delivered to Stalin by the American and British Ambassadors on August 15, fused the English and American policies into one. It displayed, moreover, a confidence in Russia's ability and will to resist that, with our prior knowledge of the nature of Hopkins' report from Moscow, reflected his findings and Stalin's assurances to Roosevelt. The message, in truth, carried in its opening sentence acknowledgment of the part played by the Hopkins report, saying:·

> We have taken the opportunity afforded by the consideration of the report of Mr. Harry Hopkins on his return from Moscow to consult together as to how best our two countries can help your country in the splendid defense that you are making against the Nazi attack.

Indicating ·that the President and the Prime Minister, as Hopkins before them, took Stalin's promise of a sustained fight at face value, the message, after reminding the Soviet leader ·of the help already dispatched him, went on to say:

> We must now turn our minds to the consideration of a more long-term policy, since there is still a long and hard path to be traversed before there can be won that complete victory without which our efforts and sacrifices would be wasted.

Thereupon, Roosevelt and Churchill put into official form the suggestion for a supply conference among the three powers at Moscow already broached to Stalin by Hopkins. Pending that conference, the signatories of the message assured the master of the Kremlin that they would "continue to send supplies and materials as rapidly as possible."

This Government, as we have seen, had announced all-out aid for Russia on August 2—the day after Hopkins left Moscow, having cabled only a skeletal and guarded report on his visit —in the exchange of letters between Welles and Oumansky. Early in the fall, Congress endorsed the policy when it overwhelmingly rejected an amendment to a new, six-billion-dollar lend-lease bill designed to debar the Soviet Union from its benefits.

Before Congress acted, the American delegation to Moscow, headed by W. Averell Harriman, a liberal multimillionaire, son of the late railway magnate, E. H. Harriman, had been selected. Although probably few Americans recalled it, Harriman's choice had an interesting historical sanction. E. H. Harriman had carried on protracted negotiations with St. Petersburg early in this century on behalf of an imperial project for a round-the-world transportation system by rail and water. Averell Harriman likewise had had business relations with a Russian Government, having worked mineral concessions in the Soviet Union until his concession was purchased by the Mineral Trust. The reason for his selection was, however, more immediate than that. As lend-lease administrator in London, he had an excellent grasp of the supply problem.

Other members of the American mission were William L. Batt, Deputy Director of the Production Division of the Office of Production Management; Major General James H. Burns, who had been assigned to help Hopkins administer lend-lease; Major General George H. Brett, Chief of the Air Corps, who was then in Europe on another errand; and Rear Admiral W. H. Standley, who, in 1942, was to return to Moscow as Ambassador. In Moscow, these commissioners met with the British delegation, led by Lord Beaverbrook, the British supply chief. Although a bit ahead of the story, it may be remarked at this point that the chief American conferees, as well as Lord Beaverbrook, returned from Moscow convinced, as Hopkins had been, of the Soviet regime's good faith, its uncomplicated will to reduce the Nazi military power, and the necessity, in terms of American and British interest, of the utmost support to Russia.

Meanwhile, the Russo-American association, foreseen in July of 1940 by Sumner Welles, overflowed into fields wider than the mere supply of war materials. The negotiations between the Premier of the Polish Government-in-exile, Wladyslaw Sikorsky, and Ambassador Maisky in London, looking to a Russo-Polish alliance, had this Government's blessing, their conclusion evoking a gratified public comment from Welles. On August 18, a few days after his return from the Atlantic Conference, Welles, under Hull's instructions, sounded Hjalmar J. Procopé, the Finnish Minister in Washington, on a peace offer the Kremlin wished to tender the Finns via this Government.

Our attempt to draw Finland out of the war and the Nazi orbit was to fail, as it would again when renewed by Mr. Hull himself early in October. This country's interest in that venture was, of course, apparent. Further Finnish successes north of Leningrad might close the most convenient line of supply from the Atlantic Powers into Russia. We had no wish to see our contributions to Russian defense against the Nazis piled up in a White Sea port or seized by an ally of the Nazis. Moreover, the Finnish forces were engaging many thousands of Soviet troops which, in our opinion, could be better disposed against the Nazis.

In the *mémoire* of his conversation with Procopé on the 18th, Welles indicated that he, too, was drawing upon the Hopkins findings. From official statements, he said, as well as "from other evidence available to this Government, the Soviet Government is not only resisting magnificently . . . but is likewise prepared to fight indefinitely against Germany and

. . . from our knowledge of the military situation there seems every reason to suppose that Russia may do so successfully and for a protracted period." Welles informed the Finnish Minister that Moscow was prepared to make territorial concessions in the interest of peace. Procopé at once "raised certain obvious questions," described by the *mémoire* as follows:

> First, in view of the experience Finland had had with the Soviet Union in 1939, what guarantees would Great Britain and the United States offer Finland that any peace treaty which the Soviet Union might now be disposed to negotiate would be maintained? Second, what assurance would Finland be given that, in the event that Germany was defeated and the Soviet Union were to become the predominant military power, Russia would respect any promises which Great Britain or the United States might have made . . . ?

Welles, not being prepared to discuss these questions but only to open the path for future negotiations, could not refrain, however, from wondering

> . . . what guarantees or assurances Finland thought she would have of retaining her own independence and autonomy if Germany . . . were the overlord of all Europe. I said that in such event Finland could look to no one for assistance whereas if Germany were defeated she would have extremely powerful friends on her side.

The argument failed to influence Procopé. American-Finnish relations steadily were to deteriorate until November, when Finland joined the anti-Comintern bloc, sending its Foreign Minister to Berlin for the somewhat *ersatz* ceremonies with which Hitler had hoped to signalize the "new order" in Europe. Finnish-American relations then came near the breaking point. Procopé professed himself bewildered by the swift reversal of sentiment which tumbled Finland from a high place in the affections of Americans to one of low esteem between the spring of 1940 and the fall of 1941. An amiable diplomat, he should have had a less naïve attitude toward the working of *Realpolitik*. Certain Americans, including Herbert Hoover, likewise found the situation difficult to assess. Yet, it was by no means complex. In the first instance, Russia had been ranged, at least constructively, against the Western World. In the second, she was fighting the common enemy of the West, and Finland's private quarrel was lost in the larger equation.

Finland's case was not, of course, helped with this Government by information that the Finnish military clique, under Field Marshal Mannerheim, a czarist general in the pre-World War I days when Finland belonged to Russia, had embraced Nazism and regarded the alliance as one of policy as well as expediency. At about this time, the State Department flatly rejected the statement of Risto Ryti, the President of Finland, that his country was self-contained, independent, and fighting Russia solely for its own reasons. In the fall of 1941, Finnish forces, with German detachments, besieged Leningrad from the North and threatened Murmansk, which port might have become the only water entry into Russia for our supplies in the event of a severe winter closing the White Sea and Archangel beyond the capacity of Soviet ice-breakers to clear channels. It was this consideration which quickened our anxiety over Finland's course as winter neared.

Meanwhile, Mr. Roosevelt, pursuing his concern for the right to worship, plus other objectives less easy to decipher, intervened on behalf of religious freedom in Russia. Few aspects of the Administration's relations with the Soviet Union have aroused so much speculation. Few have been so complex. On September 30, the President saw fit to call attention at a press conference to a letter, made public that day by the State Department, from Jan Ciechanowski, the Polish Ambassador, to the Secretary. In the letter, the Ambassador reported glowingly on the rise of Polish national forces in Russia under the Kremlin's protection, predicting that an army of one hundred thousand volunteers soon would take the field against the Nazis. The Soviet Government, he observed, was "loyally fulfilling all its engagements." Furthermore (and this was a source of especial gratification to Ciechanowski), he reported that the Soviet Government had allowed the Polish forces to have their own chaplains, that it was reopening a Polish Catholic church and a synagogue in Moscow for Polish Jews, and that it intended to give Polish communities in Russia their own places of worship and schools.

Mr. Roosevelt singled out Ciechanowski's religious passages for comment, suggesting that this meant a relaxation of policy on the part of the Kremlin. He cited Article 124 of the Russian Constitution, which guarantees freedom of conscience along with the right to propagandize against religion. That provision, said the President, squares with our practice.

> For instance, you might go out tomorrow—to the corner of Pennsylvania Avenue, down below the Press club—and stand on a soapbox and preach Christianity, and nobody would stop you; and then, if it got into your head, perhaps the next day preach against religion of all kinds, and nobody would stop you.

In the give-and-take informality of a press conference, the President failed to make clear that he was referring to a historic American practice and to what was as yet only a Russian aspiration. A good many commentators disingenuously construed his remarks to imply that Russians enjoyed the same unhampered right of religious association as Americans. Other critics suggested that the President had been trying to square the Soviet Union with the churchgoers of this country in order to sugar-coat the pill of assistance to the atheistic Kremlin. Ranging farther, still others surmised that the President's maneuver had been aimed at Moscow and other capitals more than at the United States.

To that shrewd conclusion the Russian Embassy came, wondering if the President were not engaged in political warfare, seeking, perhaps, to soften the Kremlin's antireligious line for its effect on Rome as well as on the Catholic hierarchy in Germany and the subject states of Europe. Was this not Mr. Roosevelt's means of counteracting the Nazi attempt to depict the Russian campaign as a holy war? A general assumption was that the President had Rome principally in mind, and certain Soviet sympathizers in this country suspected he was hoping to open Russia to the Roman Church as a field for proselytizing effort. That ascription of motive was probably the farthest fetched, although there can be little doubt that the President's motives were mixed.

Mr. Roosevelt's gesture can be better appraised in the light of certain representations being at the moment made by Harriman direct to Stalin. Under instructions from Washington, the chief of the American supply mission sounded the Russian leader on this delicate point. He knew, naturally, that under international law a country's domestic policy concerning religion is its own business. Hence Harriman candidly put the matter on grounds of mutual advantage. A change in Soviet religious policy would, he said, remove a subjective obstacle in America to full material aid and perhaps gain some sympathy for the Soviet cause. What would a practical man in Stalin's shoes do under such circumstances?

Stalin took the suggestion in good part, displaying understanding of the American situation and respect for the desires of the American Government, desires which he indicated a willingness to satisfy. Already, under the life-and-death stress of invasion, the rigidities of Soviet opposition to religion had been relaxed. The ideological emphasis was shifting from the scientific materialism of Karl Marx back to national patriotism, to defense of the soil of Mother Russia. In that shift a spark of the old faith had been rekindled with the approval of the Kremlin, and a prayer in one of the few Orthodox churches which had been kept open in Moscow during the dark days for religion was no longer accounted counterrevolutionary. Upon inquiry, it was discovered that the Church had been steadily, if quietly, regaining lost ground for several years past. A student of revolutions, Mr. Roosevelt had noted their organic similarity. He suspected in the early fall of 1941 that the antireligious dynamism of the Bolshevik revolution had spent its force and that a change was imminent—a change that would redound to better relations between Russia and the Western powers.

The Moscow supply conference reached its conclusion, under the chairmanship of Molotov, on October 1, with full agreement on the types and volume of munitions to be furnished by Britain and America, with Russia reciprocally furnishing certain raw materials to the Atlantic Powers. A month later Mr. Roosevelt wrote Stalin, notifying him of his approval of the Moscow proceedings and offering a loan of one billion dollars in goods under the lend-lease authority conferred by Congress. In replying, Stalin avowed his "sincere gratitude" for "an unusually substantial aid" in the "difficult and great struggle against our common enemy, bloodthirsty Hitlerism." This Government gave a blanket priority to Russia-bound requirements, the need for which had been stated at Moscow with great explicitness. The Russians had proved fairly inflexible bargainers.

Throughout the fall, the Red Army, forced back, mile by mile, held its forces together, exacting a huge price from the Nazis and making a final stand in front of Moscow early in December before launching their winter counteroffensive. Stalin's prophecy had held good.

CHAPTER NINE

The Sands Run Out—Pearl Harbor

AN "ill wind," arising from the Russian front, was, Pétain lamented in August, blowing across France, creating civil disorders and assassinations and provoking new turns of the screw by the conqueror. Although the war in the east relieved military pressure, it tightened diplomatic tension in the west. Hitler now was demanding, in addition to the African colonies, that Vichy go to war against the old ally, Russia.

Again, on August 8, Weygand flew over from Algiers under orders; again in Pétain's suite at the Hôtel du Parc, bristling, ironical, and defiant, he repeated that if the *boche* still wished North Africa, he could come and take it. "Unless, *Monsieur le maréchal*, you would prefer my resignation?" Pétain did not wish Weygand's resignation. That would come later. This time Vichy announced that the defense of North Africa was quite a different matter from that of Indo-China and would not be shared. Again, Weygand, faithful to the American convention, preserved North Africa from the Axis, a circumstance hinted at the time but only now and here able to be explicitly reported.

Less than three weeks later, Paul Collette, a redheaded, twenty-year-old pseudo volunteer in a tiny French Legion being recruited for the Nazi war on Russia, shot the evil genius of France, Laval, and Marcel Déat, the notorious collaborationist editor, as they stood reviewing the troops at Versailles. His aim was not sufficiently accurate. Not a Communist, Collette once had belonged to the Fascistic *Croix de feu*, having since turned patriot. The old marshal was at the opera in Vichy, seeing Berlioz's *Damnation of Faust*—specifically, the act in which Faust succumbs to the Devil's promises—when he got the news. He at once joined the German campaign to rid all of France of sabotage and physical violence. Soon the guillotine was hard at work.

The battle of the Atlantic likewise quickened in midsummer, with increasing sinkings of American merchantmen under our own and the Panama flag. In July the United States again extended its strategical resources, occupying Iceland in association with the British, who had been there since May, 1940. This put us in possession of both the oceanic piers of the North Atlantic bridge. And the construction of an American Naval base at Londonderry, in Northern Ireland, already had begun, with a view to securing the vital life line from North America to the British Isles.

On September 4 a Nazi submarine fired two torpedoes at a United States destroyer, the *Greer*, off Greenland. One week later the President, in the grimmest of his prewar fireside chats, announced that the Navy had orders to shoot enemy men-of-war at sight within the waters covered by our patrol. The attack on the *Greer* he held to be "piracy, legally and morally." Not a mere "localized military operation in the North Atlantic," it was a "determined step towards creating a permanent world system based on force, terror, and murder." Hence:

> My obligation as President is historic; it is clear; it is unescapable . . . let this warning be clear. From now on, if German or Italian vessels of war enter the waters the protection of which is necessary for American defense they do so at their own risk. . . . The orders . . . are to carry out that policy— at once.

This was verging on war, an undeclared naval war in the

Atlantic, and to a large part of the American public it seemed that a "shooting war" was now only a question of time.

Notwithstanding that sensational development in the Atlantic, the eyes of the White House and the State Department were turned west in the early fall rather than east; on Tokyo more than on Vichy, or even Berlin. The next great decision of the war would be made, both Mr. Roosevelt and Mr. Hull thought, in Japan. On August 14 an event occurring in Tokyo sharpened State Department apprehensions, although it went almost unnoticed elsewhere. Baron Hiranuma, a middle-of-the-roader who had been serving as Vice-Premier less than a month, received a visitor from his home town at his house in Tokyo. The visitor, producing a letter of introduction, asked for an autograph, and, as Hiranuma stooped to write, fired three shots at him. Although two bullets struck home, the seventy-five-year-old statesman chased his assailant into the arms of a guard. In Tokyo the attempt on Hiranuma's life was taken as a warning by the Black Dragons that the moderates must go. Since 1931 assassination has been a formidable political weapon in Japan. It was taken likewise as a warning that the time for action was at hand. Hiranuma resigned.

On August 6, eight days before the shooting of Hiranuma, the Hull-Nomura conversations, suspended since the occupation of French Indo-China and the "freezing" order of July 25, were resumed at the Ambassador's instance. In asking for the interview, Nomura stated that he had new proposals from Tokyo growing out of the Indo-China development. Accordingly, at the meeting, the Ambassador handed the Secretary a memorandum, which, when boiled down to essentials, contained Japan's offer to withdraw from its new conquest in southern Indo-China, after the conclusion of a peace settlement with China and at a price. The price was familiar: this country's good offices in seeking to persuade Chiang Kai-shek to make peace on Japan's terms and lifting of the embargoes.

Mr. Hull asked time to study the document, and two nights

later, on the 8th, he again received Nomura for further talk
on the memorandum. With a *fait accompli* under her belt,
Japan was not now disposed to recede. Again, however, the
Secretary urged Nomura to persuade his Government to com-
pose the "China affair" along lines of justice, renewing his
declaration that a peace leaving China under the conqueror's
heel would not be worth the parchment upon which it was
written. Again, Nomura observed that Japan could not retire
her armies from China, however much she wished. If she did,
Nomura asked, what would prevent the Kuomintang (Chiang
Kai-shek's National party) and the Communists from flying
at each other's throats. Had not the United States maintained
troops in Central American and Caribbean countries to preserve order? It had, but no longer, Hull patiently explained:
this Government had discovered that such interventions, aside
from being morally unjustifiable, only prolonged the political instabilities and immaturities they were designed to
remedy. The Secretary had no sympathy with that pretext.

At the August 8 conference Nomura first broached an arresting idea. He proposed, orally, casually, and seemingly with
no instructions on the point from Tokyo, a face-to-face meeting
between the President and Prince Konoye as a means of breaking the deadlock that had characterized the conversations since
March. By a coincidence, as we have seen, Mr. Roosevelt was
at that moment approaching the Atlantic rendezvous with Mr.
Churchill, and the American press was beginning to speculate
on certain mystifying aspects of the President's vacation cruise
in New England waters. Whether Nomura was moved by
newspaper hints of a possible meeting between the President
and Prime Minister or whether he had intelligence reports
of the impending Atlantic Conference is not known to this
Government. In any case, the timing of Nomura's proposal of
a Pacific conference is noteworthy.

Mr. Hull thought well of the suggestion. The President was,
of course, absent from Washington, but on his return the mat-

ter went before him. He, too, reacted favorably, and on August 17 Admiral Nomura was handed a note throwing open the door to a conference which might arrange a "progressive program" for peace in the Pacific area along the broad lines of the principles upheld by this Government. The Japanese reply, delivered to the President by Nomura on August 28, certified its support of the principles, "with some qualifications," as applicable not only to the Pacific area but to the "entire world."

While "gratified" by the Japanese response, Mr. Roosevelt considered it wise to obtain a further clarification of the sense in which the principles were accepted by Tokyo. Before journeying to meet the Japanese Premier, the President thought all basis for misunderstanding should be removed. He, therefore, on September 3 addressed a further note to the Japanese Government, pointing out that the Hull-Nomura conversations had been unable to reach agreement on the wide principles involved and restating them in specific terms. Implying that a "community of view" was necessary on these points before negotiation could be satisfactorily undertaken on collateral details, he asked an explicit declaration on the Four Points, which he rephrased to read:

1. Respect for the territorial integrity and the sovereignty of each and all nations.
2. Support of the principle of noninterference in the internal affairs of other countries.
3. Support of the principle of equality, including equality of commercial opportunity.
4. Nondisturbance of the *status quo* in the Pacific, except as the *status quo* may be altered by peaceful means.

A Roosevelt-Konoye conference might have been a historically important milestone in Far Eastern relations, resulting in a Pacific Charter for the peaceful, orderly, disinterested development of that vast region, had the Japanese Government been sincere. Such was not the case. On September 6, Konoye, receiving Ambassador Grew in Tokyo, assured him that he "subscribed fully" to the Hull principles. But on that same day Ambassador Nomura handed Mr. Hull a memorandum which indicated either that Prince Konoye was indulging in double talk or that his Foreign Office had a widely different understanding with which they had not troubled to acquaint him.

The memorandum of the 6th made reservations that destroyed the vitality of the four principles. Equality of opportunity, as understood in Tokyo, was to apply only to the Dutch East Indies and other regions in which it now existed and not to Manchuria, the occupied part of China, and other Japanese-controlled areas, where it did not. Further, equal opportunity in China was to be excluded from the proposed Pacific conference's consideration, since China bore a special relationship to Japan because of "geographical propinquity." This evoked the shades of the Lansing-Ishii agreement of World War I, which, unhappily, for the consistency of American policy, had accepted some such contention of the Japanese regarding their special position vis-à-vis China. The memorandum, on the whole, was an act of effrontery completely justifying Mr. Roosevelt's mistrust.

This Government's reply, handed Nomura on October 2, took a direct and unequivocal line, expressing "disappointment" at the Japanese Government's attempt to "narrow down and restrict" the principles and demanding a "clear-cut manifestation of Japan's intentions in regard to the withdrawal of Japanese troops from China and French Indo-China." Under the circumstances, it was observed that the meeting could scarcely be of value at this time. The President did not, however, close the door, expressing instead his "earnest hope that discussion of the fundamental questions may be so developed that such a meeting can be held." The exchange of views between this Government and Tokyo thereupon went back to

Mr. Hull and Admiral Nomura for further intensive exploration. With the note of October 2, the second, or middle, phase of the Hull-Nomura conversations reached an end.

Thereafter, until the arrival of Kurusu, the talks were to drone along and by October 17, when General Tojo ousted Konoye and undertook to rule Japan nakedly in the name of the Army, were stalemated. The opinion is held by some authorities in this Government that Konoye's fall resulted from his failure to win the diplomatic offensive in Washington— to gain, through Nomura, this country's validation of Japanese conquest. That might be. It might likewise be that the hour for military action was at hand, and the Kwantung army clique, now openly bestriding Japan, felt no further need for the placatory offices of Konoye. At any rate, the mood of Tokyo altered after Tojo's assumption of power, growing more exigent as if indicating that Tojo's patience was being exhausted. He also was under pressure.

Increasingly from September forward, Germany was inciting Japan to open a front in the Pacific. The Nazi timetable, having gone awry in Russia, was consequently thrown out of line elsewhere. This was especially embarrassing in Vichy and the Iberian Peninsula, where Nazi diplomats and political-warfare agents had boasted they would move south toward Gibraltar on or about October 15. In September, Hitler hopefully pushed the clock ahead to November 15; a little later it was December 15, and finally he gave up setting dates for that enterprise. The Nazi predicament here was reminiscent of the humiliation suffered by the political-warfare agents in South America when October 1, 1940, came and went without goods to fill the orders which had been "guaranteed" during the summer.

The German pressure on Tokyo had been growing in intensity since July and August, when its existence had been enough to convince Roosevelt and Churchill that war in the Pacific would not long be deferred, and early in October Ribbentrop from Berlin and General Ott in Tokyo were resorting to threats. To the Nazis the situation in the Atlantic seemed critical. More than a little surprised by the promptitude of the Anglo-American concerted aid to the Soviet Union, Berlin observed the steadily rising flood of American war supplies to Britain and Russia with growing apprehension.

The Nazis were to miscalculate still further, believing that war in the Pacific would remove the United States as a formidable factor in the Atlantic. In certain Nazi quarters such a war was regarded as a high trump capable of taking trick, game, and rubber. The time had come to play that trump. This Government, fully aware of the train of Nazi thinking on this subject, was also aware in surprising detail of the nature, exigency, and pace of the German arguments leveled at Tokyo.

As Ribbentrop and Ott put it, unless the Japanese fulfilled the tripartite agreement and attacked America and England, Germany would be bound to review her relations with her ally in the light of that failure. They constantly reminded Tokyo that the concession of Indo-China had been based on a belief that Japan would honor her obligations to the Axis. Should Japan prove a faithless ally, Germany, after the victory that the Foreign Minister and Ambassador to Japan saw as inevitable, would enter into other arrangements with other powers for disposing of the former European colonies in Asia. On the other hand, however, should Japan create a diversion in the Pacific, Germany gladly would endorse her claims to a "complete and perpetual" domination (the language is Mr. Roosevelt's) of the whole Pacific area, the Far East, the Pacific islands, and the west coasts of North, Central, and South America.

By October, as shall be seen, Nazi importunity for an attack on Siberia had subsided in line with Japan's strategic pattern. In both Germany and Japan forces intent on the defeat of the English-speaking Powers first, Russia second, were in temporary ascendancy. The Japanese had equivocated during the summer, reluctant to turn north against Siberia, which was poor in what Japan most needed—oil and rice—instead of south. The best Tokyo would promise was to hit at Siberia when the Nazis reached the Volga, an objective denied Hitler in 1941.

The activist party now counseled a bold front against Japan, seeing her not only bogged down in China but compelled to bide her time until she saw which way the Russo-German war was to terminate. As long as that conflict hung in the balance, the activists held, we were in no danger from Japan. The President was not convinced by this line of reasoning, and, as for Mr. Hull, he never underestimated the actual military menace of Japan. Moreover, Mr. Hull had noticed, "down yonder," that if two determined men happened to be contending over a sack of meal, the fellow who had his gun on him was more likely to get the meal than the fellow who'd left his gun in the cupboard at home.

The re-enforcement of Hawaii and of Manila, our neglected stronghold on the South China Sea, was going forward at a leisurely pace that failed to reassure Mr. Hull. Repeatedly at the Sunday-morning confabs, when military men were present (which was often), he pointed up his premonitions about the Pacific with homely illustrations. This anxiety over the state of our defenses gave additional meaning to the Secretary's patient examination of the much-harrowed ground with Nomura. In the phrase of his valued advisor, Norman Davis, Hull didn't want "the Japs to get their tail over the dashboard" any earlier than could be avoided.

—2—

Upon dividing the fleet in the spring of 1941, the United States Navy had, of course, abandoned the classic strategy for war on the Japanese—a frontal attack with superior mettle through the mandated islands, reducing those bases and then striking directly at Japan herself. Forced to abandon that line, both because of the divided fleet and the rising menace of aircraft to surface vessels, the American strategists, consulting with their British and Dutch opposite numbers in the summer and fall of 1941, envisaged the defense of southeastern Asia and the Indies chiefly from the air, with bombers capable of harassing the Japanese fleet and rendering the South China Sea between Manila and Hong Kong untenable for the enemy. This was to be a containing strategy, calculated to hold the enemy at bay until sufficient power could be mustered in the south and west (India and China) to propel a vast and irresistible offensive which would roll the Japanese back on their home islands. This was called the "rainbow plan," for the long, looping arcs of transport and logistics involved.

In September, a large number of flying fortresses went to the Philippines by a new, southern route, partly in the hope of escaping Japanese observation but also for the sake of opening an alternate way. The planes flew from Hawaii to Rabaul, New Britain, where the Australians had prepared a landing field, and from there to Port Darwin, which was being developed by the Australians, under American direction, for the use of American planes, with shops, gasoline stores, and spare parts. The Army had established fuel depots at both points.

From Port Darwin the flying fortresses flew up the islands to the Philippines. Later flights brought the flying fortresses' strength at Clark Field, near Manila, to thirty-five as of November 15, with others on the way. In addition, there were present at Manila some old medium bombers, a number of PBY naval patrol ships, and a group of recent pursuits.

As the Pacific skies darkened in October and November, General Marshall also dispatched to the Philippines ground re-enforcements. These included a National Guard tank battalion, a brigade of artillery, all the self-propelled 75's the American Army had at that time, and some antiaircraft units. These detachments were docked and disembarked by General

MacArthur under cover of night and the strictest censorship, but the Army intelligence had little doubt the Japanese were aware of the arrivals. By mid-November, there were about ten thousand United States troops in the Philippines. It should be remembered that on the near-by island of Formosa, General Homma had at least 150,000 men who had been undergoing intensive training for fifteen months in how to storm and take Luzon and Manila.

At this point, General Marshall notified Secretary Hull that if hostilities could be fended off until December 10 the Philippines would be in shape to make a successful conquest not only costly but hazardous. The Chief of Staff had, it is fair to say, told the Secretary and others that his force in the Philippines would be merely skeletal by the 10th: he hoped things could be kept from popping until spring, when a really strong force might be assembled in the islands.

When the Japanese struck three days ahead of General Marshall's time limit, certain of his re-enforcements were still at sea. On the day after Pearl Harbor a transport carrying pilots and ground crews for several squadrons of dive bombers and fighters arrived in Manila and were safely disembarked. However, their planes, which had been shipped separately in two freighters, failed to reach Manila. One supply ship was sunk while trying to run for Australia; the other safely reached an Australian port. A small contingent of troops that the war had caught in the mid-Pacific likewise reached a haven in Australia.

The flying fortresses in the Philippines were intended, of course, not only to prey on Japanese shipping in the South China Sea, but also to carry the attack to Japanese bases in Formosa and elsewhere. Although the actual flight from Clark Field to Japan proper with a bomb load is a bit beyond the maximum range of the fortresses, Army authorities had contemplated the possibility of shuttle flights to Siberian bases, should these be made available. A crisscrossing of air power between the Philippines, Malaya, and Borneo was also included in the plans of the ABCD Powers.

A considerable number of new airfields had been built or were under construction in the Philippines in the late fall. A few additional weeks, allowing for the arrival of more flying fortresses, dive bombers, and pursuits, with their complements, might, as Marshall supposed, have importantly altered the defense picture in the Philippines.

Meanwhile, the British likewise were adding to their strength at Hong Kong and Singapore. Farther south, the resolute Hollanders on Java were disposing their inadequate resources for war. The total armed forces available to the ABCD Powers, scattered, insufficiently trained, and underequipped, appeared somehow formidable to observers in distant Washington that fall. One reads with a pang the confident assertions of public men and journalists back in October and November to the effect that the ABCD had a safe preponderance in sea and air power in the far Pacific. Not only were the tough, hardened, jungle-trained troops of Hainan and Formosa and Indo-China, with the Japanese air force and surface strength, overlooked and underestimated during those last weeks of wishful thinking, but the military power at the disposal of the Western Powers was consistently overrated.

If the fall was a difficult time for Washington, it was likewise far from easy for Tojo and the uniformed bandits of the Kwantung clique, who now had full power over the destinies of Japan. Hard decisions had to be made—decisions in line with Japanese interest and not with the will of distant Berlin. The pathway ahead, the way of *Hakko Ichiu,* the "eight corners of the world under one roof" pattern of conquest bequeathed by the Emperor Jimmu, was by no means clear. In November, Tojo publicly reflected that Japan's situation was grave indeed, the country being "at the crossroads of a rise or fall" such as it had not encountered "in all its twenty-six hundred years of history." This was more than rhetoric. There were reasons for putting off Nazi Ambassador Eugen Ott and for agreeing to strike at Siberia only if, as, and when the Nazis reached the Volga; there were reasons, likewise, for stalling the United States until the final word could be spoken.

It had been something of a mystery why the Japanese continued to insist on pursuing the meaningless Hull-Nomura conversations into the fall, why Konoye proposed his face-to-face conference with the President, and especially why Saburo Kurusu was flown to this country in November to protract negotiations. Mysterious also was Japan's opening of the Pacific front on December 7, nine days after Marshal Semyon Timoshenko's capture of Rostov signalized the Nazi failure to break Russia in the fall of 1941. In the light of the bargain of July 2, why didn't the Nipponese go to the rescue of their Axis partner, mortally engaged with Russia? Also, why did Japan dare to strike at the Western powers with Germany "bogged" in Russia and unable to lend powerful diversionary aid, at least, in the west?

The answers to these questions are by no means clear. There are gaps, discrepancies, and contradictions, but as nearly as the design of Japanese intentions can be reconstructed from the varied and voluminous advices in the possession of this Government, received before and after Pearl Harbor, the behind-the-scenes story in Tokyo and Berlin in the fall of 1941—a catalogue of probabilities rather than of certainties—went something like this:

Since the summer of 1940, the Japanese had been pointing their military energies for a swoop on southeastern Asia, Malaya, and the Dutch Indies, striking a glancing blow at the Philippines on the way. To that end, they had established the huge training centers on Hainan and Formosa and had encroached, according to plan, on Indo-China. As a part of that strategical undertaking, they earnestly desired the neutrality pact with Stalin, bestowed somewhat gratuitously on Matsuoka in April, on the eve of his departure from Moscow. The grand strategy of Japanese advance in Asia did not include war in the north with Russia at the moment. So, with a sound and understandable aversion to a two-front war, Tojo and his satellites had no desire to see their relationship with Moscow disturbed. Hitler's drive into Russia, unexpected in Tokyo, threatened that relationship. A coolness resulted between Tokyo and Berlin, with Matsuoka, regarded as a dupe because he had brought home no word of Hitler's intentions regarding Russia, paying the penalty.

The groundwork for peaceful penetration of Indo-China had not, however, been fully laid when Hitler invaded Russia. The *Führer* still held a high card there. Hence, on July 2, the Imperial Council made the deal by which, in exchange for a bloodless occupation of the great French possession, they agreed to strike at Siberia at some time in the future. Ott was unable to make the pledge more specific, and all his subsequent efforts gained only the Japanese promise to move when the Germans had reached the Volga. In the first days of July, it will be recalled, German confidence ran high, and it would have been an unbecoming sign of weakness on the part of a Nazi diplomat during July to suppose that the Volga would not soon be reached and passed. Furthermore, Berlin knew that the Japanese could appropriate Indo-China merely by reaching for it. Japan's demand for a legalization of the conquest via Vichy—a desire growing, like the persistent discussions in Washington, out of the Japanese passion for justification—seemed a small enough price to pay for the promise to repudiate the Moscow treaty in due course.

In the inner councils of the generals and terrorists exerting the final power in Japan, there were no illusions about the principal enemy to Japanese expansion. Like Brauchitsch, Tojo saw the English-speaking powers as the "eternal enemy."

There was only a slight difference, the German putting England first, Tojo finding the United States the chief obstacle. The drive south had been settled upon in 1940 largely because the Japanese strategists expected England's fall to follow that of Holland and France, leaving no European power erect in the Far East and the United States, caught between two hostile oceans, unable to bring such strength as it then had to bear in that region. In the early summer of 1941, Tojo still believed that his German friends would be able to reduce Britain. To him, therefore, the war on Russia was a detour from the main objective, and the quicker it could be disposed of, either by destruction of Soviet power, by a truce, or by military containment on a stabilized front, the better for Japanese projects.

By October also, there is strong reason to believe, German militarists, notably Brauchitsch, had reached the same conclusion. Brauchitsch had determined that there was no further profit in the Russian campaign. The Soviet military power had been by no means destroyed, but their lines had been driven far back, their armies reduced, and their material substance expended. Brauchitsch reasoned that a truce or a stabilized front would relieve Germany of apprehension in the east, while the *Reichswehr* and *Luftwaffe* turned to the essential task of destroying England at home and in the Mediterranean and Middle East. To understand Brauchitsch's position, it is necessary to recall that he is a Bismarckian, believing in the "limited objective" theory of war rather than in the total extermination upon which Hitler was set.

Brauchitsch had been, of course, a student of Karl von Clausewitz (as had Bismarck), and to the great German military theoretician of the early nineteenth century the sole object of war was to "impose your will on the enemy." To do that you needn't utterly destroy his armies or occupy all his territories. In October, therefore, Brauchitsch wished to arrange an armistice with Stalin, stopping the war in its tracks and

striving (if possible) to patch up an entente with the Soviet
Union in the Bismarckian tradition. If an agreement with
Moscow proved impossible, Brauchitsch was willing to accept
the next best thing—retirement to a defensible winter line,
freeing the principal Nazi forces for a winter or early spring
drive toward Gibraltar or Suez and the oil of the Middle East.
Hitler, moved by political considerations and emotional impulses, preferred to fulfill *Mein Kampf's* promise of war to
the death on the Bolsheviks. He therefore ordered the war
continued into the jaws of winter. It was the *Führer*, not the
commander in chief, who decreed the second drive on Moscow
in October.

Tojo's position, maintained with an implacability irritating
to Ambassador Ott, corresponded with Brauchitsch's and had
the same underlying motivation—defeat of the English-speaking Powers. By November, Tojo's attitude began to bear
weight in Berlin, as the desirability of Japanese assistance rose
with the decline of Nazi hopes for an early decision over Russia. Even Hitler saw the advisability of making concessions to
Japan's point of view. Hence, in November, at about the time
Kurusu was dispatched to the United States, the Nazis gave
assurances to Tokyo that—win, lose, or draw—they were soon
to ease up on the Russian campaign and revert to the war on
England, against both the island base and the imperial strongholds in the Middle East, where Tojo especially wished for a
German diversion to pull British strength away from the Far
East. As Churchill was painfully to concede in the House of
Commons upon his return from the United States, even the
threat of a Nazi offensive against Suez and the oil of Iraq
and Iran served to enfeeble the British capacity for resistance
at Hong Kong and in Malaya.

A new bargain presumably was struck in November, Berlin
agreeing to prosecute an offensive in the Middle East (disposing of its Russian problem by hook or crook) and Tokyo prom-
ising to sail almost at once against the English-speaking Powers

and to the south. By mutual understanding, Siberia was relegated to second place for the time being. As an earnest of good faith, the Nazis, it will be recalled, announced the withdrawal of a number of divisions from the Russian front in November, re-enforcing the garrisons in Bulgaria and Greece and massing air power against Malta. In Tripolitania they sent heavy re-enforcements to General Rommel, Tokyo being told that he was under orders not to halt short of Suez. These moves reassured Tojo. Furthermore, the total embargoes on oil and trade generally following the "freezing" order of July 25 removed that reason for further appeasement of the West. At about this time Tojo began to manifest bellicosity in public utterances, outbursts coinciding with Kurusu's arrival in this country, all of which seemed impolitic and puzzling to the Americans.

On December 8, the day after Pearl Harbor, it will be recalled that Nazi spokesmen rather mystifyingly announced that hostilities in Russia were to be halted until spring. And three days later, declaring war on the United States, Hitler vented his whole fury on this country and England, noticcably neglecting the Soviet foe. Unfortunately for the Berlin-Tokyo bargainers, the Soviet Union refused to behave according to their wish. Stalin hurled fresh forces against the Nazi winter line; the Germans were in retreat at a dozen points by the middle of December, and, on the 19th, Hitler, who had retired to Berchtesgaden with a case of nerves, restored the Russian front to first importance.

In an unheralded and somewhat weird proclamation to the "army and the armed Elite Guard," the *Führer* announced that, in obedience to "an inner voice," he had determined to take over the supreme military command, deposing the generals who had sought to undo the work accomplished in Russia with "immeasurable heroism and heavy sacrifices." At that moment Brauchitsch, in mufti, was showing himself in Vienna, carefully informing friends of his dismissal. Other

generals had fallen and were to fall, some by death, in a purge
that startled and bewildered Europe and America. Hereafter,
Hitler notified the armies, he would rely upon his intuitions
and not upon the strategical concepts of the old *Reichswehr*
Junkers.

—4—

The sands were rapidly running out when Kurusu, making
"face," as he thought, by using American football terms in
press interviews, landed in San Francisco and flew across the
continent. On November 17, Nomura produced the "peace
envoy" at Mr. Hull's office, from which, after a somewhat
stilted twenty-three minutes of palaver, the three proceeded
across the street for a formal call on the President. On the next
day Hull, Nomura, and Kurusu talked for two and three quarter hours in the Secretary's office.

Mr. Hull recited his familiar exhortations to Kurusu:
Japan's future, as an insular, trading power, lay with the English-speaking Powers and their associates, not with the Axis.
The Secretary retraced his argument for a world of peace and
order based on justice. Kurusu cited Japan's alleged need for
Lebensraum, or, in the Japanese version, *Dai-toa Kyoei-ken*—
the "Greater East Asia Co-Prosperity Sphere." To proposals
that Japan withdraw from the Axis, Kurusu countered with
suggestions that the United States cease its support of China
and accede to Japanese occupation of whatever part of Asia
she desired, giving Japan, as a high State Department officer
put it, "an unlimited hunting license for all Asia."

On that day, the 18th, the Japanese Ministers of War and
Navy formally reported to the Diet, before which Tojo was
diligently polishing the sword, that their services had completed "all necessary preparations." On the next evening,
Nomura and Kurusu called at the Secretary's apartment for
further talk—a call repeated, at their request, on the evening
of the 20th, Thanksgiving Day. It was on this occasion that the

visitors left with Mr. Hull their notorious five-point formula, which, when simmered down, proposed that the United States abandon China, lift the "freezing" order, supply Japan with whatever oil she required, and assist her in acquiring more raw products from the Indies, in return for which the Japanese would agree not to press southward beyond the limits of Indo-China and to pull out of that colony altogether when and if peace was restored between Japan and China or "an equitable peace in the Pacific area" had been established.

Mr. Hull read the five points slowly; then, regarding Kurusu with a remote and weary glance, he "caught him up" by pointedly inquiring:

"Have you anything more to offer?"

Kurusu, having married his American secretary, understands English better than Nomura. He grasped Mr. Hull's point without delay. Not caring to defend the proposals, which had only just been received from Tokyo, he changed the subject, informing the Secretary that his Government was pressing him for a speedy composition of the differences with the United States, and begging Mr. Hull to bring the note to the attention of the President for a formal answer. After Kurusu's arrival, the Japanese representations had taken an exigent line. At each session Kurusu pleaded for haste.

On Friday, the 21st, Mr. Hull reported the incident to the President, who was about to depart for a belated Thanksgiving party at Warm Springs. At that day's meeting of the War Cabinet, including, besides the President and himself, the Secretaries of War, the Navy, and the Treasury, Mr. Hull delivered his trenchant warning that things had reverted to the status of November 7 (when he advised his colleagues that the issue was no longer diplomatic) and advised them to take care that the Japanese did not "stampede the hell out of our scattered forces" in the Pacific.

At that day's press conference, the President, showing an uncharacteristically stern countenance, parried questions deal-

ing with the Far East. Asked whether merchantmen in the
Pacific would be armed, he replied that they would not be
armed "under existing circumstances."

On Saturday, at Mr. Hull's invitation, the diplomatic representatives of the other ABCD powers—Lord Halifax, Dr. Hu
Shih, the Chinese Ambassador, Dr. Loudon, and Mr. Casey—
heard from the Secretary the tenor of the conversation
opened by Kurusu, including the five points. At the end of
the conference, Lord Halifax assured the correspondents that
he had "complete confidence" in Mr. Hull's management of
the situation.

Upon the departure of the ABCD diplomats, Mr. Hull was
informed that Ambassador Nomura had asked for another
parley that night at the Wardman Park. He accordingly received the Japanese envoys, who pressed him with some urgency to persuade his Government to accept the five points.
This, the Secretary feared, was impossible. The fifth point was
the real stickler, binding the United States "to refrain from
such measures and actions as will be prejudicial to the endeavors for the restoration of general peace between Japan
and China."

Against the background of the Hull-Nomura conversations,
accepting this point could only mean desertion of the Chungking cause at a crucial time. Kurusu insisted that acceptance
of all five points by the United States would be looked upon
only as a "temporary step": the Tokyo Government believed
that it would help prepare Japanese public opinion for a
negotiated peace in the Pacific—in short, for the comprehensive agreement desired by the United States.

Kurusu a bit breathlessly declared that his Government
was pressing them hard for an immediate decision, and Mr.
Hull divined that time was running short in Tokyo. That
night he telephoned the President his renewed impression that
we were approaching the brink. The next morning Mr. Roosevelt cut short his Warm Springs holiday and hurried back

to Washington, arriving on Monday. That day the President and Secretary conferred in a crisis atmosphere. They could not sell out China—that much was plain.

At this point began the period of the so-called "truce," the effort to find a last-minute compromise that might stave off the evil hour a little longer. At this point, the State Department's Division of Far Eastern Affairs began drafting the lengthy summation of the American position which was to be handed the Japanese on November 26, a fateful reply to the five points which the Japanese belatedly answered one hour after the bombs fell on Pearl Harbor. The President, the Secretary, and Mr. Welles took up, considered, and discarded a half-dozen formulas around the big desk in the President's office. Over in Mr. Hull's rooms at the State Department, the men of the Far Eastern Division consulted with the Secretary on the same problem. The talk settled finally on the possibility of a *modus vivendi* calculated to allow a breathing spell of three months during which, in exchange for relaxing the "freezing" order and supplying them the normal, peacetime requirements of medium octane gasoline, Japan might agree to stand still in Indo-China. As tentatively outlined, the plan called for leaving the "China affair" in a state of suspension for the term of the agreement.

This *modus vivendi,* miscalled a truce, there being no hostilities, never was to reach the Japanese, contrary to reports widely published and not until this moment corrected. There is, therefore, no way of knowing whether it had a chance of acceptance. One reason for its remaining stillborn within the womb of American and ABCD diplomacy was that the Chinese planted their feet in the sand and refused to budge. The British likewise viewed it with considerable skepticism. On Tuesday the 25th, Mr. Hull laid the proposal before the ABCD diplomats, introducing it for what it was—a somewhat desperate attempt to keep the conversations going and, at the worst, to buy a bit more time for the re-enforcement of Hawaii, the Philippines, Singapore, Burma, and the Dutch Indies.

"The military fellows are after me to hold 'em off a little longer until we can get stronger out there," the Secretary explained. Otherwise, the discussions with the Japanese were finally "stranded," as he put it. Mr. Hull was by no means enthusiastic: he would rather fight than palaver when the time came to fight. On the other hand, he liked the odds as nearly even as possible.

The British Empire representatives, Halifax and Casey, taking a planetary view similar to that of the Americans, thought rather favorably of the possibility of purchasing more time, although they had strong misgivings. Dr. Loudon's views coincided with Minister Casey's. But Dr. Hu Shih, a world-famous philosopher, a poet of charm and sensibility whose gift to China of a vernacular literature had contributed to cultural unity, bowed his back. To Dr. Hu Shih, the Japanese were a present, not a future, enemy—cruel, treacherous, and under no circumstances to be trusted. The Chinese doubted that the Japanese would enter into such an understanding in good faith, suspecting they would ignore its obligations. Moreover, they opposed making any agreement so long as Japanese troops remained on Chinese soil.

Mr. Hull invited the Chinese Ambassador to his home that evening for a further discussion. He found him immovable. Meanwhile, T. V. Soong, the former Chinese Finance Minister and soon to be named Foreign Minister *in absentia*, exerted himself with friends of China in the Administration. Dr. Soong, a brother-in-law of Chiang Kai-shek, and an able, forceful statesman, backed the Ambassador's views with emphasis and conviction: any accord with Tokyo represented a selling out of China. He was on suggestible ground there, neither Mr. Roosevelt nor Mr. Hull being willing for an instant to be put into that position.

Overnight, the friends of China and those supporting a

more active policy vis-à-vis Japan were beating the drums against a "truce" purchased with concessions tantamount to blackmail. They stimulated opposition in the press and in the Administration. One difference between Mr. Hull and the activists was that he expected Japan to fight, and at once, whereas many of them believed Tokyo, as usual, to be running a bluff that only needed to be called. The Washington Sunday papers of December 7 published two lengthy articles, one by an admiral, proving that Japan was inhibited from opening a war with the Western powers, both because of the uncertainties over Russia and her own bogged-down condition in China.

Mr. Roosevelt received Dr. Hu Shih and Dr. Soong on the morning of the 26th, endorsing their view, having previously found Mr. Hull agreed that no "truce" would be acceptable in the face of Chinese opposition. When the Chinese left the White House, the Secretary came over with the text of his answer to the five points. This note first restated the principles Mr. Hull had so patiently elaborated with the Chinese.

In a second, activating section, the note proposed a seven-power, nonaggression treaty among the United States, Great Britain, China, Japan, the Soviet Union, the Netherlands, and Siam. It also suggested that the above powers, minus Russia, sign an agreement to respect the territorial integrity of Indo-China, the implication being that the colony be placed under the administrative control of these six Governments, pending the postwar reorganization of France. As between Japan and the United States, the note further proposed that Japan withdraw in force from China and Indo-China, that both powers abandon their claims to extraterritorial privileges in China (using their good offices to persuade other powers to do the same), and that the commercial treaty that expired by American denunciation in January, 1940, be renewed.

That afternoon the memorandum was handed to Ambassador Nomura. Although this communication, labeled "strictly confidential, tentative, and without commitment," indicating in the idiom of diplomacy that it had not risen to the dignity of a note, completely rejected the Japanese conditions of the 20th, it was by no means ultimative. The oral accompanying remarks described it simply as "one practical exemplification of a program which this Government envisages as something to be worked out during our further conversations." Again the door was left wide open.

When the memorandum was out of his hands, however, Mr. Hull had a feeling that it somehow put an end to the grueling, anxious year and a half since Sedan, the period of the diplomatic defensive during which the White House and the Department of State, lacking military might, had deployed this country's moral suasion and economic strength around the globe in an effort to keep war from our shores. Mr. Hull regretfully thought he might have kept the peace a little longer without sacrifice of vital interests, but the issue of war or peace had been taken out of his hands. Soon it would be entirely out of this Government's grasp. The question was controversial then; it is academic now, and its final determination must await a longer view.

By the end of November the national spotlight had been firmly focused on Japan and the Pacific area. A prediction credited to an anonymous "high official" that the chance of peace was only one in ten received widespread assent. The official was Sumner Welles. War was expected, but war aimed only obliquely at us in southeastern Asia, in Siam or Malaya, and not directed toward the heart of our power in the Pacific. After November 26, the State Department believed war in that corner of Asia a virtual certainty, the only uncertainty being the time factor. In the next ten days, daily press reports told of ever-increasing Japanese troop movements into Indo-

China. From Hainan and Japan proper, as well as from Chinese ports, the great transport convoys steamed south, no longer attempting any concealment. Meanwhile, in Tokyo the warlike utterances of public men and the press rose to a screaming pitch, Tojo sounding a shrill key when he charged that "Britain and the United States desire to fish in the troubled waters of East Asia," adding grimly:

> For the honor and pride of mankind, we must purge this sort of practice from East Asia with a vengeance.

In these final days of peace, this country's insular position between its two wide oceans strikingly was brought home. Trouble brewed in the Atlantic area also. Amid a rising toll of American and Panamanian vessels sunk by U-boats, France, the intermittent danger spot, was put under further pressure by the Nazis and yielded on one crucial point. America lost a friendly ally, the Atlantic cause a bulwark, in North Africa.

On November 17, Maxime Weygand, now seventy-four, but spry as a sparrow, alighted at the Vichy airdrome with his staff. Again sent for by Pétain, again he declined to transcend the armistice terms at the behest of the Nazis. Weygand lunched and dined with the marshal, had an interview with the object of his special detestation, Darlan, and saw Admiral Leahy. At dusk of the 19th he left Pétain at the Hôtel du Parc and went for a walk along the Allier river front. There he was observed by a member of the American Embassy staff, pacing slowly and alone. The next day, Pétain announced Weygand's resignation as Delegate General to North Africa, his retirement to the Riviera.

The United States, advised of Weygand's impending removal, responded on the day of the announcement, November 20, with a public statement, charging that Vichy had "acquiesced to the express demand of Hitler . . . thus permitting a German control over French authority entirely outside the provisions of the armistice." In consequence, this Government reviewed its French policy. It at once suspended the North African agreement, contemplated shipments of mixed cargoes from an American port being canceled. A Red Cross ship loaded at Baltimore with powdered milk and vitamins for children in the unoccupied zone was divested of its cargo, which went into a warehouse.

Although the exact effect of Weygand's dismissal could not be calculated at the time, Ambassador Leahy had received assurances on this point from the little general and from Robert Murphy and United States consular missions in North Africa. Weygand had carefully disseminated his point of view among civil and military commanders and their subordinates in Algeria, Tunisia, and Morocco. The Nazis insisted upon placing General Alphonse Juin, a war prisoner paroled for the purpose, in command of the North African forces, estimated at 200,000 effectives but riddled by idleness and short of equipment. His release and elevation were taken as evidence of a sound conversion to the Nazis' "new order." Yet Juin found himself surrounded by Weygand men, and his conduct belied expectations that he would take orders slavishly from Paris and Berlin.

Soon after Weygand's dismissal, Vichy circulated hints that the third of the face-to-face meetings of high French and Nazi officers of state was about to occur. The first, it will be recalled, brought Pétain and Laval together with Hitler at Montoire; the second involved only Darlan and Hitler at Berchtesgaden. Each produced extraordinary pressure for the fleet and bases. It was assumed that Hitler again would foregather with the French, but the *Führer* had his hands full on the central front in Russia, where his desperate second drive on Moscow was petering out amid the autumn snows. Instead, on December 1, Hermann Goering, the ferociously affable hogshead of a man, aglitter with Nazi decorations, met the Marshal of France, Darlan, and a large suite on a rail siding at the hamlet of Saint-Florentin-Vergigny, 110 miles southeast of Paris and 140 miles north and east of Vichy. The place of meeting had, as was natural in wartime, been kept secret, and even Pétain did not know his destination until safely on the train and in the custody of Darlan.

The real reason for this third high Vichy-Nazi session could not be discerned through the plethoric verbiage of the Vichy explanations. The Nazi account, issued through an official spokesman at Berlin, was more succinct but likewise vague. Indicating that Franco-German relations had been reviewed in the light of "three factors which have come into the foreground recently [*sic*] regarding the . . . European community of destiny," the statement specified these as: "First, the Bolshevik danger; second, the British blockade, which affects all European nations, and finally American attempts at intervention." None, of course, was new.

Under the first heading, Goering tepidly renewed efforts to muster France into an all-out military campaign against Russia. With a million and a half French prisoners of war still in Nazi camps, this project, although it had Darlan's obedient support, encountered the disdainful realism of Pétain. Goering failed to press the matter. The British blockade brought out familiar arguments from the Nazi side for using French convoys of merchantmen through the Anglo-American patrol. As to the third "factor," Goering, the editors of the Nazi-owned French-language press in Paris asserted, sought to bring Vichy within the terms of the Axis pact by asking Pétain to make war on the United States should that country become involved in the general war.

While Pétain and Goering talked at Saint-Florentin-Vergigny, Japanese carriers were steaming toward Hawaii. Did the *Reichsmarschall* inform the French of the impending blow, the surprise attack which automatically would align the United States against the Axis? A reading of the Parisian press might support such a hypothesis. The State Department, which had what it considers an accurate précis of the Vichy-

Nazi conversations a few hours after their termination, insists that Goering did not communicate the Japanese secret to the French. It has been assumed, in view of corroborating circumstances, that Goering knew the hour for a Japanese offensive in the Pacific was at hand. What then of the Paris press, broadly hinting that France had been solicited to join the Axis against the United States and agitating for that wholly unnatural step? Typical in its fulminations, the *Nouveaux Temps* observed that "the hour for a final choice has sounded." Not only had the United States "unceasingly provoked Germany and France," but now the transatlantic Republic was "engaged in a bitter political conflict with Japan." The editor found a reasonable identity between the Nazi and Japanese "policies toward Anglo-American imperialism," hence:

> If war comes, it will be a world war, in the Pacific as well as the Atlantic, in Africa as well as Asia. Can there be any neutral power? If so, can France stay neutral? An objective examination of the situation forces a negative reply. Europe will not be remade without France, but France will be European or will not exist.

Strong ground may be found for believing that Goering's reticence on Japan's plans and the press campaign in Paris formed part of one whole. The utterances of the journalists constituted an assurance to Japan that Germany was enlisting Vichy on their side against the English-speaking Powers. As part of the bargain by which Nippon opened a Pacific front on behalf of the Axis, the support of France would have had a more than sentimental value. Madagascar lay in the forefront of Japanese strategical thinking, as it did in that of Britain and Australia also. It would be no surprise to Washington if postwar revelations were to disclose false Nazi assurances to the Japanese that Vichy had been persuaded to surrender Madagascar at the December 1 conference. Why did Goering not take Pétain into his confidence, as the Japanese no doubt expected he would, respecting the imminence of the new front? This Government holds that Goering had reason to fear the secret would reach Washington, if divulged to Pétain, in time to frustrate the foul blow. The State Department considers it highly probable indeed that Pétain would have warned Leahy had he been privy to the underhanded assault.

Actually, the meeting of December 1 considered routine matters: the treatment of war prisoners, financial arrangements between Vichy and the occupying forces, and the like. It ratified the reduction of occupation expenses from eight to six million francs a day, a *quid pro quo* granted Vichy in exchange for Weygand's dismissal. Actually, no new factors were introduced. The Nazi regime, as has been seen, was at the moment torn internally, the generals wishing to call a halt in Russia, Hitler meditating the purge which came two weeks later. The long-awaited drive through southwestern Europe toward Gibraltar and North and West Africa was in abeyance.

The conference failed to upset the balance of forces at Vichy. Leahy reported that the marshal, having surrendered in Weygand, stiffened otherwise. Far from moving to the support of Japan, Pétain manifested his sympathy with the United States over Pearl Harbor, officially avowed Vichy's neutrality, and, with Leahy, initiated steps toward restoring Franco-American relations to a workable basis. Within ten days of Pearl Harbor, the North African agreement was renewed upon the earnest request of the British; also, a new neutrality agreement covering the French possessions in America was negotiated between Admiral Robert, Vichy High Commissioner, and Admiral Frederick J. Horn, on behalf of the State Department, at Fort-de-France, strengthening this country's hand in the Caribbean.

—6—

With the beginning of December, Washington's anxiety over Japan's southward movement deepened. On the 2nd, Mr.

Roosevelt directed Mr. Welles to inquire of Ambassador Nomura the meaning of re-enforcements so obviously in excess of "common defense" requirements. Three days later, only two days before Pearl Harbor, Nomura handed the State Department a reply, subsequently described by the President as "evasive and specious," calling reports of the troop movements "exaggerated" and ascribing them to the necessity of taking "precautionary measures" against Chinese troop dispositions "along the northern frontier of French Indo-China." The communication insolently ignored the gist of Mr. Roosevelt's inquiry, which dealt not with the northern, but the southern end of Indo-China. Grossly deceived at the time about the true strength of Japan in Indo-China, our best estimates put the troop totals at about 125,000. In reality, they were double that number.

In that final week, Washington's eyes were focused upon Siam. Japanese forces massed along the Indo-China-Siamese border made threatening gestures. The Siamese Premier, Colonel La ung Bipul Songgram, sent reserves to the Mekong River frontier, the Bangkok radio steadily warned of invasion, and in the west, the powers discussed what should be done in such case. In the American press, editorial writers and columnists innocently speculated upon the various courses open to the United States when and if Japan struck south: a breaking of relations with Japan, arming United States merchantmen in the Pacific, acceleration of help to China, and a blockade.

Japan's movements toward Siam were genuine enough, yet they served the purposes of a ruse, the great Siamese ruse, which, during the first week of December, removed the gaze of Americans, including some of the responsible officers of both services, from the danger to Hawaii and the Philippines. In his eleventh-hour appeal to Hirohito on Saturday, December 6, the President, it is true, reflected the apprehensions of the people of the Philippines as well as of Malaya, Siam, and the

Netherlands Indies, but the country continued to assume, and most members of the Administration considered it probable, that the Japanese would at the outset by-pass this country and its Pacific possessions. Assuring the Emperor that the fear of these peoples was "legitimate," Mr. Roosevelt pronounced continuation of the menacing situation produced by the troop concentrations in Indo-China as "unthinkable," adding:

"None of the peoples whom I have spoken of . . . can sit either indefinitely or permanently on a keg of dynamite."

Few, if any, high officials believed, however, that the United States would, or could, stand aside for long if the Japanese struck at the East Indies or Malaya, or even thrust into Siam. For at stake were not only immediate interests vital to us, but resources and strategical positions affecting our long-term security as a nation. The question perplexing many high officials was how, in the absence of a direct Japanese attack on the American flag, to summon the nation, divided as it then was on questions of foreign policy, to the strong action which they believed essential. There had been considerable discussion of possible methods. Under these circumstances the American response probably would have been some form of blockade. In planning how best to protect American interests, officials were hampered by political dissension within the nation. It was commonly supposed that the Japanese were too smart to solve this problem for the President by a direct assault on the American flag—especially at Hawaii, which even the extreme isolationists recognized as a bastion of our security.

Nevertheless, the danger that the Japanese would attack anywhere, or several places simultaneously, was not overlooked. The most remote possibilities, as well as the probabilities, had been weighed again and again by the responsible officials in Washington. The President and Secretary Hull had kept the Army and Navy fully informed of the gravity of the trend of events. Both had every reason to believe that our armed forces in the Pacific were on the alert and ready, in so far as their strength permitted, to meet any contingency. The defenses of the Philippines were known to be weak—although it was not anticipated that the Japanese would succeed in destroying two thirds of our air forces there on the ground in one afternoon, hours after the assault on Oahu. In the Hawaiian Islands, our naval and air and ground forces were ample to throw back any attack which the Japanese could launch.

The first bombers over Pearl Harbor caught more than the military and naval establishments at Hawaii off guard. They caught the entire United States napping. Why were the Japanese able to perpetrate so immense and crushing a surprise? The answers, being largely subjective, will be endlessly debated. There are, of course, all the surface reasons set forth in the Roberts report.

Yet, the fundamental reasons for our trancelike unawareness of peril must lie deeper. They bear on the all but universal feeling that the Japanese would not dare strike at the United States, an underrating of the enemy's might that gave rise to the confidently widespread assertion in the first days after Pearl Harbor that the Nipponese had committed hara-kiri by their presumptuous act. This attitude may be attributed to a national sense of sufficiency, a smugness based upon a continental state of mind, an indifference to and ignorance of the world about us, as well as to a consciousness of the rectitude of our own intentions toward other peoples.

There is an additional reason, simple, kindly, and going to the heart of the American character. In one of his books, Hermann Rauschning, apostate Nazi, Junker intellectual, and former President of the Danzig Senate, notes that the Anglo-Saxon peoples have, unlike continental Europeans, striven hard to exorcise evil *qua* evil. Those peoples, American and British, which have during long generations enjoyed, above all others, the blessings of the earth, have likewise, Rauschning postulates, sought to banish the ancient concept of abstract evil as a principle of life as well as of superficial conduct, by ignoring its existence. To that optimistic characteristic, the East Prussian Rauschning attributes the torpid awakening of the American and British people to the reality of the reactionary lapse to barbarism animating the members of the Axis. Conquest, rapine, loot, the machine-gunning of civilians from the air could happen in Poland, in France, in Russia, and in Rotterdam; it could not happen in Honolulu, Manila, or nearer home.

Furthermore, those who upheld the isolationist side of the public debate raging throughout the prewar months from Sedan onward helped disarm the American people psychologically. Returning grimly to their self-elected task after each defeat in Congress and with the people, the forces personified by Lindbergh and Wheeler dinned the public's ears with assurances of our immunity from danger. Implicit in their protestations was the suggestion that we make common cause with the enemies of the West or, at least, condone their predatory behavior. Such arguments, taking little cognizance of the basic elements of American self-interest, were superficial and romantic.

The national policy, evolving through the year and a half after France went down, was founded on the complex of America's geographical position and strategical necessities as well as underlying historical motivations. Supported at all times by a large majority of Americans, the national policy realistically took account of the security of this country and, by extension, of the entire Western Hemisphere.

We might better have gone to war earlier, on our own volition, rather than have waited for the physical attack. The fact is that, unlike Britain and France but like Russia, we became a belligerent only after our soil was violated and our flag fired upon. The last pros and cons in this matter will not be said for long years to come. Less debatable is the proposition that

American policy clearly followed the national interest in both the Atlantic and Pacific areas, shrewdly balancing war and peace against the survival of the America which remains "the last best hope" of a world in which so many issues fateful to mankind are yet to be resolved.

CHAPTER TEN

Postscript: The Grand Alliance

On Monday, December 8, 1941, Mr. Roosevelt, wearing a long, blue Navy cloak, motored unceremoniously to the Capitol where, before packed, grim galleries, he asked Congress to recognize the first war ever brought to the American people by treachery. Except for a lone professional pacifist from Montana, Representative Jeannette Rankin, the Congress acted with prompt unanimity.* The great, democratic debate over war and peace was at an end. Hereafter Americans would dispute only over ways and means of winning the war. Somewhere in *Mein Kampf* Hitler remarked with grudging admiration the unity of the American people in World War I. This time, as the prime author of America's righteous, embattled anger, he was to witness a closing of the ranks more solid than in 1917.

The warlike act at Hawaii established political as well as military fronts. Politically indeed, this Government was better prepared for war than in a military sense. The lines of wartime policy followed curves plotted, as we have seen, with sound realism before Pearl Harbor. As in the case of the earlier climactics, the fall of France, Britain's stubborn resistance, and the invasion of Russia, Japan's stroke produced a reshuffling

---

* Miss Rankin also had the distinction of voting against the declaration of World War I. George Norris, the venerable Senator from Nebraska who opposed the declaration of April 6, 1917, voted aye this time. In the galleries in 1941 as in 1917, Mrs. Woodrow Wilson again saw the country formally enter a world war.

of world forces and a reconsideration of strategic objectives. Our belligerency brought a spate of war declarations from friend and foe. In the first hours after Pearl Harbor the President and his foreign-policy advisors meditated whether to take the initiative in declaring war on Germany and its European satellites or await their anticipated action. The discussion evoked from Mr. Hull a characteristically apposite story about a bucking mule. Said Mr. Hull:

> Down in our country we had a Negro boy who was prone to admit that he was the best mule trainer in the county. He boasted that he had never been thrown and he could break the roughest mule that could be brought to him. The other boys finally got tired of his boasting and they fetched in a scientific, double-back action mule. Two minutes after the self-constituted champion mounted this mule he was picking himself up out of the plowed ground. He wasn't feazed, however. Brushing himself off, he said: "That's the way to break a mule. When you figger he's going to throw you, you just get off."

This Government allowed the Axis to buck first, the question being academic.

The swift manifestations of inter-American solidarity arising in Central and South America gratified Washington, attesting as they did to the strength of the hemisphere policy. Certain of our neighbors betook themselves to war even ahead of the United States in point of chronology and by June, 1942, all of North America, from the Pole to the Isthmus, was uniformly engaged with our enemies. Moreover, in the great southern continent, only Argentina and Chile still maintained diplomatic relations with the Axis, and these relations were impaired by the united agreements reached at the Rio de Janeiro conference of January-February calling for the rupture of economic relationships and joint action against the political agents of the enemy States.

Except for the arbitrary and intrusive act of Ramón Cas-

tillo, acting President of Argentina, in repudiating his own
Foreign Minister's commitments at Rio, the conference would
have brought about a unanimous break in diplomatic ties between the New World and the Axis. Sumner Welles, laboring
at Rio with sympathy, good humor, and a patience bordering
on the saintly, described the conference as a "success." His
verdict won the concurrence of disinterested observers. Under
the searching conditions of a universal war involving the
chief American power, the principle of hemispheric solidarity
had stood its first major test. The recalcitrance of Castillo and
his Chilean followers solidified the forces of unity in the other
countries, and it is noteworthy that the severest censure visited
on the dissidents came from below the Rio Grande. Without
such Pan-American cohesion, as Mr. Welles once said to the
authors, our wartime situation would have been "infinitely
dangerous." Moreover, as the Under Secretary has publicly
observed, the systematic good will exemplified in inter-American relationships affords a model and a frame of reference for
all efforts to create larger associations among the nations of
the world.

Once the United States became embroiled, the necessity for
a world-wide league of belligerents was plainly indicated: a
league embracing the Big Four—Britain, Russia, China, and
the United States—as well as the Dominions and India, the
governments-in-exile, and the American republics moving to
war in the train of their northern neighbor. The advisability
of such a vast alliance of the sovereignties opposing Axis
aggression, committed to wage war unitedly until victory came
on behalf of the principles of the Atlantic Charter, had been
intensively discussed at the White House and State Department before Pearl Harbor. As the fountainhead of lend-lease,
with strong links already running to the embattled democracies, Washington seemed the logical seat of such a combination of forces. Britain and Russia already were in bilateral
alliance, pledged against a separate peace. With the United

States a belligerent, Chungking ranged itself more formally on the anti-Axis front. That made a quadrilateral of Great Powers. The entrance of the United States into the war served as a catalyst.

On Sunday morning, December 14, one week after Pearl Harbor, Secretary Hull called in several of his advisors to discuss the composition of the document which was to formalize the grand alliance. At Mr. Hull's suggestion, Maxwell Hamilton, Chief of the Division of Far Eastern Affairs, already had made some tentative drafts. These were discussed at the December 14 conference. Mr. Hull charged Adolf Berle, Dr. Herbert Feis, advisor on International Economic Affairs, and Hamilton to proceed with the preparation of a text. Thereafter, although numerous consultants took a hand, the Berle-Feis-Hamilton draft remained at the core of the declaration. Several changes in language were made by the President after the draft was placed in his hands early in the afternoon of December 19.

A brief document, the Declaration of Washington committed the subscribing Powers to the Atlantic Charter's principles before pledging them to an all-out effort and against a separate peace by any signatory. As a concession to the Soviet Union, which was not at war with Japan, the compact was given a limited character, binding the powers to fight only such enemies as they were then engaged with. In what was construed by some observers as a *quid pro quo,* the Russians agreed with the Western democracies that "complete victory over their enemies is essential to defend life, liberty, independence and religious freedom. . . ."

The high contracting parties were uniquely represented in the Washington of December, 1941. Winston Churchill came at Christmastime for conferences of the first importance. Maxim Litvinov, bearing high prestige as a former Commissar for Foreign Affairs, arrived as Soviet Ambassador on December 7, being at lunch with Joseph E. Davies when the word came from Hawaii. Chiang Kai-shek, increasing the rank of his representation, appointed T. V. Soong Foreign Minister of China *in absentia*. These three, with the President, signed the United Nations declaration on January 1, 1942, at the White House. The declaration came first. It was comparatively simple to arrive at the broad statement of principles. The name came harder. In frequent discussions between Mr. Roosevelt and his house guest, the Prime Minister, they failed up to the night of December 30 to find a satisfactory label for their league of belligerents. They joined in opposing the World War I designation, "Allied and Associated Powers." That Wilsonian terminology, awkward on the tongue, had implied a faint moral condescension on the part of this Government. Mr. Roosevelt wished an inclusive description, enrolling all the anti-Axis nations in one unreserved undertaking. He rejected the term alliance, however qualified. So the urgent matter rested when the President and Prime Minister retired on the night of the 30th. On the 31st, the document had to be prepared for the signature of the allied statesmen.

The name came on the morning of the 31st. Mr. Roosevelt was awake earlier than usual. Running over the alternatives in bed, he fixed on the phrase "United Nations." Its pertinent simplicity recommended it. Rising, the President went in search of Mr. Churchill for his before-breakfast opinion. He found the Prime Minister in his tub. Advancing to the door of the bath, the President hailed his guest.

"How about 'United Nations'?" he called out as Churchill brought his soapy head above water. The Prime Minister ducked again to rinse the last of the soap from his eyes, shook his head, and turned a dripping gaze on the President.

"That," he said, "should do it."

Upon Mr. Churchill's return to London, he remarked to the House of Commons that he and the President were on such a candid and friendly footing they could "say anything to each other however painful." He might have added "anywhere."

The other twenty-two nations signed the declaration on January 2, as of the day before, in the office of Assistant Secretary Berle at the State Department. By June 14, the original twenty-six had, by the adherence of Mexico and the Philippine Commonwealth, been enlarged to twenty-eight. Running as an invisible thread through the United Nations was the fact of lend-lease, its objective quality as a conveyor belt of assistance from the "arsenal of democracy," and its utility as a diplomatic instrument in reaching postwar economic aims. Despite the President's aversion to alliance as a title, the press soon was warming memories of the Napoleonic era by dubbing the United Nations pact the Grand Alliance.

——2——

The waking hours of the President and the Prime Minister during the Christmas visit were crowded with political problems as well as the more obvious decisions involved in the establishment of unified commands for the various theaters of war and collateral questions of supply. There was the amazingly complex matter of spreading the promises of the Atlantic Charter across the Pacific as well. That connoted India, to which Sir Stafford Cripps was soon to be dispatched. India, in signing the declaration of the United Nations through the person of her first diplomatic representative to the United States, advanced in some degree toward the status of the Dominions. Then there was the irruption of the whole Vichy-Free French situation through the Christmas Eve appropriation of Saint-Pierre and Miquelon, French islets hugging the coast of Newfoundland, by Admiral Muselier and a party of De Gaulle French, who landed from the submarine *Surcouf* and three corvettes.

A tempest in a teapot, the Saint-Pierre expedition prejudiced this Government's good faith with Pétain, furnishing propaganda ammunition for the collaborationists in Paris and Vichy and rendering difficult situations more difficult. The State Department had just renewed and strengthened its "gentlemen's agreement" with Admiral Robert at Martinique covering all the French possessions in America. At Ottawa, Muselier had talked with Jay Pierrepont Moffat, the American Minister to Canada, concerning a proposed forcible transfer of sovereignty at Saint-Pierre from Vichy to the De Gaulle committee. The United States, recognizing Vichy, had no diplomatic relations with the De Gaulle committee in London, although it co-operated, as we have seen, with the Free French via the British and dealt with them informally in French Oceania and Brazzaville. In the light of the Robert agreement, this Government could not approve the projected descent upon Saint-Pierre. Moffat so advised Muselier, obtaining from him what he took to be a promise not to execute the plan. As the United States was the senior military power in the American waters, it was assumed that the Free French would not care to counter its wishes.

The news from Saint-Pierre on Christmas surprised the State Department, which was unprepared and scattered for the holiday. For three days this Government had no official word from the island, its only intelligence being that cabled by a correspondent with Muselier to his newspapers. At first, it was believed that the expedition was unauthorized, a filibustering adventure carried out by individuals. On that supposition, a subordinate drafted a press release at the State Department which described the flotilla as being composed of "so-called Free French vessels." The description was arbitrary and lacked diplomatic finesse. Partisans of the Free French in this country, who had been steadily critical of the Government's Vichy policy, seized upon the characterization as a further weapon in their campaign. In the main, they were unaware of the background, the Moffat-Muselier conversations, the renewed Robert understanding, and the fear, soon confirmed, that the pro-Nazi forces in France would make telling use of such a development. Incessantly, on the radio and in the press, the collaborationists charged that the seizure of Saint-Pierre was but the beginning of a dismantling of the French empire by the perfidious Anglo-Saxons in disregard of solemn agreements between this country and Vichy. Roosevelt and Pétain had exchanged reassurances on this point less than two weeks before. There was no doubt that the Saint-Pierre incident strengthened the hand of the pro-Axis elements in France, and the State Department believed the political disposition of the few hundred souls on the islands a matter of slight consequence in view of the larger issues which it affected. To Mr. Hull the action of Muselier was like that of a man who carelessly touched a match to a dry prairie. "The match," he said, "doesn't count, but the fire may be disastrous at a point many miles away."

When the smoke cleared, it seemed apparent that Muselier had acted on authorization of some kind from his superiors in London and that, moreover, he had set sail from Halifax with the approval, or at least the connivance, of Canadian authorities. A controversy thereupon arose, reaching a peak at the White House in a discussion between Mr. Churchill and Mr. Hull, the President standing aside. The Secretary, holding that the Free French admiral had acted in contravention of American understandings with both the British and Canadian Governments, asked that the British induce him to leave Saint-Pierre, themselves putting a guard over a small radio station on the island to see that no use was made of it beneficial to the Axis. The Prime Minister felt that expulsion of the Muselier party would jeopardize his relations with the Free French movement. To this the Secretary replied that the presence of the Muselier group jeopardized our relations with Vichy, Admiral Robert, and the authorities in French North Africa. At the end, however, it was agreed that the retirement of Muselier should not be demanded, but that both London and Ottawa should join in applying moral suasion.

This Government's relations with De Gaulle and the Free French National Committee in London subsequently were clarified. On July 9, 1942, the President designated Admiral Harold R. Stark, Commander in Chief of American Naval Forces in European Waters, and Brigadier Charles L. Bolte, Chief of Staff of American Army Forces in the United Kingdom, to consult with the French National Committee on all matters relating to the conduct of the war. At that time the official attitude toward the Free French was restated in a State Department memorandum. This Government recognized General de Gaulle and his committee as a center and symbol of "French resistance in general against the Axis powers." It did not recognize the Free French as a provisional government entitled to formal diplomatic recognition, the French National Committee having subscribed to the view of the British and United States Governments that the political organization of France must be determined by free expression of the French people after the war. This Government reaffirmed its policy and practice of dealing with Free French officials in their respective territories where they were in effective control, and of giving lend-lease aid to the military defense of these areas.

A far more perplexing political issue cropped up in the Roosevelt-Churchill conferences from Moscow by way of London, a perplexity that reached the light only in June, 1942, after the announcement of the Anglo-Russian treaty and the U. S.-Soviet accord. In July, 1941, Britain and the Soviet Union forged a wartime alliance forbidding a separate peace. Admittedly, this was a temporary expedient, to be followed in course by a more comprehensive convention dealing not alone with war policy but with what was to come after victory. In December, Eden went to Moscow charged with exploring the ground for a long-term understanding. Eden found Stalin highly

amenable to a Russo-British compact ending the long con-
straint between the two powers. He also found the Kremlin
firmly committed to postwar settlements which would fix the
Soviet Union's western borders at somewhere near their position after the occupation of the Baltic republics—Estonia,
Latvia, and Lithuania—and portions of Rumania. The Kremlin considered the restoration of these lands, all in Nazi hands,
as a minimum condition of military security in the postwar
world.

Eden's report aroused deep misgivings at the White House.
Making full allowances for the sincerity of the Russians in
asking for the return of a territorial safeguard that had served
them well in the face of Hitler's unprovoked attack, Mr.
Roosevelt at once apprehended the difficulties into which such
a treaty would plunge him and the American war effort. A
Soviet demand for sovereignty over its weak neighbors in the
West would, the President knew, affront the ingrainedly anti-
imperialistic sentiment of this country, arouse mistrust of the
Soviet Union's good faith, and be interpreted as a repudiation
of the self-determination article of the Atlantic Charter. With
this Churchill agreed.

To the White House circle it seemed that the Kremlin's
manifestation of skepticism regarding the durability of the
next peace was premature. There would be, it was thought,
time enough for Russia again to advance her borders if the
postwar system seemed likely again to subject her to peril.
The White House conferees by no means condemned Stalin's
motives. Even more poignantly than Roosevelt, the Prime
Minister understood the genuine fearsomeness actuating a
Government fighting for its nation's life against the demonic
malice of Nazidom.

—3—

Five worrisome months followed Eden's visit to Moscow.
Mindful of the part that the secret bartering of territories

played during World War I in undermining Wilson's Fourteen Points, Mr. Roosevelt never wavered in his opposition to a recognition of the Kremlin's demands. The President has been at all times determined to avoid the pitfalls of Versailles. In this he was stoutly seconded by Secretary Hull in the face of pressure steadily applied by Moscow and London during the spring of 1942. Stalin declined to accept any compromise. At Whitehall, Eden's fears overbore his resolution. Churchill was compelled to retreat, being outvoted by his War Cabinet, and at times the representations of the British weakened the fortitude of certain of the President's foreign policy advisors.

In April, the British and American Governments invited Vyacheslav M. Molotov to visit London and Washington, the White House hoping that the security alternative offered by the British, a specific alliance for war and peace, might seem more desirable to the Commissar for Foreign Affairs if he could be assured of the good faith of the English-speaking Powers on the ground, so to speak. The White House's hopes were justified. When Mr. Molotov reached London late in May he submitted the Kremlin's security program in undiluted form. The President, presenting his views to Ambassador Litvinov in frequent consultations and through Ambassador Winant in London, was shaken but not dismayed. Three days after Molotov's arrival in London he signed the treaty, which not only omitted any mention of territorial safeguards, but likewise contained a pledge against "seeking territorial aggrandizement for themselves and of noninterference in the internal affairs of other States." After so brief a consultation between Molotov and the Kremlin, Stalin had accepted the assurances of the English-speaking Powers at face value. Whatever was to happen in the future, the record had been kept clear for this time. Whether or not the Russians finally abandon their claims to the boundaries of 1939, these claims had not been recognized as part of a wartime bargain between London and Moscow. In this connection, significance also may be read into the disclaimers of Eden and Molotov that the London agreement contained secret clauses.

The news of the Anglo-Russian alliance and the collateral understanding between the Soviet Union and this country was made public simultaneously in London, Moscow, and Washington. At one stroke the Atlantic Charter had been upheld in its first crisis, the hands of the peace conference left unfettered and the small nations of Europe reassured. The Treaty of London, expressing a twenty-year alliance committing the British and Russians first to victory, then to military security and economic collaboration in the postwar world, acknowledged the Atlantic Charter and professed itself in harmony with the Declaration of Washington.

In exchange for the *cordon sanitaire* desired by the Kremlin, Churchill and Eden gave them a long-term pledge characterized by Molotov in his report to the Supreme Soviet as "clear and categorical." In Washington, Mr. Roosevelt, confirming with Mr. Molotov in their historic White House conferences what the Russian statesman termed a "fighting collaboration," likewise had reassured the Soviet Union regarding its postwar security. The Roosevelt-Molotov accord agreed with the London treaty makers on the urgency of a second war front, bespoke enlarged shipments of supplies to the Soviet Union, and vowed the peacetime "co-operation of the two powers.

Unlike the Quadruple Alliance of 1814, the Grand Alliance of the United Nations, anticipating victory, had prepared for peace. That preparation resulted from the foresight of Mr. Roosevelt, Mr. Churchill, and certain of their advisors, but primarily Mr. Roosevelt and Secretary Hull. In invading Russia, Hitler ran the risk of duplicating Napoleon's experience in drawing the Bear back into Europe on his heels. Actually in June, 1942, a year after Hitler's invasion, Russia re-entered the West as a decisive diplomatic factor for the first time since Czar Alexander I on April 1, 1814, promised the French on his own authority an easy peace if they would but repudiate the Emperor. In the diplomatic vacuum following the destruction of Bonapartism, Alexander was able to improvise the peace of Paris, overshadow the Congress of Vienna, and enforce a new spoliation of Poland. This time, owing to the forethought expressed in the Atlantic Conference, the organization of the United Nations, and the diplomatic uses being made of lend-lease, Russia found upon entering the West a pattern of postwar aspiration and behavior already formulated and endorsed by the West itself.

Two years and a day before the news of the London treaty and the Washington accord, Mr. Roosevelt, contemplating the defeat of France and Mussolini's infamy, foresaw at Charlottesville danger to the United States in a "world-wide arena." He therewith affirmed this country's solidarity with the nations resisting aggression. On that June night, as we have seen, the President was confronted with the implications of his utterance and the central position and productive power of America: the likelihood that events would call him to lead the liberal forces of the West against Hitler. On June 11, 1942, evidences of such leadership were abundantly at hand.

As the most gratifying by-product of the London and Washington conversations, Russia, Britain, and the United States had achieved a high level of mutual trust. Insofar as Russo-American relations alone were concerned the work of Ambassador Davies at Moscow and in wartime America and the Russian policy of Sumner Welles had borne prime fruit. It can scarcely be accounted an accident that Under Secretary Welles stated this Government's peace views at Arlington during the visit of Mr. Molotov and his associates. The Commissar for Foreign Affairs was reported "delighted" by Mr. Welles' characterization of this as a "people's war," his forthright declaration against imperialism, and his insistence upon loyalty to our allies in wartime and upon a policing of the peace by the victors until an international organization may be formed to preserve the security of all lands.

If this book has fulfilled its promise, it has made clear the idealism, the consistency, and the strength of American foreign policy in peace and war since the fall of France threatened to reduce the entire West, with its high and brave tradition, to an ignominious dependence upon Nazi dominion. Whatever may be said of Mr. Roosevelt's domestic policies during his unprecedentedly protracted administration, it can scarcely be doubted that his conduct of foreign affairs has followed a firm and elevated course, serving the vital interests of America and the hemisphere which the Good Neighbor policy has bound into one voluntary, benevolent, and enlightened political entity. It should be apparent also that the outlines of foreign policy, the global strategy of defense improvised in 1940 and 1941 under the impact of Axis aggressiveness, have been filled in and matured since we were thrust into a "shooting" war. American wartime policy has developed along lines clearly visible in the prewar Russian *rapprochement,* the Good Neighbor practice, the enunciation of the "four freedoms," lend-lease, the Atlantic Charter, and the pragmatic complex of attitudes expressed toward the divided French. The year and a half between Sedan and Pearl Harbor was an immensely creative period in foreign policy, as creative as that earlier period at the beginning of this century when the Atlantic and Open Door policies were made articulate. If we wish insight into the probable course of this country in foreign affairs after this war we could do worse than to project the major lines of policy as they have been set forth in this record. Those curves of policy are likely to remain constant, however circumstances shift, flowing, as they do, out of this nation's sturdiest political, cultural, and strategical traditions.

Index

[NOTE: An asterisk indicates a footnote reference.]

ABOUT THE AUTHORS

FORREST DAVIS' experience as a newspaper correspondent, magazine writer, and author of books spans the whole period between the two World Wars. From 1922 to 1935 he was a New York newspaperman, first on the staff of the HERALD TRIBUNE, then on the WORLD TELEGRAM. From 1935 to 1937 he served as general correspondent for the Scripps-Howard press. Twenty years ago, he covered the Washington Arms Conference. He studied inflation and its effects on the Weimar Republic. He watched the British Isles trying to readjust themselves to peacetime conditions after the last war. During the 1940 presidential campaign, Mr. Davis served first as advisor to Senator Taft of Ohio and then to Wendell Willkie's running mate, Senator McNary of Oregon. He is the author of WHAT PRICE WALL STREET, a history of the speculative market in America, of HUEY LONG: A CANDID BIOGRAPHY, and, most recently, of THE ATLANTIC SYSTEM, which tells the story of Anglo-American control of the seas from 1890 to the present day. He writes regularly for national magazines.

ERNEST K. LINDLEY has covered Franklin D. Roosevelt since the Albany days. Like Mr. Davis, a native of Indiana, Mr. Lindley is a graduate of the University of Idaho. He attended Oxford as a Rhodes Scholar, receiving his B.A. degree there in 1923, having majored in international relations. The next year he got his first newspaper job on the WICHITA BEACON but soon came to New York as a reporter for THE WORLD. In 1928 he began representing that paper in Albany; in 1931 he became a political writer for the New York HERALD TRIBUNE, moving to its Washington Bureau in 1933. In 1937 he became Washington correspondent for NEWSWEEK and he has written a syndicated Washington column since 1938. More recently he has commented on the news for the National Broadcasting Company. He is the author of FRANKLIN D. ROOSEVELT—A CAREER IN PROGRESSIVE DEMOCRACY; THE ROOSEVELT REVOLUTION—THE FIRST PHASE; HALF WAY WITH ROOSEVELT; and—in collaboration with his wife—A NEW DEAL FOR YOUTH.